REVIEW 10

REVIEW

Volume 10 1988

Edited by

James O. Hoge
*Virginia Polytechnic Institute
and State University*

James L. W. West III
The Pennsylvania State University

University Press of Virginia

Charlottesville

THE UNIVERSITY PRESS OF VIRGINIA
Copyright © 1988 by the Rector and Visitors
of the University of Virginia

This journal is a member of (CELJ) the Conference of Editors of Learned Journals

First published 1988

ISSN 1090-3233
ISBN 0-8139-1217-2

Printed in the United States of America

The editorial assistants for volume 10 of REVIEW are LaVerne Maginnis and Robert M. Myers, both of The Pennsylvania State University.

PENNSTATE

Funding for *Review* is provided by the generous gifts of Mr. and Mrs. Henry J. Dekker and Mr. Adger S. Johnson to the Virginia Tech Foundation, and by a grant from the College of the Liberal Arts, The Pennsylvania State University. Additional support is provided by the *Review* Association, a group of major universities which support the aims and purposes of the series. Member universities are as follows:

      City College of New York
      Columbia University
      University of Colorado
      Duke University
      University of Minnesota
      University of Virginia

Contents

The Culture of Priapism   1
  by James Grantham Turner
    Review of Aphra Behn, *Love-Letters Between a Nobleman and His Sister;* Claude Reichler, *L'Age libertin;* Harold M. Weber, *The Restoration Rake-Hero: Transformations in Sexual Understanding in Seventeenth-Century England*

The Theory of American Literature, Once More   35
  by Thomas M. Leitch
    Review of Russell Reising, *The Unusable Past: Theory and Study of American Literature*

Richard Ellmann and the Art of Biography   51
  by Jerome H. Buckley
    Review of Richard Ellmann, *Oscar Wilde*

The Collapse of a Critical Model: 59
Or, Was There a Rise of the Novel?
  by Maximillian E. Novak
    Review of Geoffrey Day, *From Fiction to the Novel;* Michael McKeon, *The Origins of the English Novel, 1600–1740;* Paul Salzman, *English Prose Fiction 1558–1700: A Critical History*

Realism, Naturalism, and the   73
New American Literary History
  by William E. Cain
    Review of Walter Benn Michaels, *The Gold Standard and the Logic of Naturalism*

The Dreiser Surge 85
   by Philip L. Gerber
      Review of Richard Lingeman, *Theodore Dreiser: At the Gates of the City, 1871–1907;* Thomas P. Riggio, ed., *Dreiser-Mencken Letters: The Correspondence of Theodore Dreiser and H. L. Mencken, 1907–1945*

Samuel Johnson and the Printed Word 97
   by Walter J. Ong
      Review of Alvin Kernan, *Printing Technology, Letters and Samuel Johnson;* Robert DeMaria, Jr., *Johnson's Dictionary and the Language of Learning;* Richard L. Harp, ed., *Dr. Johnson's Critical Vocabulary: A Selection from His Dictionary*

The Riot of Gorgeousness: 113
The Poetry and Prose of Marianne Moore
   by Sidney Burris
      Review of *The Complete Prose of Marianne Moore*, ed., Patricia C. Willis; Taffy Martin, *Marianne Moore: Subversive Modernist;* Grace Schulman, *Marianne Moore: The Poetry of Engagement;* John M. Slatin, *The Savage's Romance: The Poetry of Marianne Moore*

The Attenuated Self and Meta-Memoir 125
   by Panthea Reid Broughton
      Review of Virginia Woolf, *Moments of Being: Revised and Enlarged Edition,* ed., Jean Schulkind

Making Taliaferro Famus 137
   by Carl Ficken
      Review of Raymond C. Craig, ed., *The Humor of H. E. Taliaferro*

Documentary Editing: Critical, Noncritical, Uncritical 149
   by T. H. Howard-Hill
      Review of Mary-Jo Kline, *A Guide to Documentary Editing*

Contents ix

The Figure in the Carpet Bombing: 155
Pynchon's Patterns of Chaos
   by Dwight Eddins
      Review of Kathryn Hume, *Pynchon's Mythography: An Approach to* Gravity's Rainbow; *Thomas Moore, The Style of Connectedness:* Gravity's Rainbow *and Thomas Pynchon;* David Seed, *The Fictional Labyrinths of Thomas Pynchon*

The Evasion of Consensus 171
   by Jeffrey M. Perl
      Review of Gerald Graff, *Professing Literature: An Institutional History*

Historical Poe, Theoretical Poe 177
   by James M. Hutchisson
      Review of Dwight Thomas and David K. Jackson, *The Poe Log: A Documentary Life of Edgar Allan Poe, 1809–1849;* I. M. Walker, ed., *Edgar Allan Poe: The Critical Heritage;* J. Gerald Kennedy, *Poe, Death, and The Life of Writing*

The Lives of Sterne 193
   by W. G. Day
      Review of Arthur H. Cash, *Laurence Sterne, The Later Years;* Kenneth Monkman, *Sterne's Memoirs, A hitherto unrecorded holograph now brought to light in facsimile*

Thomas Wolfe and His Biographers 203
   by Richard S. Kennedy
      Review of David Herbert Donald, *Look Homeward, A Life of Thomas Wolfe*

Glimpses of the Henry James Who Earned His Living 211
   by Hershel Parker
      Review of Michael Anesko, *"Friction with the Market": Henry James and the Profession of Authorship*

G. Bernard Shaw: Losing or Saving Him 219
  by A. E. Wallace Maurer
    Review of Dan H. Laurence, *Bernard Shaw: A Bibliography*; Stanley Weintraub, ed., *Bernard Shaw: The Diaries, 1885–1897*

Studying the Studiers: A History of the 241
History of American Literature
  by James J. Martine
    Review of Kermit Vanderbilt, *American Literature and the Academy: The Roots, Growth, and Maturity of a Profession*

Crisis and Conversion in Jewish American Literature 251
  by Andrew Gordon
    Review of Mark Shechner, *After the Revolution: Studies in the Contemporary Jewish-American Imagination*

Jacobitism and Alexander Pope 267
  by Vincent Carretta
    Review of Douglas Brooks-Davies, *Pope's* Dunciad *and the Queen of the Night: A Study in Emotional Jacobitism*

Through the Looking-Glass, Shrewdly: 273
C. L. Dodgson and the Marketing of Lewis Carroll
  by Barry Menikoff
    Review of Morton N. Cohen and Anita Gandolfo, eds., *Lewis Carroll and the House of Macmillan*

A New Biography of Sherwood Anderson 285
  by James Schevill
    Review of Kim Townsend, *Sherwood Anderson: A Biography*; Hilbert H. Campbell, ed., *The Sherwood Anderson Diaries 1936–1941*

Correspondence 297

Contributors 303

Editorial Board

Felicia Bonaparte
City College, CUNY

Jerome H. Buckley
Harvard University

Paul Connolly
Yeshiva University

A. S. G. Edwards
University of Victoria

Ian Jack
Cambridge University

Robert Kellogg
University of Virginia

James R. Kincaid
University of Southern California

Cecil Y. Lang
University of Virginia

James B. Meriwether
University of South Carolina

Hershel Parker
University of Delaware

Martin Roth
University of Minnesota

George Stade
Columbia University

John L. Sharpe III
Duke University

G. Thomas Tanselle
John Simon Guggenheim Memorial Foundation

Stanley Weintraub
The Pennsylvania State University

The Culture of Priapism

James Grantham Turner

Aphra Behn. *Love-Letters Between a Nobleman and His Sister*, with a new introduction by Maureen Duffy. Virago Modern Classics. London: Virago, 1987. xviii, 462 pp.

Claude Reichler. *L'Age libertin*. Collection "Critique." Paris: Editions de Minuit, 1987. 137 pp.

Harold M. Weber. *The Restoration Rake-Hero: Transformations in Sexual Understanding in Seventeenth-Century England*. Madison: University of Wisconsin Press, 1986. x, 254 pp.

These three books, utterly different from one another, nevertheless represent useful materials and concepts for constructing a history of sexuality in the "libertine age." They deal only with the illicit side of sex—Behn fictionalizes the scandalous affair of Lord Grey and his sister-in-law, Reichler looks at *libertinage* in French literature, Weber examines the rake in English Restoration comedy—and thus make little use of the official discourse of marital sexuality or the emerging ideal of "companionate marriage." Within these limits, however, they throw light on an important phenomenon, or in Weber's terms a "transformation of sexual understanding," that took place during the seventeenth century. Extramarital sexuality emerges from the grotesque subculture, and becomes *heroic*. The seducer is no longer an ugly whoremaster, but a "Rake-Hero," genteel, dashing, and sublime; transgression is glorified by means of a heroic ideology and an elevated diction borrowed from Romance. In the words of one comedy-heroine, "Sublime Deserts may justify Desires."[1]

Behn's ill-fated lovers, for example, write of "glorious ruin," "mighty passion," "pleasures vast and unconfin'd," "the flight of generous love ... elevated above what we have seen yet on earth," and the "awful ceremony" of copulation; extremity and excess are the supreme good, dullness and confinement the greatest evil (pp. 20, 37, 39, 53, 66, 81, 97). So deeply did this mode of thinking permeate the English mind that even the sober William Petty, calculating methods of boosting the population by state-controlled polygamy, uses "The Great Man" and "The Hero" for the male to whom four wives would be assigned.[2] The military and political situation was obviously different in France, but there the ideology of "greatness" was even more developed, explicitly to justify and glorify the king's *amours* and those of his courtiers, from whom a certain symmetry was expected: conquests in the field and in the boudoir were equally *de rigueur*.[3] This equation of the "greatness" of passion and the "height" of refinement allows the emergence, not only of the masculine "Rake-Hero" and "libertin honnête," but of a female-authored sexual discourse—a perspective that neither Reichler nor Weber takes into account.

Space will not allow me a full analysis of Behn's novel, once immensely popular but more recently condemned and neglected. A detailed study of the *Love-Letters* is currently being undertaken by Judith Kegan Gardiner, who will relate them to Behn's whole *oeuvre* and draw out their implications for literary history. I will confine myself to passing references, suggesting that Behn's concerns are central to the history of libertinism. The remainder of this essay will thus concentrate on the work of the scholars Reichler and Weber.

Though they are primarily students of literature, both authors espouse a historical and cultural approach, and claim to uncover something distinctive about the period (Weber runs from Jacobean drama to *Les Liaisons dangereuses*, Reichler from de Viau to de Sade). Both assume that libertine history is a complex phenomenon. Weber's oft-asserted "complexity" and "ambivalence" rest on a rather simple binary model, however: firstly, the rake's passions struggle to be free, and society tames him; secondly, those passions are either sexual or aggressive, and the rake is good or bad according to which of the two predominates. Reichler's approach is more sophisticated. Although his references to Foucault are slight and noncommittal, he has absorbed the most important idea in Foucault's *Volunté de savoir*: that the history of sexuality cannot be written just in terms of "liberation" and "repression." For him the problematic and contradictory essence of libertinism belies its etymology; in trying to free the subject from the "representations" that alienate and repress, seventeenth-century libertines underestimate the power of those representations and fail to realize how deeply they are internalized. And the apparent triumph of sexual freedom in rococo France is a fiction, projected by *homo libertinus* to mask a deep sense of incompleteness. Weber on the other hand claims his affinity to Foucault prominently in the introduction, but operates entirely within the Whig or neo-Rousseauian model that Foucault has exploded, assuming a self-evident virtue in "freeing" the inner, natural, sexual self from the unhealthy constraints and repressions imposed by external authority.

Reichler's intellectual coherence is impressive, and his refusal to separate the seventeenth and eighteenth centuries is an important step forward; this involves not just the union of two periods, but the establishment of common ground between two meanings of "libertinism," anti-religious skepticism and sexual license. His method is to isolate the "conceptual kernel" within a variety of anti-authoritarian and amorous texts. Reichler's goal is not to write a history of ideas or to exemplify a theory of the "libertine text" (p. 10), but to discover the symbolic matrix or "modélisation" that underlies and explains the distinctive period and form of libertinism. As we shall see, the danger with such a bold project is that historical explanation and structuralist/anthropological analysis may come into conflict.

Reichler proposes a three-part history of French libertinism, each stage representing a different way of dealing with "man as subject of representations" (p. 9; the subject is always assumed to be male). For the first stage the central figure is Théophile de Viau, openly outrageous before his trial in 1623 and ostensibly compliant for the last three years of his life. (In his "Préambule" Reichler cites the Paduan materialists and even Calvin [though not Aretino] as starting-points of libertinism, but this sixteenth-century material conspicuously fails to reappear in the book itself.) This early stage, liberationist and confrontational, fell victim not just to external repression in "the first modern totalitarianism" (p. 17), but to internal contradictions—"the perverse dynamic of introjections and projections which leads the subject to devote himself to his own misfortune" (p. 19).

The second generation of libertines, compelled by Richelieu and Louis XIV to "s'affranchir sous le masque de la soumission" (p. 9), tried to subvert authority by miming its external forms while keeping their inner space ("for intérieur") independent, hedonistic, and untamed. At a crucial moment, then, libertine sexual discourse such as that of Nicolas Chorier, whose heroine advises strict dissimulation in order to guarantee unlimited secret pleasure, coincides with the hegemonic theories of *honnêteté* and the dominant values and procedures of polite society—*bienséance, vraisemblance, complaisance,* respect for the social game of conversation, the "retreat" or masking of the inner self (even though, paradoxically, it is only by penetrating the masks of others that one can truly bend oneself to their pleasure). The libertine's supple, detached conformity to social and stylistic expectations, the ease with which he slipped from place to place in a "verbal geography" (p. 27), effectively redefined *all* beliefs as local customs and all truths as received opinions, without actually running the danger of defying official ideologies. Nevertheless, Reichler argues, this apparent solution generated its own "problematic." The self may cleave to its mask, losing the capacity to distinguish the authentic but veiled interior from the ironically compliant exterior. Inverting the error of the first stage, this second generation gave so much weight to social representations that their autonomy was threatened, the inner self collapsing into "its own vacuity" (p. 37). Being and seeming converge. Such, to quote the title of Chapter 1, are the "paradoxes of conformism."

The third stage of libertinism, in the eighteenth century, acts out the problems implicit in the previous stages until a "double impasse" is reached. On the one hand, Reichler argues, excessive trust in the autonomy of the self leads to a fantasy of mastery and a complete denial of the social bond; on the other hand, the excesses of simulated compliance—surrender to role-playing, dependence on an audience, mechanical rehearsal of what should have been supple and spontaneous—reduce the self to a set of "characters in the social theatre" (p. 38). The cynical seducers and flimsy *petits-maîtres* of French fiction (and, we might add, Richardson's Lovelace) suffer from both these extremes at once, and thus reveal them as two sides of the same logical coin. Reichler's second chapter, named after Valmont's proclamation that "Conquérir est notre destin," explores this double impasse, beginning with the sense of emptiness and psychic mutilation that underlies the eighteenth-century libertine's illusions of conquest. He identifies a cycle of idealization, mastery, and disillusion in a number of sexual initiation novels, and connects it to the construction of "woman" as an unattainable object, an unknowable mystery. This theme spirals out into sections on female fainting, on heroines of obscure birth, on incest and enclosure in pornography—all ingeniously if tenuously linked to the central theme, the sense of "incompleteness" in the masculine imagination.

The individual sections of Chapters 1 and 2 are thought-provoking even when they seem tangential, and Reichler's account of the eighteenth-century stage is particularly convincing—perhaps because it is anchored in the analysis of a single author, Crébillon *fils*. It is refreshing, too, to see de Sade correctly placed as the *terminus* of ancien-régime libertinism rather than as a heroic precursor of modernity. But a history so schematic, confidently sketched on the basis of highly selective and diverse evidence, is bound to provoke some objections. His chronological stages, for example, may be undermined by significant counter-examples. Deceitful conformism (or "Nicodemism") was already associated with the religious "Libertines" attacked by Calvin in the sixteenth century, and Garasse gave it a prominent place in his 1623 assault on de Viau and his circle. And in the generations after de Viau some libertines do confront the authorities and die impenitent, like Ferrante Pallavicino in Italy and Claude Le Petit in France; others, with less risk, cultivate a deliberate incivility of language and behavior to reinforce their privileged or "franchised" status—the circle of Charles II is an obvious example, but obscene burlesques like Bussy-Rabutin's *Comtesse d'Olonne* (c. 1670) or Alexis Piron's "Ode à Priape" (c.

1740) show that de Viau's outrageous manner did not die out in France. Indeed, French erotic dialogues like *L'Ecole des filles* (1656) or Chorier's *Satyra Sotadica* (1660–68), cited to prove the ethos of dissimulation, revel in a stylish rudeness that could hardly be assimilated into polite "conversation"; Rochester's oxymoronic praise of Sedley, as a poet "mannerly obscene," better describes this characteristic libertine effect. Given the pioneering boldness of Italian libertinism and the constant cultural exchange between England and France, Reichler would have done better to admit more non-French materials into his reading list.

Another problem created by Reichler's range and virtuosity is that of defining libertinism too broadly. A figure like Descartes, with his motto *larvatus prodeo* and his theory of an essential divide between extension and inner cognition, would seem to fit the second-stage criteria exactly, and yet who would classify him as a libertine? (Perhaps for this reason, Reichler does not mention him.) And surely the cycle of idealization, disillusionment, and pursuit of the unattainable is not specific to libertinism? Yet such a "structure" is proposed as a diagnostic criterion, "at once formal, thematic, and historical," of whether a given text is libertine or not (p. 49).

Reichler's model of libertinism is powerful and suggestive, but it does not really account for an important preoccupation of the period, the representation of female sexuality. He insists, rightly, that libertinism is constituted by its problematic, its anguish, its ambivalence, and yet he describes a quintessentially libertine test like Nerciat's *Félicia* (1775) as if it were wholly devoid of "équivoque" or "ontological problematics," expressing nothing but a free-floating "epicurism of the heart and the senses" (p. 72). I would refer this to the semantic instability of the word "libertinage" itself, which covers a large range of trangressions from mass murder to the "petits libertinages" permitted at home on Shrove Tuesday.[4] Reichler's solution is to divide libertine narration into two kinds. In one the narrator (often female) shows "total confidence in the epiphanic capacity of language": her sexual experiences, her descriptions, and her real self are identical and equally "transparent" (p. 78). (His examples include *Fanny Hill*, in a French version, but he seems unaware of the important passage at the start of Letter 2, when Fanny laments the difficulty of finding varied language for an experience that is all the same "at bottom.") In the other mode, the narrator is the unsatisfied lover, trying in vain to close the distance between himself and the unattainable, thickening the "mystery of woman" the more he tries to pierce it. Language brings instead "another knowledge," a compensatory and imaginary meaning that is projected into the empty space. But is this really a dichotomy? Reichler does say finally that the male author's quest for the "secret of woman" (and the use of female narrators) is actually a key to open "his *own* intimacy" (p. 78). But he does not explore the connection between this masculine self-referentiality and the creation of female libertine narrators, fantasies of untroubled confidence in sex and language. And in sidestepping this question he also avoids another complication of his chronological scheme: the female narrator/initiatrice did not appear with *Fanny Hill* or *Félicia*, but was the central figure in virtually all the erotic dialogues from Aretino's *Ragionamenti* onwards.[5]

Indeed, apart from a brief reference to *La Princesse de Clèves* Reichler examines no female-authored texts, and most of the time he talks of female characters in male fiction as if they were real "women."[6] At the same time, he discusses a figure like Suzanne in the pornographic *Portier des Chartreux* as if she were subject to the same inner vacuities as men, as if male and female libertines were the same, even though all the constituent conditions he identifies (the compulsion to pursue sex as knowledge, the cycle of illusion, conquest, and disgust, the polarization of the opposite sex into Virgins and Whores) are specific to the situation of the male in a culture that lives by the double standard. Reichler does occasionally show a political awareness of gender, an awareness that reality is structured differently for men and women according to their different relations to power and sexual ideology, and that all dealings between the sexes, including those imagined in literature, must be inescapably determined by considerations of power. He sees that the whole idea of female mystery is "constructed" (p. 60), and that the cult of clandestine knowledge is an act of aggression: the libertine "parades this mysterious knowledge before the doors of the Gynecaeum" (p.

77). The exploration of the supposed nature of women is understood as a gesture *against* them, but at the same time the central tenet of this ideology, the Mystery, is reaffirmed in the image of a "gynécée" with closed doors. At several points, in fact, he lapses into an "essentialist" language, speaking as if woman actually *is* a mystery.

Reichler's third chapter, "Le Corps au Péril des Images," is the most wide-ranging. It begins, promisingly, with the representation of the body in sexually explicit fiction, and assumes throughout that body and text are closely related; on the one hand "the body is only intelligible when it is represented," on the other hand representation is inseparable from the phenomenological "transformation" it produces (p. 111). The main threads of the book are continued in this analysis: representing the body in words reenacts the tension between public and private, and manifests the "fantasme de maîtrise" and the "relation d'incomplétude" already identified with the masculine-libertine imagination (p. 81). Rather than tracing this theme through the erotic dialogues of the seventeenth century, where the relation between bodily reality and imagination is of central importance, Reichler works more selectively, picking out a few paradigmatic scenes from *Thérèse philosophe* (1748) and *Le Portier des Chartreux (L'Histoire de Dom B.)* (1742), and constructing on this basis a matrix-diagram of the deep structure of representation. Between the pornographic fragments and the structuralist diagram displayed at the end of the chapter, Reichler undertakes an ambitious journey through ancient and modern literature, following themes only loosely related to the opening analysis: *Beauty and the Beast*, the dream-vision of a dead mother who cannot be grasped, the meeting of Isolde and the lepers. Only two of these texts come from libertine authors, an obscene sonnet by de Viau and a striking letter in which de Sade describes his dream of Petrarch's Laura.[7] Clearly Reichler wants to bring in the great canonical names and so claim a more general significance for his essay, but in thus universalizing his topic he runs the risk of losing his grip on "l'age libertin" itself. The material is too diverse to throw light on the period, and one suspects that historical curiosity has been sacrificed to the scientific urge, the

The Culture of Priapism

Casaubon-like desire to find the deep structure that underlies all myths and all texts.[8]

Reichler certainly does isolate some of the important polarities in libertine representation. In the voyeur-scenes of *Thérèse philosophe*, for example, he rightly identifies an "opposition" between the grotesque Father Dirrag (described in a style as strained and metaphorical as the Father's own approach to seduction) and the "natural" fondlings of Thérèse's enlightened mentors (which she presents in a more plain and relaxed style). On this basis he makes the Noble/Vile antithesis one of the fundamental axes of his diagram. But this essential dichotomy is treated symbolically rather than historically, in isolation rather than in context; Reichler does not recognize that it recapitulates the central theme of a century of libertine texts, from *L'Ecole des filles* to La Mettrie's *L'Ecole de la volupté*—the distinction between the high voluptuary, who turns sex into a conscious work of art, and the low debauchee who is little better than an animal. An essential condition for the evolution of a heroic or sublime form of libertinism, in fact, is that both clandestine pornography and *précieux* love-discourse agreed on this distinction. In Behn's *Love-Letters* for example, a text hovering between scandal and romance, Philander despises the "hot brute" driven by mere physical desire, while exalting his own equally sexual love as "a nobler fire," and Behn herself, as narrator, endorses this hierarchy if not the character who utters it: "Love in a mean unthinking soul, is not that glorious thing it is in the brave" (pp. 92, 261).

Again, Reichler correctly stresses the imitative reciprocity between "natural" image and sexual act in these mid-eighteenth-century erotic texts, but he does not pursue its ramifications, being impatient to launch into Homer and Proust. Thus he does not give full weight to the extraordinary ending of the *Portier des Chartreux*, when death and mutilation suddenly flood into the narrative, producing a grimly literal image of the boredom and vacuity that appear from time to time beneath the strenuous copulation; the relation between seeing and doing must suddenly be reinterpreted when we learn that the narrator is a eunuch. Nor does he do justice to the narrative pattern of *Thérèse philosophe*. The book ends when Thérèse, who has allowed the Count every favor but the last, wagers that she can spend days in his library and art gallery without succumbing fully. (The library is itself a recapitulation of the canonical texts of erotic libertinism from Chorier onwards.) These images produce in her, not exactly an imitation (since she is still a virgin), but an erotic reverie that blurs the distinction between representation and reality; she cries out for her lover, who appears, like an embodiment of the picture that entrances her, to consummate their affair. Only *then* does she begin the narrative of her life, which in turn (she tells us at the beginning of the book) will form the "backdrop" to future embraces. Sexual fulfillment thus opens up a mutually generating cycle of representation and action. But the other narrative embedded in the text, that of Thérèse's friend Bois-Laurier, puts this idyllic arrangement into question. It suggests a quite different relation between erotic wholeness and narrative authority, since Bois-Laurier, the procuress and erotic metteuse-en-scène, was born without sexual organs.

These criticisms merely show that Reichler's briefly sketched insights do indeed have a historic resonance when they are closely applied to the texts of the period. But in elaborating the second deep polarity of his diagram, Reichler runs the risk of distorting libertinism itself. Put briefly, Reichler distinguishes representations of the body into two fundamental kinds, according to whether they originate as responses to "l'Interdit" (prohibition) or to "le Deuil" (grief, abandonment, death). Libertinism adheres mostly to the former kind, producing images that run from innocent voluptuousness (Noble) down to bestial violence (Vile). Romantic representations belong mostly to the latter kind, ranging from the Sublime (the ghosts of the departed in Hades, the mother who returns in a dream) down to the mortifying (the lepers who embrace Isolde).

This grid holds true for the examples selected to prove it; but in fact, as I have suggested, the most important movement within libertinism would confound it. I mean the attempt to locate sublimity, not in evanescence or disembodiment, but *within* sexuality itself—in a free and heroic image of love that remains frankly physical and extramarital. The court entertain-

The Culture of Priapism 11

ments of Louis XIV, for example, glorify his sexual conquests in the vocabulary of quasi-divine Greatness, and the incestuous couple in Behn's *Love-Letters* elevate their forbidden desires into a glamorous and sublime transgression:

> Your beauty should . . . force all obligations, all laws, all ties even of nature's self: you, my lovely maid, were not born to be obtained by the dull methods of ordinary loving. . . . Let us (born for mightier joys) scorn the dull *beaten road*, . . . let us look forward to pleasures vast and unconfined. [pp. 3, 4, 20]

Examples abound in Reichler's own area of reading: the ending of Fanny Hill's *Memoirs* is clearly an exercise in sublimity, as is Diderot's article "Jouissance" and the whole of La Mettrie's *La Volupté*, which explicitly aspires to "la sublime de la poésie."[9] It is Laclos's Marquise de Merteuil, in fact, who sums up the erotic sublime when she contrasts the insipid embraces of the Présidente (as she imagines them for Valmont's benefit) with the libertine idea, "cet entier abandon de soi-même, ce délire de la volupté où le plaisir s'épure par son excès" (*Les Liaisons dangereuses*, letter 5). Reichler recognizes the Sublime in the storm that carries off the modest Virginie, a force opposed to sexuality (p. 109), but not in the innumerable equations of sexual passion and tempest that run through heroic drama and love-theory. He does discover sublimity in one of his priapic texts—de Viau's sonnet, from the early "offensive" stage—but his own system of oppositions forces him to identify this as an "aberrant hybrid."[10] On the contrary, it is central to the libertine age.

Many of Reichler's perceptions can be fruitfully applied to English libertinism too, even though we must recognize important social and political differences that separate England from France. The idea of cultural "geography," for example, is even more relevant to England than to the more stratified culture of France; a figure like Rochester can slide between different self-representations—the brilliant courtier, the drunken hooligan, the City moralist, the devoted country squire—precisely because the social structure of England (and particularly London) provided different "worlds" in close proximity, each with its own character and style.[11] The three-stage model of libertinism, progressing from naive confrontation to assimilation and then to fantasies of Titanic mastery, is also useful for analyzing the English material, though a different political history means that these chronological stages are delayed or conflated. In England the weak hegemony of Charles I, and then the Puritan revolution, created a reactionary and compensatory "Cavalier" hedonism that, for several observers, reproduced the fanatical extremism that it ostensibly opposed.[12] We should be careful not to assume that English libertinism is a purely Restoration and Royalist phenomenon, however; Aubrey's description of the regicides Henry Marten and Thomas Challoner shows that the "English Revolution" could produce its own libertines.

The authority structure in England was also quite different, as a consequence (or perhaps a cause) of this upheaval. Whereas the French courtier had to live under an absolute monarch who was simultaneously the supreme repressor and the ultimate libertine (as Reichler shows in his last chapter), a figure like Rochester suffered because "he found no Body of Quality or Severity so much above him, to challenge a Deference," and served a king who restlessly "rolled about from whore to whore" and had to be provoked into exerting the power of royal displeasure.[13] A similar uneasy mixture of acceptance and rebellion governed submission to the rules of polite society. Etherege's Dorimant, for example, is obviously held up as a model of up-to-the-minute gallantry, and yet his conversation (particularly with women) is more violent and provocative than would have been tolerated in the *salon*. The excessive conformity of polite conversation is thus less of a problem in England, where a more "biting" and assertive style prevailed. (Parson Yorick would later say that the civility of the French eroded their individuality, like coins worn smooth by too much handling.) But if the English *beau monde* did not fear the loss of self in general conformity, it certainly dreaded another of the dangers that Reichler has identified in libertinism—that of mechanization, stereotypy and routinization. Such a fear clearly underlies the constant satire against Foplings and Witwoulds in the comedy. Despite his cultivated brutality, a figure like Dorimant still shares many features of Reichler's "libertin honnête," such as the supple triumph over mechanical imitation, or the mastery of ironically civil dissimulation that guarantees his private world of freedom and pleasure. Wycherley's Horner does the same, but in a far coarser way; he does not make use of the forms of polite conversation, as Dorimant does, and so must be regarded as a low or grotesque version of the topos.

All the tensions that Reichler discovers in French libertinism rise to memorable expression in Richardson's Lovelace, who grasps in a moment of despair that there is nothing to distinguish the active rake-hero from the passive fopling or *petit-maître*: he is "*compelled* to be the wretch my choice has made me," and he is therefore no more than "a machine at last, and no free agent" (Everyman edn., III. 146). What Reichler says of de Sade may be applied also to him—that he sums up the libertine tradition but also turns it into madness, just as Don Quixote had done for chivalry (p. 48). Lovelace embodies perfectly the "double impasse" of the third-stage libertine, simultaneously too confident in his inner powers and too ready to throw the blame onto the way of the world, unable to escape the circle of idealization, mastery and disillusion except by entering another endless path, the quest for an unattainable object. And his deadlock with Clarissa may be understood in terms of Reichler's fruitful suggestion—made in the course of a rather risky speculation on why Crébillon left his novels unfinished—that the desire for a neat and harmonious ending to the libertine quest, the comic reclamation of the rake that Clarissa and her friends deceive themselves into hoping for Lovelace, is actually *unrealizable* in serious fiction (pp. 50–51). Reichler also recognizes the dilemma that paralyzes Lovelace, that the triumph of libertine knowledge is inextricably linked to pain—not for the woman alone, as one might expect, but for the disillusioned rake himself.[14]

This Richardsonian view of English libertinism is not shared by Weber, who devotes only a few words to Lovelace. The reference comes in the last chapter, "Sexual Discourse in the Eighteenth Century," where he is cited to show the persistence, or recrudescence, of a "demonic" view of sexuality. Lovelace is thus *contrasted*, rather than aligned, with the "Restoration Rake-Hero" of Weber's title, since the "demonic" vision belongs to the first half of the seventeenth century, and the quintessential libertine emerges only when this archaic religious conception is thrown aside.

The stages of libertine history, as Weber interprets it, are reflected in his chapter headings. First comes "The Rhetoric of Demonic Sexuality in Jacobean Drama," where Weber argues that not just the drama, but the whole "Renaissance" period, equates sexuality with Satanic possession and thus locates it outside the true self. Then comes the first and most important "transformation in sexual understanding," pioneered by the comic seducers of the 1670s and 1680s; spurning the hated restrictions of marriage, glimpsing for the first time a secular vision of unlimited sexual pleasure in which they invest their entire identity, they bring health and vitality to a repressive society. This sexual revolution is itself subdivided into two stages, according to a hint borrowed from Maximillian Novak: in the 70s we see "The Hobbesian Libertine-Rake" (Chapter 2), and in Congreve we arrive at "The Philosophical Libertine: 'Artist in the Science of Voluptuousness'" (Chapter 3). As the refinement of the libertine increases with these stages, so apparently do his problems; either the aggressive impulse grows at the expense of the pure sexuality that defined him in the first place, or else he loses both sex and power to become a sort of eunuch. In Chapter 4 we switch to a parallel history, that of "The Female Libertine" in drama, which likewise passes from the demonic Jacobean period to the free Restoration, and thence to an over-aggressive decadence. The fifth and final chapter, as we have seen, takes us into the eighteenth century, where all the previous themes (Satanism, hedonism, aggression, refinement) recur in abundance. What is distinctive about this later period is that, whereas before only one mode operated at a time—the entire seventeenth century is now, rather confusingly, labelled "demonic"—in the eighteenth century we encounter a proliferation of different styles or "discourses." There is, however, a general tendency to replace sex with economics: "Horner's generous desires to 'spend' and exhaust his supplies of china have been converted into Moll [Flanders]'s relentless desire to horde [sic] her substance" (p. 199).

Weber assumes that the sexual appetite of the rake represents an unbridled "individual will," whereas the role of "society" is to clamp down these desires and restrict each man to one woman in a nuclear family. (Until the fourth chapter these noble victims of societal repression are always assumed to be male.) The individual who refuses to be tamed is either expelled as a criminal or (if he is talented or high-born) made into a "rake-hero," threatening the orderliness of "society" but at the same time infusing it with a much needed vitality (pp. 5–6, citing Freud). This polarity may have made sense in nineteenth-century Vienna, but it is clearly inapplicable to Restoration England, when the King's ministers were *advised* to take mistresses so as not to appear disloyal. The fashionable world expected the man to indulge in conquests—though respectable women were of course held to a different standard—and such attitudes soon spread through the minor squirearchy: Fielding's Squire Western, the fanatical preserver of his own daughter, assumes that the young fellow will naturally get bastards and that "the women will like un the better for 't" (*Tom Jones*, IV.x). It is precisely "society" and social expectations that force Valmont to ruin the Présidente, and which reduce Lovelace to "a machine"; though at first he uses the rhetoric of "imperial will" to glorify his illicit intentions, he comes to realize that to reform, to breach the libertine character expected by his "confraternity," would be the *real* act of individuality.[15] Consequently it is misleading to present the rake-hero as a radical figure, and to label objectors such as Blackmore "conservative" (p. 7). Historically, the moralists represent a new Whiggish order, and the rake, despite his modishness, is a throwback, a boudoir version of the old absolutism.

It is even more perilous to claim, as one's principal thesis, that "the rake's career on the Restoration stage initiates the modern 'discourse' on sexuality, for the rake represents the initial attempts of English culture to transfer control of sexuality from the divine to the secular world" (pp. 10, 179). Firstly one must ask how "English culture" can be deduced from a handful of comedies; Weber's selection of texts is far too limited to warrant such representative claims—he gives disproportionate space to drama, and his non-dramatic material often seems filtered through other scholars.[16] Secondly one must recognize conflicting models of the secularization process. Why, for example, was it the *Puritans*, not the rakish Cavaliers, who first transferred marriage from the ecclesiastical to the civil law (p. 51)? And why did a contemporary like Butler see Restoration libertinism not as a secular movement, but as an inverted form of religious fanaticism?

Weber's entire case rests on his contention that the "demonic" dominates the conception of sexuality before the Restoration, and that the advent of the rake "released" England from its grip. Satanic imagery continues to be widespread, of course (Weber himself shows how pervasive it is in *The Double-Dealer* and *The London Merchant*, and he might have added Etherege's depiction of Dorimant as a fallen angel), but it has somehow become fragmented, removed from its primary status as an expression of belief. Weber's account of "Jacobean thought" often rests on unsupported generalizations, however, such as "Renaissance psychology and medicine treated erotic love as a disease," or "theologians occasionally envisioned an Edenic state *sans* sexual intercourse" (pp. 17, 48). In fact medical theory treated any humoral imbalance as a disease and prescribed sexual intercourse for certain conditions, while all theologians held that Adam and Eve would have enjoyed a full sexual life if they had not fallen so soon; many Jacobean divines encouraged married couples to recreate the happiness of Eden and the Song of Solomon, "erring" and "being ravished" in their sexual "due benevolence."[17] Satan could be associated with sexual perversion, but only an extremist like James I would openly associate the Devil and the genitals (p. 25), and he presumably forgot this while he was fondling the Duke of Buckingham's codpiece. Weber's grim picture is created by selective quotation, ignoring the coexistence (in both life and art) of religious and secular attitudes, ease and discomfort, fear of sex and delight in it. When the prosecutor condemned the Earl of Castlehaven for multiple rape and buggery, he compared him not to Satan but to the Emperor Tiberius.[18] For every Penitent Brothel there is a Falstaff or a Doll Tearsheet, for every White Devil a Rosalind. Weber recognizes that the comedy of this period celebrates sexuality in a festive spirit (pp. 35, 68), and yet he draws all his evidence from a few

The Culture of Priapism

dark Jacobean plays, hybrids between comedy and satire, with strong infusions of tragedy. Even his chosen examples show that sexuality could be conceived in many different ways—as an evil possession, as a farcical pantomime, as "Ambrosia of Delight," or as an expression of freedom.[19] No one doubts that there was a *drift* towards more secular attitudes, but Weber's attempts to universalize his claim and to homogenize the earlier period involve some sleight of hand; on page 17 sex is associated with the demonic only "at the furthest range of metaphor," on page 18 Jacobean society "normally" made the connection, and by page 19 sex is "invariably" seen as demonic or divine.[20] To this fabricated consistency he adds an argument from hindsight—that demonic associations "inhibit" or "prevent" the development of the rake-hero, and "displace" his sexual energies.

Weber's secularization thesis does have one advantage, however: it refers to libertinism as an attempt to *"control"* rather than to liberate sexuality. This obviously contradicts the Dionysiac model that he assumes elsewhere, and reminds us that orderliness, method, and scientific rationalization, far from being imposed on the libertine from without, lay at the heart of his enterprise. When Rochester promises his wife that he has "a sence of what the methods of my Life seeme so utterly to contradict," true feeling is associated with married life in the country and "method" with the libertine sexuality of London.[21] The libertine was faced with the problem of retaining all the advantages of Method while avoiding the pitfalls of Mechanization. Behn's *Love-Letters* express this effectively, by splitting the seducer role into the sublime Philander, who rails against "the dull methods of ordinary loving," and the mean villain Brilliard, who "fancied himself a very *Machiavel*" (p. 148)—though each turns out to be equally corrupt. Weber does try to assimilate the calculating and dominant aspect of libertinism into his model, by distinguishing the true sexual hero (Horner) from the "frigid Machiavellian" (Dorimant), in whom the aggressive urge to control has grown so strong that it threatens to swallow up his natural libido. It should therefore be Dorimant who confronts a recently seduced mistress with his intention to sleep with all her friends and threaten them with blackmail, as the only effective way to "silence censorious women"—crowning his threat (which he proceeds to carry out) with the boast that "I am a *Machiavel* in love." But in fact it is Horner in *The Country-Wife* (IV.iii).

The principal distinctions within Weber's Restoration section may thus be brought into question. On what basis, for example, does he distinguish the first, "Hobbesian," type of rake from the second, "philosophical," type? (Actually the first and commonest stage libertine, like Etherege's Sir Frederick Frollick, is neither one nor the other, but a Hooray Henry who throws stones through whores' windows [cf. p. 78].) How can a character named after a major philosopher be *opposed* to the "philosophical" type? Since the main feature of the "philosophical" rake is his assimilation of *honnêteté* (p. 96), why should the elegant Dorimant be classed as a Hobbesian rather than a *libertin honnête*? It is in the 70s, not in the 90s, that Shadwell's rake-hero quotes Lucretius and Wycherley's Horner confronts the ladies with "the second Part of the *Escole des Filles*," that is, *La Philosophie des Dames*; it was the 70s that another stage-rake called "this quick-sighted Philosophical Age, wherein whoring is improv'd to a liberal Science."[22] The relation between sexuality and philosophy, which continued to fascinate the comedians of wit, was never simply a question of refinement. In Vanbrugh's *Provoked Wife*, for example, the suffering wife blames "old foolish Philosophers" for loading women with "fine notions of Virtue" that prevent her from taking a lover (I.i), whereas the French maid evokes philosophy to justify complete sexual abandon:

Lady Fancifull. Why sure you wou'd not sacrifice your Honor to your Pleasure?
Mademoiselle. Je suis Philosophe. [I.ii]

In Behn's *Love-Letters*, again, "philosophy" is linked to "the arts and politics of love," the cynical but realistic analysis that the high-born libertines, male and female, share with their servants; it represents the lower stratum of sexual understanding, in contrast to the high rhetoric of "immense passion" and ecstatic excess they present to each other (pp. 143, 181). To the extent that the rake becomes heroic in this fiction, it is by embracing the libertine sublime and concealing the "philosophy" that dictates fickleness and new conquests for the man, dissimulation and survival for the woman.

Weber seems unconcerned with these tangled associations, and (despite his taxonomic labels) uninterested in exploring the connections between the stage-rake and intellectual history. His references to "the naturalism of Machiavelli and Hobbes" (p. 53), and his attack on marriage as "an unnatural arrangement that undermines people's attempt to locate themselves in a Hobbesian state of nature" (p. 111), suggest that he is unfamiliar with these authors; why would people *want* to make their lives nasty, brutish, and short? To document the second stage Weber cites general statements from Blount, Temple, and Saint-Evremond about pleasure—*not* about sexual love, which for Saint-Evremond formed an exception to his general rule of moderation—and then abandons almost entirely his attempt to link the rake-hero to a new "philosophical" mentality.[23] His analysis of the "perverse refinement" of *The Way of the World* is a refreshing exception, however.

Weber ironically misses the relevance of what Hobbes *does* offer, namely an irreducibly political and semiotic analysis of the human condition, in which all passions are shown to be reducible to "signs of Power." To this extent Horner *is* a Hobbesian. Like everyone else in the play, he seems obsessed with "signs" and compelled to find some infallible hermeneutic device to tell "right" women from unavailable ones: "One knows not where to find 'em, who will, or will not" (I.i). Interestingly (in view of Reichler's analysis), Horner feels that this trickery is forced upon him because fashionable civility is now indistinguishable from the look of amorous willingness; the poor male finds himself adrift in a sea of appearances, unable to penetrate to the sexual interior. He could stick to acknowledged whores and established mistresses, of course, but he evidently regards them with horror (his eunuch trick is designed as much to rid him of these "Duns" as to make new conquests). This suggests that his primary motivation is not sexual appetite, but the game of deciphering and the triumph of unmasking. The case of Horner confirms Reichler's assumption that sex and the body are always apprehended as *representations*. Indeed, Reichler offers a clue to the "philosophical libertine" in general, precisely because, unlike Weber, he looks for the philosophic implications *immanent* in the act of sexual pursuit itself, rather than treating philosophy as something additional or superficial: he detects, beneath the apparent aimlessness and compulsive repetition of the seducer, "un besoin de savoir insatiable, une compulsion de vérification; la rationalité tactique introduite dans les rapports entre les sexes apparaît comme une force d'enquête jamais apaisée" (p. 59).

Neither Reichler nor Weber, however, fully grasps the necessity of reading libertinism politically, according to Hobbes's insight that *all* ideals and *all* professed motives can be analyzed into power relations. Weber does pursue what Behn calls "the arts and politics of love," but intermittently. He does read Congreve's *Love for Love* as an attack on a corrupt society (though regarding Miss Prue as a symptom of this malaise may seem far-fetched), and he does devote an interesting chapter to "The Female Libertine on the Restoration Stage." Weber recognizes that women relate differently to the prevailing ideology, that under the double standard they are more restricted in their sexual roles and more vulnerable to ruin, even in the supposedly free Court society. (He could have made this point more effectively, however, by reminding us of the lack of contraception and the horrors of childbirth, or by citing the evidence of women themselves; Behn's *Love-Letters* make it clear that the errant woman will be "loathed, undone and infamous as hell, despis'd, scorn'd . . . lampoon'd, perhaps diseased"—and as the story develops abandoned by her seducer during her pregnancy [p. 72].) Weber understands, in the case of the professional actress, that an apparent freedom for women may enclose them still further in male-imposed sexual categories. He acknowledges the masculine need to boost a "disintegrating Self" by forcing negative images onto the opposite sex, and he brings in Mary Astell and Sarah Fige [Egerton] to prove that women themselves could counter such charges. Weber shows that new images of female freedom generate fear and loathing as well as fascination, though his "de-demonization" thesis leaves him at a loss to explain why virulent attacks on female sinfulness, and the imagery

The Culture of Priapism

of the "common sewer" (p. 135), actually increase in Restoration lampoons and misogynist satires.

Weber's important insights into male representations of female sexuality are not consistently applied to the texts themselves, however. Like Reichler, he will slip into an essentialist language of gender. He speaks as if the female libertine actually existed, as if male-ordered female characters are real women and their assertiveness somehow equivalent to the self-assertion of women themselves. He will sometimes assume that qualities projected onto female characters are intrinsic properties of the sex: in an otherwise sensitive account of Southerne's *Sir Anthony Love* and *The Wives Excuse*, for example, he asserts that the fear and trembling of Viola show "essential femininity" or that the expulsion of a female libertine "reveals the depth of her depravity, both her antisocial nature and . . . her vicious conception of freedom" (pp. 166, 176). On the other hand, he will assume that "the rake" constitutes a single essence with a single history underlying the difference of gender. Thus Southerne's Mrs. Wittwould "most fully reveals the degraded nature of the rake-hero," and Horner's sexual generosity is "converted into" the parsimony of Moll Flanders. (Weber than digs himself deeper by weighing Moll's "many female traits" against her "essentially masculine nature.") Such essentialist treatment of literary characters is hard to reconcile with the frequent assertion that the female libertine is a mere "male fantasy."[24]

I know it is hard to summarize plots without slipping into the convenient shorthand of gender labels, but we should always be aware that male-authored "females" are *representations* in the complex sense developed by Reichler or the New Historicists. They are ideological theses, projections, compounds of satire, didacticism, fantasy, and realistic observation. They may be rejected (as feminist critics of the time were quick to do), but they may be powerful and plausible enough to be internalized. Such representations *relate* to the world rather than reflecting it or concealing it: to treat them as pure fantasy is to distance them from their own "reality-effect"; to treat them as direct evidence of the condition of women is to ignore their ontological complexity, their Pygmalionesque status as ideology made flesh. Male-authored females ("I's" in drag, as Nancy Miller calls them) may embody pertinent criticism and valid psychological observation, and they may develop a certain animation and autonomy beyond what their author would license in "real life"; Pygmalion may become Frankenstein. But they cannot be separated from sexual politics. The same is true for the characters of women writers, though their political situation is obviously different: when Behn creates a female libertine more sublime and at times more resolute than her deceitful male counterpart, prouder of her "glorious ruin" and more contemptuous of the "dull" routine of marriage, it must be seen as an expropriation, as a critical response to a heroic ideology that hitherto served only the male.[25]

Weber's book, then, suffers from a divergence between its political insights and its working assumptions, between its historical backgrounding and its literary analysis. In a section on the status of women, for example, he mentions that seventy-two female-authored plays were produced in London between 1660 and 1720 (p. 151). But he does not examine any of them—not even Behn's *The Rover*, which he dismisses as "conventional" while devoting many glowing pages to its source, Killigrew's *Thomaso, or the Wanderer*. Behn did not simply rescue the workable scenes from Killigrew's sprawling closet drama, however, but reblocked it to give the female parts greater prominence. She created a new female character to match the masculine rake, a virtuous heiress who is nevertheless "very free and witty," and whose part includes lines that in Killigrew were confined to the underworld of prostitution.[26] Behn also makes the courtesan Angellica stronger and more sympathetic, whereas in Killigrew she is accused of "moral corruption" (p. 156), and she provides new scenes of female initiative such as the Carnival scene (I.ii), where the double standard is temporarily suspended. In short, *The Rover* is crucial for the understanding of libertinism, disguise, and sexual freedom from a female point of view. Surely we would expect a more detailed comparison of the two texts? Nor does Weber deal with the undisputed classic, Mme de Lafayette's *Princesse de Clèves*, which again focuses on the troubled female response to a magnificent libertine, and her eventual decision to reject him because his libertinism must lead to her betrayal—a powerfully moving scene that survives even in Nathaniel Lee's adaptation. This omission is particularly glaring because Weber lavishes attention on Lee's grossly inferior stage version, in which Nemours's high libertinism degenerates into a bizarre mixture, part verse-speaking romantic lover and part prosaic stage-rake.

Though his analysis of individual plays can be persuasive, Weber's claim to trace major historical changes—"transformations in sexual understanding"—is weakened by the selectivity of his reading and by his unwillingness to give full weight to gender, class, and literary genre. Differences in period can only be convincing if like is compared to like. Weber's Restoration examples are restricted to "a single genre, the comedy of manners" (p. 183)—the sexual overreachers of heroic drama are barely mentioned—but the key texts from the Jacobean and Augustan periods are not comedies at all. Thus he takes a murderous prostitute from lower-middle-class tragedy (Millwood in Lillo's *London Merchant*) and compares her to breeches-part heroines from upper-class comedy, in order to show how "the rake" has changed between the pleasure-loving Restoration and the business-obsessed eighteenth century. Or else he asserts that the figure who comes closest to Moll Flanders (the female *picara* from the underclass of literature and society, forced to choose between hedonism and economic survival) is Vainlove, the over-delicate fopling of Congreve's first comedy. In this process of simplification Weber obscures a genuinely fascinating issue, the tangled relationship of "business" and "pleasure" throughout the Restoration and eighteenth century.

In trying to persuade us of a fundamental difference between the Age of Sex and the Age of Money, Weber sometimes distorts the texts that are most central to his study. Describing attitudes towards sexuality in Gay's *Beggar's Opera*, for example, he exaggerates the contrast between the mercenary Peachums and the libertine highwaymen. Polly is tarred with the same brush as her father, and Peachum's attack on marriage is quoted as if economics were his sole concern, whereas in fact he says that Polly should guarantee her pleasure by *not* making herself "a property" (p. 204). (The same issue is in any case central to the Restoration: for Dorimant, the world is divided into people one enjoys as "friends" and those one uses as "properties" [V.i], and both Sylvia and Philander, in Behn's *Love-Letters*, make her lesser admirers into "a property" [pp. 110, 162, 252].) The highwaymen, on the other hand, are treated in the most glowing terms, at least until Macheath's betrayal. Like Horner, they are motivated by "a generous desire to spend their substance." Macheath is "one of the most erotically powerful of literary creations" (this in a book that gives only half a sentence to Lovelace and never mentions Don Giovanni), who triumphs over the vulgar consumerist mentality when he declares that "I must have women. There is nothing unbends the mind like them. Money is not so strong a cordial." When Macheath distinguishes "his eight women" by name and offers them a choice of wine or gin, this shows that he respects their individuality and their right to full enjoyment. When he struts about like a rooster by the barn door, this demonstrates that "he possesses the wisdom and morality of a creature who has not been corrupted by human vanity," and when he denounces women as "Beasts, jades, jilts, harpies, furies, whores," he reveals an attractive vulnerability. In a wonderfully comic moment at the end of the play, when yet another abandoned mistress comes on stage with a bastard, he turns away and announces that he would like to be hanged after all; for Weber, this ending proves that Macheath is the quintessential rake-hero who "values his erotic satisfactions above all else" (pp. 207–10).

The problem is, in fact, that Weber's book disproves its own thesis. He wishes to define the rake-hero in terms of "overwhelming desire for sexual pleasure," "immense and indiscriminate appetites" (p. 3), a healthy (if compulsive) libido that is at the same time generous to women because it recognizes their own erotic needs. Aggression, trickery, and economic survival play a part in his character, but they are subordinate to pure sexuality and form an equilibrium with it—a balance that is destroyed in subsequent aberrations. In practice, however, Weber finds virtually no characters for whom sexuality stands out as a distinct and predominant force (p. 70); is thoroughly infused with power, distaste, humor, epistemological insecurity ("la besoin de savoir"), the hatred of hypocrisy, the desire to impress or bond with other men by "womanizing," the need to enforce an ideology of gender. Even his most ebullient specimens have something else on their mind. Southerne's Valentine acknowledges the sexual favors he receives from Sir Anthony Love (he is "charmed with the certainty" that she is a woman in disguise), but what really keeps them together is a shared fondness for "Roguery" and "Jest."[27]

Lee's Nemours, again, is held up as an example of overwhelming passion for "*all* flesh" (pp. 71–74), but he suffers from the general disease of the rake, the collapse of appetite after the act of yielding—"Willingness spoils all, . . . it palls the Appetite like Sack at Meals; give me the smart disdainful she"—and it is for this reason that the widowed Princess refuses him even though she loves him. As Weber himself notes (without explanation), what Nemours actually longs for is "variety" and a state of mental excitement that carries him *beyond* the limits of the flesh. In comic mood he admits (to his own mistress, incognita) that what he really values in sexual pursuit is "the freedom, Wit and Roguery, and all sorts of acting, as well as Conversation" (far from praising his generosity, however, she is furious). In a more romantic mode he defines his goal as "Inspiration, Extasie, and Transport." He is related to the sublime overreachers of Lee's heroic plays—when rushing to an assignation he exclaims "the Heroick Vein is upon me"—and like his tragic cousins he turns eroticism into a transcendent or Titanic gesture: he wants to "enter the Closet of the Gods, and to lye even with the Fates themselves, . . . and Death I defy thee!" Once "the Fury of Wine and the Fury of Women" is understood as a means of defeating mortality, a sort of displaced religion, then Nemours's conversion to a more serious mode (after the death of the Prince in Act IV, not at the very end) becomes more plausible.[28]

This leaves us with Horner, Weber's supreme example of the healthy and balanced rake-hero, "the life-force triumphant" (p. 55). Horner differs from the Dorimant-type because he channels his aggression only towards other men, and refuses to mingle the imagery of warfare with the pursuit of sex. His sexuality is "joyous," and he emerges from the bedroom bursting with "enthusiastic eroticism." His metaphorical equation of food and sex shows a natural understanding of human needs. He may enjoy exposing the hypocrisy of the "women of honor," but the drinking scene in Act V (when the City wives all throw off their masks and admit their sexual misdeeds), far from being the coarse misogynist satire that critics have thought it, is actually a sort of encounter group. Whereas the City husband "fails to recognize the powerful sexual urges" that steer humanity, Horner demonstrates them abundantly, and thereby reveals his "just appreciation of women." Inspired by this, Fidget, Dainty, and Squeamish gradually "come to terms with the nature of [their] desires" and "finally talk honestly," gaining the ability "to admit their sexual natures, not just to Horner but to each other." By such "forthright acceptance of [their] own sexual needs" they fling off "the social illusions that so hamper the freedom of the other characters," and "free" themselves from conventions that "have little to do with their true natures." For a brief moment the little group forms an ideal community, breaking away from a society that "can offer only the most limited images of sexuality." Weber does acknowledge the dark side of Horner after this scene, particularly his betrayal of Alithea to protect his secret affair with Margery, which is presented as a refusal to change society according to his vision of freedom. By the next chapter, however, such covering-up has become a virtue; Mirabell's trick to protect his cast-off mistress's reputation "reveals the generosity towards women previously seen in Horner."[29]

Unfortunately this portrait of Horner is almost completely imaginary. Dorimant is certainly aggressive, and takes pleasure in snubbing the mistress he is tired of, but on the other hand he seems genuinely excited by Harriet, and does not try his fan-breaking tricks on her; as we have seen, Horner takes equal pleasure in getting rid of previous mistresses, whom he dreads as "insatiable" debt collectors, and he has no Harriet to match him. As for his enthusiastic eroticism, it is shown only before the event, and then only to Margery in boy's clothes. Before copulating with Lady Fidget in the china scene (a feat that cannot take more than two minutes), he does nothing but jeer at "Bigots of Honour" with the doctor, and afterwards he finds not a single

The Culture of Priapism

word of affection, not even in whispered asides (IV.ii). After consummation with Margery he wants only to get rid of her. He calls her "Dearest" and "my life" through clenched teeth, in a manner that offends her, and the minute he has shoved her away he exclaims, "A silly Mistriss is like a weak place, soon got, soon lost, a man has scarce time for plunder" (V.iv). This appears to be a metaphor of warfare, and in the absence of any post-coital love scene it must stand for his entire attitude. Thenceforth he devotes to her only two strangled exclamations, "damn'd, damn'd loving Changeling" and "Peace, Dear Ideot"; he has assumed the diction of Pinchwife as well as his habit of locking Margery up.

As for his multiple fornications with the "virtuous Gang," we have already seen his ugly "*Machiavel* in love" attitude, and in the boozing scene (Weber calls it an "elegant dinner-party" [p. 208]) his tone towards them is always insolent, never affectionate. His food metaphors here, far from showing an easy naturalism, present sex as a gross scramble for the best bits in a common ordinary. The lines that Weber quotes to prove Horner's generous acceptance of female sexuality are actually the maxims of traditional misogyny: "All the difference I find betwixt we men, and you women, [is that] we forswear our selves at the beginning of an Amour, you as long as it lasts" (p. 63). In fact his pseudo-misogynist persona in Act I, and the real self revealed in Act V, agree entirely on this; as he predicted, the ladies only come to his lodgings for sex, and their "Virtue is [their] greatest affectation" (I.i). (If there were any doubt that the author shared Horner's scorn, the dedication to *The Plain Dealer* would dispel it—but for some reason Weber does not deal with this powerful and disturbing play.) Many of Weber's genuine insights could in fact be applied to Horner here. It is clear that sexual adventure offered women only a dubious freedom of the kind that he discovers in the position of actresses, who are free to confirm men's opinion of them as whores. Elsewhere, too, Weber describes the rake's obsession with other men's wives, and his inability to feel desire without an obstacle, as a serious failing (p. 173). When a Jacobean character declares that even the most virtuous-seeming women "sure will sinne behind a Skreene," this is assumed to reveal a grim disorder of the masculine psyche, an inability to "generate an exalted Self without a female Other to worship or destroy" (pp. 141–42). Why is this not true in Horner's case?

The caricatured City wives do not come to any realization or growth experience in the unmasking scene (apart from the obvious one that Horner has cheated all of them); warmed by drink and masquerade, they reveal what they always thought, what had always been their secret working assumptions. Their reasons for concealment were tactical, not psychoanalytic, and given the reality of marital punishment and ostracism they had every reason to maintain their virtuous front. Wycherley does not regard their situation with sympathy, however, and puts into the mouth of his ideological puppets, both Horner and the "women" themselves, the crudest possible insult—that respectable ladies are different from common whores only in that they charge more (p. 59). Again, *The Plain Dealer* and Wycherley's poems attack the "mercenary" woman *ad nauseam*.

As for Horner's understanding of women's needs and Sir Jasper's "failure to recognize" them, they both share the identical "understanding": that woman is a bag of quivering lust who will explode at the least opportunity, that the entire male population is plotting to provide such an opportunity, and that husbands must lock up their wives or confide them to eunuchs. What could be more "limited"? The shared ideology of both libertine and official morality was that women are wholly defined by their sex (Lovelace spends hundreds of pages trying to prove this of Clarissa), and in such a context to seduce a respectable woman is not a gentle release but a sadistic triumph. Even if Horner did not sneer at his victims, it would be wholly apolitical and anachronistic to equate his activities with "warm and generous sexuality." Wycherley no doubt wanted us to think of him as a good fellow and a clever fox, despite his betrayal of Alithea and stifling of Margery, and by giving him the last word in the comic conclusion he endorses the view that Horner seeks "by women to be priz'd." This makes the play more rather than less disturbing, however, since it enforces the ideology that there is only one way to relate to women, only one activity that could have any meaning or value between a man and a woman. On looking back, we may reflect that the play has indeed showered contempt on every kind of *social* relation between the sexes, as fit only for impotent men and superannuated servants.

The perspective of a female author like Behn is particularly important to our understanding of the libertine character, if we are to unmask the ideology of the rake without missing the genuine dash and energy that make him attractive. Behn's *Rover* manages this nicely. Her rake-hero Willmore is allowed to capture both the glamorous courtesan and the dazzling heiress, but he is flanked by companions who help to define, and to limit, the achievements of libertinism. In Killigrew the three Cavaliers are more or less on a level, but Behn makes one far grosser and adds a more gallant and respectful young man to the group. Of the former she says in a stage-direction that he "struts and cocks" with vanity (p. 23); she is certainly not impressed by the natural wisdom of the barnyard rooster pose, and takes evident pleasure in having him cheated, robbed, and dropped in a common sewer (her addition to the original). The nobler friend is on hand to curb the rake's more questionable attitudes. When he appeals to his friends to help free his beloved from captivity, for example, Willmore suggests that such "obligations" could only be repaid by her sleeping with the whole group: "Thou know'st there is but one way for a woman to oblige me" (p. 26). But this exclusively sexual definition of woman is rebuked as "profane." Behn's play also allows us to see the class aspect of sexual pursuit, when Willmore curses the possibility that the free-seeming woman he met at the Carnival (actually his future match in disguise) might have been "some damned honest person of quality"; this equation of sexual availability with lower-class status is normally given to more oafish characters.[30]

The libertine sublime, for Behn, may be a genuinely heroic attempt to transcend the "arts and politics of love," or else it may be a façade to hide predation and deceit. The distinction is rooted in her sense of the inequalities of gender. In the *Love-Letters*, for example, both Sylvia and Philander translate their passion into sublime terms, and both are eventually perceived as willful and corrupt. But their trajectories, and our sympathies, are quite different. The man at first seems authentically passionate and heroic, and potentially appreciative of such heroism in women: he could have found his wife's affair with the Duke of Monmouth "bold" and "noble," if she had "generously" acknowledged it and not sunk to dissimulation (p. 11). But his credibility is rapidly undermined by farcical episodes of impotence and transvestite disguise, and by his political rebellion; it is less surprising that he abandons Sylvia for another intrigue within a few months. She, on the other hand, only gradually builds up a heroic image of her transgression, as she struggles with the alternative heroism of traditional virtue, and only gradually loses her dignity after her betrayal. Behn never lets us forget the different situations of the man and the woman. Sylvia is inspired by an egalitarian vision of the love bond between "two souls touched with equal passion" and "equal judgments," a higher relationship in which "both undertake to take and pay," whereas in marriage "I've nought to do, but dully give a cold consenting affirmative" (p. 109); but at the same time she knows that she is going to her ruin, and her lover does indeed abandon her for the masculine-libertine principle of variety. When Philander sinks to the same dishonesty he condemned in his wife, Behn herself intervenes with an indignant attack on the double standard (p. 321). Though Sylvia also dissimulates, lying is "infinitely more excusable in her sex"; in a man, "whose most inconstant actions pass oftentimes for innocent gallantries, and to whom it is no infamy to own a thousand amours, but rather a glory to his fame and merit," it is utterly base.

Elsewhere, in a memorable poem, Behn explicitly confronts the rakish need for variety. Far from interpreting it as a generous urge to spend his substance, or a universal aspect of the human condition (*pace* Weber, p. 101), she sees it as a specifically male neurosis with disastrous consequences for women. "Alexis" had written a philosophical poem on the vanity of fruition, inspired by Montaigne: "Our boundless vast desires" drive us from one hollow satisfaction to another. Behn responds by challenging this sublime conception, suggesting that it is the feebleness rather than the vastness of man's libido ("charms [that] like lightning flash and are no more") that makes him abandon mistress after mistress. The ethos of libertine conquest, however,

The Culture of Priapism

is a social construct, acquired and not innate: "'Tis a fatal lesson he *has learn'd*, /After fruition ne're to be concern'd" [my emphasis]. And it is a contradictory social attitude that forces women to make "Man" their entire "business" and "aim," to "put Attraction on," only to be inevitably rejected after "one betraying enterview." Behn is particularly troubled by the double jeopardy imposed on the woman, who is "undone" whether she complies or not:

> They fly if Honour take our part,
> Our Virtue drives 'em o're the field.
> We lose 'em by too much desert,
> And Oh! they fly us if we yeild.

At the heart of libertine eroticism, then, Behn discovers a philosophical principle that displaces the erotic: "Inconstancy," rather than enjoyment, is "the good supreme."[31]

Notes

1. Francis Fane, *Love in the Dark* (London, 1675), p. 7; cf. my "The Libertine Sublime: Love and Death in Restoration England," *Studies in Eighteenth-Century Culture*, 19 (1989), forthcoming.

2. *The Petty Papers: Some Unpublished Writings*, ed. the Marquis of Lansdowne (London: Constable, 1927), II. 52–54; Petty also proposes that a "Great Rich Woman" should have five husbands, that marriages should be dissolved every few years (did Richardson know this manuscript?), and that paternity claims should be abolished. These arrangements he called "Californian marriages."

3. Cf. Philippe Beaussant, *Versailles, Opéra* (Paris: Gallimard, 1981), *passim*, esp. pp. 57–61, 112–13. I am grateful to Martha Pollak for this reference.

4. Furetière's *Dictionnaire*, s.v. "Carême-prenant"; for "libertinage" used for soldiers' burning a town to the ground, cf. Michèle Fogel, "L'Amour de la guerre ou la confiscation," *Nouvelle Revue de Psychanalyse*, 33 (1986), 272.

5. The exceptions, Antonio Vignali's *La Cazzaria* (before 1541) and Antonio Rocco's *Alcibiade Fanciullo in Scuola* (1652), confirm the impression that the libertine dialogue shies away from heterosexual initiation, since the central characters in both are homosexual males.

6. Reichler also cites three supernatural tales by women in Chapter 3, but (as I say below) these are tangential to libertinism.

7. See pp. 103, 96; de Sade calls out to Laura, from whom his family supposedly descended, "O ma Mère!" The other readings in this chapter come from Homer, Virgil, Apuleius, Beroul's *Tristan*, La Fontaine, eighteenth-century fairy tales, Bernadin de Saint-Pierre, Baudelaire, George Sand, Flaubert, Proust, Freud, Bataille, Klossowski, Genet, and Barthes.

8. The problem of ahistoricity is felt also when Reichler evokes parallels with Biblical myths (libertine initiation is a secular Fall, the idealized woman is a Virgin Mary) without touching upon those writings that may have formed a historical link between Christianity and its opponent (e.g., the ideas that desire is central to the definition of man and that sex has a special relation to knowledge, which belong to Augustine as well as to "modernity" [p. 52]). The fourth and final chapter, "The King's Leg," does return to the close analysis of a specific historical representation—of Louis XIV by Rigaud and Saint-Simon—but again the effect is rather thin, since Reichler's analysis turns into a set of structuralist variations on the relationship of "high" and "low."

9. Cf. my "'Illustrious Depravity' and the Libertine Sublime," *The Age of Johnson*, 2 (1988).

10. See p. 103. Reichler's grid-model does allow for diagonal relations, so that the grotesque Father Dirrag (lower left) could theoretically be opposed to the sublime Laura (top right); in the original text the description is manifestly antisublime, since Dirrag is given a hypocritical speech about the sublimation of carnal desires. But if the Interdit/Deuil dichotomy can be crossed so easily, how can it be a fundamental coordinate?

11. For the concept of a geography of decorum, see my "The Properties of Libertinism," in Robert P. Maccubin, ed., *Unauthorized Sexual Behavior During the Enlightenment*, Special Issue, *Eighteenth Century Life* 9, n.s. 3 (May 1985), 75–87.

12. According to Samuel Butler, Restoration libertines behaved as if they "had no other Way but Sin and Vice / To be restor'd again to *Paradise*," and devoted themselves to the "forc'd Hypocrisy of Wickedness" and to the "Mystery / Of moral secular Iniquity," *Satires and Miscellaneous Poetry and Prose*, ed. René Lamar (Cambridge: Cambridge Univ. Press, 1928), pp. 41–42.

13. Thomas Rymer, cited in David Farley-Hills, ed., *Rochester: The Critical Heritage* (London: Routledge, 1972), p. 166; Rochester, "A Satyr on Charles II."

14. I am not suggesting that eighteenth-century French libertinism is a *source* for Richardson, but rather that both derive from a common stock of seventeenth-century Anglo-French topoi and problems; Rochester's "Absent from thee I languish still" expresses the self-defeating cycle of libertinism better than any of Reichler's examples, and his *Satyr [Against Mankind]* expresses the unnecessary miseries brought by consciousness (though here, as several scholars have shown, his sources include the early French *libertin* Des Barreaux).

15. Cf. my "Richardson's Lovelace and the Paradoxes of Libertinism," in

The Culture of Priapism

Margaret A. Doody and Peter Sabor, eds., *Samuel Richardson: Tercentenary Essays* (Cambridge: Cambridge Univ. Press, 1989).

16. Weber cites David Foxon's essential study of "Libertine Literature in England," for example, but (apart from a brief phrase from Thomas Stretser's *Merryland*) pays no attention to these formative texts, even though his hero Horner alludes to *L'Ecole des filles*. Various minor technical problems suggest his unfamiliarity with scholarly research: on the few occasions that he cites seventeenth-century editions, he reproduces obsolete typography without the usual editorial tidying (prose is printed as verse, "i" "v" and "u" are not standardized) and quotes the entire title page even down to the words "Printed for"; he cites a Latin title in full, including the number of books; he does not recognize the eighteenth-century abbreviation for pounds; he refers to London landmarks by their old names ("the Mail"); he treats French accents arbitrarily (Abbè, Bouce).

17. Cf. my *One Flesh: Paradisal Marriage and Sexual Relations in the Age of Milton* (Oxford: Clarendon Press, 1987), chs. 1 and 2.

18. *The Case of Sodomy, in the Tryal of Mervyn . . . Earl of Castlehaven* (London, 1708), p. 8; not a single participant in this 1631 trial mentions the Devil.

19. The praise of the strumpet's freedom in Dekker's *The Honest Whore* (p. 140) is cited again to illustrate the wholly admirable Fanny Hill (p. 211); for "Ambrosia," cf. Marston, *The Dutch Courtezan*, V.i, translating a passage in which Montaigne proposes turning sex into an elaborate art (*Essais*, III.v). Weber's discussion of this essay, an important foundation of philosophical libertinism, is quite minimal (pp. 41–42).

20. Weber's case for a "transformation" depends on the idea that the demonic conception of sexuality is universal and ubiquitous before the Restoration, intermittent or "inconsistent" afterwards; though he asserts this in many places (and assumes it throughout), he nevertheless claims on page 27 that "I do not, of course, mean to suggest that demonic eroticism represented a quotidian understanding of sexuality; eroticism was not consistently or even usually comprehended as a satanic passion. What it indicates instead are beliefs on the margins of discourse."

21. Nevertheless Weber cites this letter (p. 92) to prove Rochester a quintessential rake-hero.

22. Thomas Shadwell, *The Virtuoso* I.i; Wycherley, *The Country-Wife* I.i; Fane, *Love in the Dark*, p. 14.

23. See pp. 92–95. Saint-Evremond, who attacked the new "sublime" valuation of excess and vastness, praises the greatness of love in modern tragedies and includes "l'excès de la joie" in a depiction of ideal love; cf. *Oeuvres choisies*, ed. A. C. Gidel (Paris: Garnier, 1867), p. 102, and Theodore A. Litman, *Le Sublime en France (1660–1714)* (Paris: Nizet, 1971), pp. 145–57.

24. E.g., pp. 172, 209, 211, where he cites Nancy Miller's "excellent essay " 'I's' in Drag" and attacks Leo Braudy's idea that in Cleland sex "makes all men and women equal."

25. "If there be no boldness like that of love, nor courage like that of the lover, sure there never was so great a heroine as *Sylvia*. Undaunted, I resolve to stand the shock of all; . . . it is below the dignity of my mighty passion to justify it farther" (*Love-Letters*, pp. 81–82). When Philander uses "mighty passion" (p. 53) he is compensating for a fit of impotence.

26. Ed. Frederick M. Link (Lincoln: Univ. of Nebraska Press, 1967), p. 27 and *passim*.

27. Thomas Southerne, *Sir Anthony Love* (London, 1691), pp. 49, 64.

28. Lee, *Works*, ed. Thomas B. Stroup and Arthur L. Cooke (New Brunswick: Scarecrow Press, 1955), II. 186, 190, 203. Weber's distinction of the "Hobbesian" rake Nemours from the "philosophical" type illustrated by the life and death of Petronius (p. 95) is undermined when Nemours himself is compared to the dying Petronius (II. 218).

29. Weber, pp. 50–63, 67, 81, 124; contrast p. 19: "The Restoration does not mark the beginning of a long 'liberation' of sex that culminated in our own halcyon days."

30. Behn, *Rover*, p. 27; Willmore brings out the paradox that, since her style was "free and witty," she could not be free. Cf. the dupe Golding in Southerne's *Sir Anthony Love*: "I have a villanous Suspicion, that when I see this Lady, I shall take her for a civil Gentlewoman [and fail to seduce her]; Abuse her, away, she does not deserve: Think too well of her, and lose my labour!" (p. 48).

31. Both poems appear in Behn's *A Miscellany of New Poems*, appended to her *Lycidus* (London, 1688), pp. 127–31; Richard E. Quaintance suggests they might both be by Behn herself ("Passion and Reason in Restoration Love Poetry," Ph.D. dissertation, Yale Univ., 1962, p. 141).

The Theory of American Literature, Once More

Thomas M. Leitch

Russell Reising. *The Unusable Past: Theory and the Study of American Literature*. New York and London: Methuen, 1986. xii, 290 pp.

Throughout the introduction to his important new book, Russell Reising emphasizes the novelty of his project, even at the risk of making it seem marginal. His book, he acknowledges, is "tertiary" (p. 1) in the sense that is neither a work of imaginative literature nor a study of such works, but rather a study of earlier studies of American literature. Unlike the theorists he considers—a series including D. H. Lawrence, Perry Miller, Yvor Winters, F. O. Matthiessen, Lionel Trilling, Richard Chase, R. W. B. Lewis, Charles Feidelson, Leslie Fiedler, Leo Marx, Richard Poirier, Sacvan Bercovitch, and John T. Irwin—Reising proposes "to offer no new definition of what American literature means, what its Ur-theme(s) may be, or what makes it 'American' as distinct from any other geographic, political, social, or cultural category.... I offer, in short, no new theory of American literature. I do offer a theory of the theories we now have" (pp. 1, 8).

Reising's program may sound forbiddingly metacritical—a book about books about books—but in fact its focus places it at the heart of American studies. After quoting a wide range of pronouncements about the Americanness of American literature, Reising announces that "one of my assumptions in this study is that these claims are *significant*" (p. 3). This apparently remarkable conclusion—for why shouldn't such theories be significant?—is explained by the peculiarly unanimous emphasis, in surveys of American literature over the past hundred years, on its uniquely American character. This assumption itself is remarkable. When we pick up Walter Allen's study *The English Novel* or Martin Turnell's *The Novel in France*, we expect a survey of the material, not an argument about its Englishness or Frenchness. One might say, as F. R. Leavis once said in reviewing Van Wyck Brooks's work, that the preoccupation with the Americanness of American literature was merely a sympton of nationalistic anxiety which led to a relaxation of critical standards.[1] But Reising, in accepting the significance of this preoccupation, assumes an intimate connection between American literature and the conditions of American life.

Indeed it is precisely this connection that he finds earlier theorists, despite their avowed intentions, to have neglected. His leading argument is that "theorists of American literature have not situated . . . [its] tradition in sufficiently social a terrain. . . . Their mythic, symbolic, rhetorical, romantic, or psychological rubrics deflect the social and political significance of American literature" (pp. 47–48). In his three central chapters, he argues that studies of Puritan influences on American literature, cultural theories of American literature, and stylistic or self-reflexive theories of American literature all operate and justify themselves by discounting in similar ways the social matrix of the works they address:

> Whether their declared interests are historical, linguistic, cultural, or psychological, what these prevailing perspectives on American literature tend most consistently to exclude or to marginalize is . . . a "social" tradition. By social tradition I refer to three specific areas of literary practice: (1) writers, texts, and even genres that reflect a direct, often critical apprehension of the historical, social, economic, and political contexts of American culture; (2) the broader assumption that all literature mediates social reality; and (3) criticism that grants the importance, if not the centrality, of such social concerns, one that takes itself seriously as a form of social knowledge. [p. 34]

Because of his pervasive criticism of the ways in which earlier theories have impoverished American literature by privatizing American social experience, Reising's emphasis on "how those theories define the canon of American literature and how those definitions [of its Americanness] influence our understanding and teaching of that canon" is explicitly ideological (p. 1). Just as Brooks, writing in the 1930s, had rejected the genteel tradition enshrined around the turn of the century, theories of American literature most influential since the war, Reising contends, have been written against the earlier political criticism of Brooks, V. L. Parrington, Granville Hicks, and others, and have justified themselves by excluding or marginalizing these critics, their concerns, and the works and authors (including Garland, Sinclair, and Dreiser) they found most compelling. Reising's call for a new canon of American literature is therefore, like similar calls from H. Bruce Franklin, Paul Lauter, and Nina Baym, politically programmatic; his aim, like theirs, is not only to encourage the inclusion of Kate Chopin and Frederick Douglass in the American canon but to force a reassessment of the present canonical writers, and of American literature generally, in the light of such inclusions. Only through such an enlargement and a corresponding reassessment of the American canon, including works and writers and areas now dismissed as "unusable," can theorists again recover the power of American writers to change the perception and behavior of their audience.

This summary will scarely do justice to the scope and comprehensiveness of Reising's study. Despite the selectivity of his analysis—some of his omissions are noted, others (e.g., studies by Alfred Kazin, A. N. Kaul, David L. Minter, and Tony Tanner) are not—Reising surveys an extraordinarily wide group of earlier critics and manages to map their positions in consistently illuminating ways. Although his tone is generally critical, he can be sympathetic even to theorists he is taking to task, and his readings of earlier critics are pointed and economical, as in his discussion of Richard Poirier's argument that the stylistic goal of the great American writers is to create a world elsewhere:

According to Poirier, the central American tradition consists of American authors' trying to free their characters from the rigidity of social definitions and historical circumstances, regardless of the admittedly inevitable failure of such an attempt. The problem is this: a persistent strain in American literature beginning with the Puritans' struggle to achieve an equipoise of individual and society, of internal belief and external conduct, and finding full expression in the works of Hawthorne, James, and even Eliot, suggests a tradition exactly the opposite of Poirier's. Hawthorne and James are, perhaps, the clearest examples. Who could argue that characters like Goodman Brown, Wakefield, Reuben Bourne, the man of adamant, Ethan Brand, and the numerous other Hawthorne characters alienated from humanity or some of James's solipsists such as John Marcher, Spencer Brydon, George Stransom, and a host of other artists, aesthetes, and egotists divorced from human connections do not suggest that American writers, contrary to Poirier, are actually very concerned with exposing, not endorsing, the posturings of solipsistic characters? In other words, the *real* American tradition could just as well be to socialize American characters, not to create a world elsewhere for them. [p. 197]

Passages like these indicate that despite Reising's description of his book as tertiary, it is neither theory-ridden nor overloaded with jargon; in fact, it is as readable as most of the works it discusses.

Although he disclaims any pretense at reinterpreting either American literature as such or particular literary texts, Reising occasionally tests his readings of earlier critics, as in this passage on Poirier, by remarks on canonical American writers, and even more occasionally offers extended readings—of Hawthorne, of Mark Twain, and, in his closing chapter, of Frederick Douglass. These readings are highly variable in quality. Reising glosses the conclusion of "Ethan Brand," in which Bartram breaks Brand's skeleton into fragments of lime, with a strikingly unpersuasive assertion: "The tale concludes . . . not on a note of shallow pastoral affirmation, but on Hawthorne's dramatizing of the human reduction of other humans into commodities, an indictment of capitalism's perversion of social relations, not simply of mechanization or of Faustian egotism" (p. 149). On the other hand, his defense of the final quarter of *Huckleberry Finn* as foregrounding "the contradictions of an economic and political complex predicated on propriety, religiosity, family unity, and racial violence" (p. 156) is both more successful and more pertinent to the argument he is advancing about earlier critics' celebrated debate about the ending: "Jim's imprisonment and the very real danger

The Theory of American Literature

he faces as well as the cruelty of Tom's strategies . . . can be defined as 'a falling off' only if one mythicizes, marginalizes, or disregards the question of slavery and freedom in the novel" (p. 157). At such points Reising's metacritical project does not preclude his establishing his own place among earlier critics of American literature.

Other similarities between Reising's book and the books it considers are less fortunate. In his introduction, Reising writes: "I claim no perspective immune from the ideological blindness that I uncover" (p. 8). The warning is well-taken, though in the heat of debate Reising himself often forgets it. Just as earlier theorists of American literature have frequently been at pains to make Hawthorne and Melville say what they wanted them to say, Reising's premise requires him to present the ideas of a critic like Lionel Trilling somewhat selectively. Following Gene Wise, Reising identifies Trilling as a counter-Progressive: "Whereas Progressives wanted to understand what, *in fact*, was the reality of history, counter-Progressives stressed the primacy of how people *felt* about reality and how their myths, images, and symbols dramatized these feelings. In other words, the human mind and its responses (aesthetic and otherwise) came to constitute 'reality' for the counter-Progressives. They transferred the grounds of reality from economic and political *systems* to human *psyches*" (p. 95). Although "Trilling would like to abolish . . . [Parrington's] simple dualism of reality versus mind," Reising contends that "his solution, the 'literary idea,' actually reinstates the same opposition, though on a subtler level" (p. 99).

In one sense this is an apt criticism. Trilling's definition and etiology of ideas in "The Meaning of a Literary Idea" are indeed close to those developed by Allen Tate in his New Critical essays on Emily Dickinson and Elizabethan satire—a conception of ideas whose potency is dramatically contained within a given work. But Trilling's emphasis in the same essay on the notion of piety recalls Kenneth Burke's overtly political use of the same term.[2] Despite his suspicion of writers like Dreiser and Dos Passos whose minds have been violated by the ideas they profess and his preference for writers like Hemingway and Faulkner whose hallmark is negative capability rather than allegiance to a systematic ideology, Trilling is not condemning the appearance of ideology in prose fiction but rather the uncritical acceptance of any given ideology. Trilling's criticism of American writers in "Manners, Morals, and the Novel" is precisely that their doctrinaire approach to reality reduces its power by preferring abstract analysis to the kind of engagement offered by particular manners, habits, and circumstances.

Hence Reising's contention that "Trilling's standards are, finally, formal rather than ethical" (p. 104) is acute but limited. It is true that Trilling characteristically sees the novel as recapitulating social problems in psychological terms, as when he observes that in *Don Quixote* and subsequent novels, "the shifting and conflict of social classes becomes the field of the problem of knowledge, of how we know and how reliable our knowledge is."[3] On the other hand, Reising's formulation fails to come to terms with Trilling's larger cultural concerns. When Trilling asserts that "in proportion as we have committed ourselves to our particular [ideologically abstract] idea of reality we have lost our interest in manners," he is expressing a lament "not only over a waning form of art but also over our waning freedom."[4] Reising's attitude toward this freedom is different from Trilling's own because currently influential political theories would dismiss it as illusory: we are all obliged to see the world ideologically, whether or not we are aware of our biases. But Trilling's call for a self-conscious critique of one's own beliefs surely has as much relevance to an ideological conception of literature as a commitment to a particular purpose or program would have. Reising acknowledges this relevance in a generous but backhanded summary:

By repeatedly championing the integrity of individual consciousness and the complexity of social reality, Trilling verged on a critique of ideology far ahead of his time. What he offers in a schematic form seems to be nothing less than a critical method which, though never explicitly or systematically formulated, is capable of comprehending the various strategies humans use for processing reality, for unscrambling the chaotic barrage of media impressions which saturate our existences. Not reducible to an opposition of "reality" versus "consciousness," Trilling's focus *could have been* on the interrelationships between self and society. [p. 100; my emphasis]

The reason that Trilling fails to achieve such a focus is not only because of his own implicit political commitments—in condemning Dreiser he is reacting as much against his Communist sympathies as against his novels—but because his conceptions of both social and individual reality are politically parochial, forcing him to ignore what Reising calls "a material analysis of social relations and of the relationships among economics, history, and consciousness" (p. 102) and what David Hirsch calls "the ordinary facts of human existence."[5] Trilling would surely claim, however, that Hirsch's "ordinary facts" were themselves ideologically tendentious and that the whole business of the novel was to attend both to the buzz and hum of social intercourse and *thereby* to its underlying political implications. Trilling's emphasis on the power of individual consciousness in the novel has been exaggerated both by critics like Marius Bewley who agree with him and by critics like Nicolaus Mills who do not, and Reising seems often more attentive to later versions of Trilling—the schematic, anti-American Trilling of Mills and the revisionary Trilling of Hirsch and William T. Chace—than to Trilling himself.[6]

More generally, perhaps inevitably, Reising's accounts of sharply different theorists often make a disconcertingly similar use of them. Each of the principal figures with whom Reising deals tends to begin with a position with promising social and political implications but then denies or privatizes any possibilities of political action which might be released by either the work at hand or the critic's own position. Thus Reising's summaries of different critics use revealingly similar rhetorical strategies. "Like other mythic and psychological critics," he contends, "Lawrence locates the same struggle between blood and mental consciousness in every text, reducing a text's specific historical status to a backdrop for the primary, ahistorical drama of consciousness" (p. 166). This tendency to recast social conflicts in self-limiting formal or psychological terms, which vitiates Trilling's work as well, turns up in most of the critics Reising analyzes, even those he most admires. "The implications of Feidelson's work are exciting, posing a method for investigating the constitutive function of language," writes Reising. "A historicized version of Feidelson's tactics could pursue any number of cultural inquiries. Assuming that specific discursive practices crystallize at specific moments under specific pressures, a method such as Feidelson's would be capable of revealing how and why language attempts to transcend various social determinants as well as what impact those social pressures have on cultural discourse" (pp. 179–80). Unfortunately, "several of Feidelson's theoretical tenets . . . deflect attention from such potential. . . . By severing the work from any reality outside its textual borders, and by defining the intra-textual world ahistorically, Feidelson locks American literary studies into what Fredric Jameson calls 'the prison house of language.' . . . In fact, Feidelson's understanding of the 'thinking ego and brute fact' grants the polarized terms the very validity he wishes to deny; he sees them in a static opposition rather than in a dynamic contradiction wherein one side inhabits the other" (pp. 180, 182, 185). After praising Bercovitch's progress from *The Puritan Origins of the American Self* to *The American Jeremiad* by emphasizing the "dynamism that Bercovitch attributes to jeremiad rhetoric" and observing that "what had appeared as a notion of the American Self that existed only in a relatively static, mythic realm is now more fully historicized, subjected to social pressures and scrutinized under changing forms" (p. 84), Reising concludes: "Bercovitch has situated Puritan rhetoric both historically and politically. What remains now is to free his inquiry from its narrowly canonical bias, its positivistic notion of literary politics, and to forge a critical method capable of elucidating the adversarial elements that may not be compromised by the ambiguities of jeremiad rhetoric" (p. 88).

The obvious limitation of such summaries is that they tend to simplify the critics with whom Reising is dealing in order to make them fit the pattern of Reising's argument. This problem is natural and perhaps unavoidable in any work of thesis criticism. Although one could wish that Reising had paid closer attention, for example, to Feidelson's later essay "James and the 'Man of Imagination,'" in which James's increasing internalization of the relation between consciousness and social reality is treated more critically and in more clearly dialectical terms than Reising's Feidelson ever uses, this omission is a minor flaw in Reising's argument.[7] A more serious problem is that Reising, whose most frequent criticism of earlier theorists is the positivism that undermines their analyses, is not immune from the charge of positivism himself. Concluding his discussion of Winters, Chase, and Fiedler, Reising remarks dismissively that "much of the literary work we have been discussing is superseded" by the work of "materially minded historians" (p. 67). A few pages later he explains:

> In so far as they make Puritan religious doctrine decisive or fail to locate it in a precise social context, Puritan origins theorists distort the actual reality of Puritanism. I draw on recent historical writing not to invoke a naive distinction between historical truth and literary (or critical) fabrication. Puritan history is, of course, still being written and debated, but these insights do help fill out a more realistic picture of Puritan culture by reminding us that the Puritans, too, lived in a complex social world and that their ideas are inseparable from their lives in that world.
> [p. 69]

Reising seems to forget this general disclaimer, however, in saying that the work of Winters, Chase, and Fiedler has simply been "superseded," just as he seems to forget his generally even-handed tone toward the subjects of his criticism in the more dismissive section headings within his chapters. Thus the section on Trilling is headed "Unreality in America"; on Lewis, "Parties of one"; on Feidelson, "Making the world safe for symbolism." It is often amusing but sometimes painful to watch Reising's courtesy to critics whose intellectual energy he regards as wayward or misdirected, as in this passage on Leo Marx:

> Marx's elucidation of the social and political implications latent in the theme of the machine in the garden is important [sc. *acceptable*], as is his insistence on placing the study of literature in a political perspective. But his thesis that the works themselves do not present explicit critiques or offer any but "virtual resolutions" rests on some inadequately developed literary assumptions. His method, too—indebted as it is to Trilling's ideas as well as to those of consensus historiography in general, and bound, as it is, to largely conventional readings of canonical texts—prevents him from advancing a more trenchant [sc. *approved*] analysis.
> [p. 145]

Over and over Reising seems to be grading earlier theorists up or down—mostly down—according to how closely they anticipate his own social and political program.

This criticism may seem unfair, since every critic has a right to his or her presuppositions, and Reising expounds his own with commendable explicitness and defends them with more than customary diplomacy. It is not entirely clear, however, why Perry Miller, whose "approach has limitations, owing chiefly to his polemical context" (p. 54), should not have as great a right to his polemical prejudices as Reising does to his. If the right to one's critical or methodological bias is earned by the original insights that bias enables, Miller's position in American criticism is secure; his proportion of useful and illuminating ideas to disabling biases is at least as high as Reising's own. In exposing the narrowness, the contradictions, and the inadequacies of postwar theories of American literature, as he often does with surgical skill, Reising tends to impute an imperialistic power to his own analysis. He allows his readings of Trilling, Feidelson, and Poirier to be dictated too completely by revisionists like Mark Krupnick and Barbara Foley. More generally, his argument rests perhaps too uncritically on Jameson's assertion that "the political perspective" is "the absolute horizon of all reading and all interpretation."[8] Although Jameson himself presented his argument in the most tendentious terms possible, as if he expected to outrage his audience, Reising, writing only six years later, takes it as an article of faith. When he concludes that in Lawrence and Fiedler, "the literal level of American literature is reduced to mere evasion, significant only in so far as it alerts the perceptive critics to the deeper level which it distorts" (p. 134), or when he notes that the mythic paradigm of the machine in the garden "attenuates the historical thrust of Marx's argument by defining the conflict between industrialization and pastoralism in America as merely one more manifestation of a trans-historical psychic tension" (p. 148), he is privileging the political dimension of American literature in much the same way that his subjects had privileged a mythic or psychological dimension.

Whether the ultimate reality of American experience is material is impossible to determine, partly because a phrase like "ultimate reality" begs so many questions. Reising aptly notes that "though an appreciation and understanding of the aesthetic nature of literature is necessary, a primarily aesthetic apprehension of literature—if such a thing is even possible—is antithetical to any study postulating a theory of American literature" (p. 223). We cannot, after all, talk about the Americanness of American literature without talking about the social and political realities of America, even if those realities leave distinctive formal or stylistic traces in the works which rehearse them. Reising's most powerful indictment of earlier theorists is that, however clearly they have seen the connection between social reality and literary performance, their theories repeatedly lose sight of the first in analyzing the second. Perry Miller frankly disdains the importance of economic and social circumstances; Winters, Lewis, and Marx allegorize these circumstances and the conflicts they arouse; Trilling, Feidelson, Poirier, Bercovitch, and Irwin privatize them by recasting social conflicts in psychological, hermeneutical, or rhetorical terms.

This indictment would be more persuasive, however, if it were not for two omissions which would implicate Reising's own project more deeply in the political matrix he takes for granted. The first is a consideration of the politics of academic publishing. Although Reising observes that "one would have to rely on a truly naive belief in the freedom of academic inquiry from political and economic pressures to posit an unhampered and relatively autonomous position for literary studies within the American system" (p. 40) and proceeds to an adroit and suggestive analysis of the marginalization of social ideas within the academy by such pressures, he shows little awareness of the political forces peculiar to the American higher education as such. Reising assumes that critics write at all times with the goal of telling the truth as they see it, or occasionally to pay off political scores (as Trilling does in condemning Dreiser). But the imperatives of the critical establishment change dramatically during the period on which Reising is focusing, a period during which theories of American literature become less the province of novelists like Lawrence or social historians like Parrington and Hicks—that is, writers who have chosen to write on American literature freely, from a sense of gratuitous commitment—than the province of professional readers of literature. A good deal of the interpretive and canonical inertia Reising ascribes to New Criticism arises instead from a related but distinct development: the need of critics who are also teachers to earn promotion, tenure, and further eminence by choosing an area for themselves (e.g., Poe, the Gilded Age, the American short story) within a recognized field and publishing critical books and essays which will establish their mastery of that area. Given the relatively recent establishment of American studies (and indeed of American literature) as an accepted field of study in the academy, it is hardly surprising that critics like Matthiessen, Feidelson, and Chase should attempt to defend the legitimacy of their subject by emphasizing its Americanness even as their analytical tools remained primarily aesthetic.

Furthermore, the political realities of teaching, which frequently involve annual encounters with a set of prescribed texts, place a premium on original insights into those same texts. Reising, discussing Marx's 1953 review of Trilling's and T. S. Eliot's readings of *Huckleberry Finn*, observes that, "whereas this earlier essay argues for a frankly *social*, vigorously *public* reading—one in which the distinction between a personal and a social or political morality is crucial—Marx's rereading in *The Machine in the Garden* ten years later complicates these matters" (p. 154) without considering the extent to which Marx's later mythopoetic reading might be influenced by a professional imperative to extrapolate his earlier analysis into a more complex and comprehensive system. Marx's emphasis on "largely conventional readings of canonical texts" (p. 145), which Reising attacks as a weakness of his book, is determined not only by his decision to focus on the theory of American literature rather than the explication of particular texts—a decision to which Reising thinks he has a perfect right himself—but also by his pedagogical experience and the requirements of academic recognition. More to the point, the requirements of scholarly publishing, which stipulate a combination of new insight and recognized area of study, virtually guarantee a torrent of studies on a few familiar figures—new lights on Hawthorne and Henry James—rather than a reconsideration of the rationale for the existing terrain.

In that case, we might ask, how could Reising's book, which does call for such a reconsideration, have appeared at all? This question is easy to answer if we rectify Reising's second omission by inserting his own analysis into history, including institutional history, instead of assuming that it stands outside or above it, as his positivism sometimes suggests. For Reising's own book can be seen as a response to the same historical pressures that inspired most of his subjects—the need to get ahead in the profession, to establish a reputation, by producing a book that is at once novel in its analysis and acceptable in its scope and rationale. The book responds to current fashions in literary theory by wedding revisionary readings of earlier critics to a premise which sees politics as the essential framework for literary analysis—or, as Reising says, by attempting "to review and revise the major theories of American literature in light of these new directions in critical practice" (p. 6). One can imagine a latter-day Reisingian analyst of Reising pointing out that the economic realities of scholarly publishing in the 1980s favored literary theory and metacriticism, especially political theory, over the kinds of analytical surveys which had heretofore dominated American studies (the characteristic influence of Methuen's New Accents series, under whose imprint Reising's book appears, would doubtless be instanced here); suggesting that his political framework had no more a priori justification than the Freudian or formal or allegorical frameworks it sought to displace—that is was in fact an allegorical framework itself—and adding that despite Reising's obvious commitment to a materialist view of reality, his book did nothing to change the political realities of the academic marketplace and was in its own way as politically regressive as any of the books it considered.

This conclusion would no doubt infuriate Reising, who would be quite right in seeing his study as politically committed given the circumstances of its composition and publication. But the inevitable situating of his own study within a history which is material as well as textual and interpretive does not prevent him from treating his subjects almost exclusively as a series of isolated texts whose primary operations are interpretive rather than material. His argument about earlier theorists is finally, in his own interpretive terms, unsuccessful, for his book does not succeed in "correcting their derealization of American literature" (p. 48); it works instead by substituting a more updated rationale. Reising's argument that the major theories of American literature have substantiated their claims by rendering a vast part of American writing an unusable past is finally less revealing than his implicit demonstration that the American literary past is variously reusable, rich, and varied enough to support the requirements of repeated waves of readers.

Readers who are interested in a challenging and engaging supplement to earlier theorists of American literature rather than a correction of their faults will, however, find Reising's book almost continuously rewarding. Reising argues that "the worth of a theory lies in its ability to account for as much of its subject as possible. In this simple sense, a theory of American literature that can incorporate twenty authors is better (other things being equal) than one that deals with five, ten, or fifteen writers" (p. 222). In terms of this program, Reising's polemical reading is impressive, because his charge that postwar theorists of American literature have postulated frustratingly narrow definitions of Americanness, literary value, and the American canon is far more persuasive than the implication that he is above any such narrowness. Reising's title is well-chosen because it emphasizes the strongest aspect of his argument. Whether the more comprehensive past Reising indicates without fully describing is more usable than the parochial conceptions of the American Renaissance or Eight Classic American Writers is of course open to question, but there is no doubt that Reising adumbrates *a* usable past, a notion of American literature which may well be more responsive to our present needs than those he considers.

In sum, Reising is not so much summarizing and bracketing a critical debate as continuing it, marking a new chapter in the evolution of the theory of American literature. His continuity with earlier theorists is based not only on the formal similarity of his project to those of Matthiessen and Fiedler, but on the surprising way in which virtually all theorists of American literature since Winters have been at heart metatheorists whose primary interest was less in providing new readings of a small array of classic texts than in setting their forbears straight. Trilling corrects Parrington on reality and Eliot on *Huckleberry Finn*; Marx

The Theory of American Literature 49

joins the debate on *Huckleberry Finn*, and a host of critics—Richard Chase, A. N. Kaul, Joel Porte, Nicolaus Mills—correct Trilling, all in different ways. Matthiessen tries to balance Granville Hicks with New Criticism; Feidelson corrects Matthiessen; Perry Miller raps Feidelson's knuckles in a brief review. The fact is that in focusing on theories of American literature rather than on American literature itself, Reising is subscribing to a tradition nearly as old as American literary theory itself.

This may sound like faint praise to a writer of Reising's aspirations. But to continue and valorize the debate whose terms were established by Matthiessen, Trilling, and Feidelson is no small achievement, and the attempt to redefine the terms of that debate, though eminently in keeping with academic tradition, is itself an ambitious undertaking. Whatever the persuasive power of his book on isolated readers, the results of Reising's call for critics to re-theorize and re-canonize American literature by conceiving it as more responsive to, and more influential on, social and political reality remain to be seen.

Notes

1. See Leavis, "The Americanness of American Literature," in *Anna Karenina and Other Essays* (New York: Simon and Schuster, 1967), pp. 138–51.
2. See Trilling, "The Meaning of a Literary Idea," in *The Liberal Imagination* (New York: Viking, 1950), pp. 299–300, and Burke, *Permanence and Change* (2d rev. ed., 1954; rpt. Indianapolis: Bobbs-Merrill, 1965), pp. 71–74.
3. Trilling, "Manners, Morals, and the Novel," in *The Liberal Imagination*, p. 209.
4. "Manners, Morals, and the Novel," pp. 216, 222.
5. Hirsch, *Reality and Idea in the Early American Novel* (The Hague: Mouton, 1971), p. 36.
6. See Bewley, *The Eccentric Design* (New York: Columbia Univ. Press, 1959), pp. 13–21, and Mills, *American and English Fiction in the Nineteenth Century* (Bloomington: Indiana Univ. Press, 1973), pp. 3–31. One example: Trilling remarks of the modern American novel that although "life in America has thickened since the nineteenth century," still "we do not have the novel that touches significantly on society, on manners," because "Americans have a kind of resistance to looking closely at society" ("Manners, Morals, and the Novel," p. 213). Bewley's analysis instead emphasizes the social "deprivation" of the great

American novelists, "the sense of being without certain kinds of reality that men ought to have" (*The Eccentric Design*, p. 17). And Mills, in arguing against Trilling, attributes to him Bewley's view that "social thinness sets into play forces that produce the American rather than the English novel" (*American and English Fiction in the Nineteenth Century*, p. 23). In general, what Reising calls the "dialectical" quality of Trilling's premise is simplified by both Bewley and Mills and dismissed as "not a dialectic in any sense" by Reising himself (p. 106).

7. Feidelson, "James and the 'Man of Imagination,'" in *Literary Theory and Structure: Essays in Honor of William K. Wimsatt*, ed. Frank Brady, John Palmer, and Martin Price (New Haven: Yale Univ. Press, 1973), pp. 331–52. Reising also neglects the later work of Trilling (especially "On the Teaching of Modern Literature" and *Sincerity and Authenticity*) and Fiedler (especially *What Was Literature?*).

8. Jameson, *The Political Unconscious* (Ithaca: Cornell Univ. Press, 1981), p. 17.

Richard Ellmann and the Art of Biography

Jerome H. Buckley

Richard Ellmann. *Oscar Wilde.* New York: Alfred A. Knopf, 1988. xvii, 680 pp.

Completed shortly before Richard Ellmann's death in 1987, *Oscar Wilde* marks a fitting culmination to a distinguished career. A large handsome book, well illustrated and written with spirit, it takes its place at once beside Ellmann's *James Joyce,* which, since its first appearance thirty years ago, has set an exemplary standard for modern literary biography.

Oscar Wilde clearly transcends all earlier lives of Wilde, many of them merely self-serving and fiercely partisan reminiscences by friends, enemies, and sometime disciples. It takes account of such memoirs and of countless published anecdotes, but it measures every item against a fresh study of actual records and available primary sources, assembled by scrupulous research and carefully assessed. Ellmann has an admirable sense of place and time, a feeling for the ambiance of mid-Victorian Dublin, of Oxford in the 1870s, of a variously rowdy and genteel America in the early eighties, of "Aesthetic" London, of *fin-de-siècle* Paris. He presents a gallery of colorful late Victorians and develops a full context of ideas, prejudices, and changing values. Yet he keeps his subject sharply in foreground focus as a distinct individual dependent on the public he exploits, ready always to flout its taboos but intent ultimately on what seems nothing less than a willful self-destruction.

Near the beginning Lady Wilde, the flamboyant Speranza, foreshadows her son's attitude and conduct. When told of a "respectable" young woman she might receive, she firmly replied, "You must never employ that description in this house. It is only tradespeople who are respectable. We are above respectability" (p. 9). Whether the term implied Philistine propriety or simple mediocrity, Oscar from the outset was concerned to establish his Wildean difference, if only at first in his taste as a schoolboy for scarlet and lilac flannel shirts or in demonstrations of his extraordinary prowess as speed-reader. He soon made his intellectual attainments likewise conspicuous; at Trinity College, Dublin, he proved himself a superb classicist; at Oxford he won the Newdigate Prize for poetry and "was awarded a rare double first" in Greats (p. 98). His dress, whether velveteen coat and breeches or dandified evening wear, attracted amused attention. His lordly extravagance, especially when in debt, as collector of beautiful expensive objects was a perpetual affront to middle-class prudence. And the repartee with which he dominated dinner tables and which he later re-polished for his plays was as often as not a calculated assault on respectable complacency. The zeal, however, with which he half-concealed and half-advertised his homosexual preferences and liaisons became a far more dangerous defiance of convention. Ellmann traces all aspects of Wilde's rejection of the commonplace, his floating joyously above respectability and his falling shabbily beneath it, the pathetic trajectory from a high acclaim to a cruel debasement. In the sorry aftermath of his prison term Wilde appears as the vagrant Sebastian Melmoth abjectly wandering the streets of Paris, begging a handout from the great Madame Melba, whom in happier London days, when he could call himself "the Lord of Language," he had saluted as his "Queen of Song."

Throughout the biography Ellmann maintains a steady balance of judgment tempered with quiet irony and patient compassion. Only a few slips, contradictions, and redundancies creep into the text. Tennyson's 1885 play which Queensbury attacked was titled *The Promise of May*, not *The May Queen* (p. 388). Chatterton forged late medieval poems rather than Jacobean dramas (p. 284). Constance Wilde is said to have been "shy yet fond of talking" (p. 234), then "never a fluent talker" and "almost mute beside her husband" (p. 255), but again is reported to have interrupted Oscar at dinner parties, corrected his stories, and finished them herself (p. 267). We are told twice (pp. 32, 88) that the philosopher Baumgarten coined the word "aesthetic" in 1750; Ruskin's Oxford lectures on Florentine art are assigned twice, within two pages (pp. 48, 49) to Michaelmas term 1874; and the second citations of a number of other details appear as if for the first time. Finally the index, which is full and wide-ranging, is sometimes inaccurate in page references (I suspect inadequate transfer from the English to the American edition). But these, except perhaps for the matter of the index, are quite minor blemishes in a major work, echoes and errors which an alert copy-editor might have caught.

"What is true in a man's life," Wilde insisted, "is not what he does, but the legend which grows up around him. . . . You must never destroy legends" (p. 44). If the serious biographer must distinguish between fact and legend, Wilde quite deliberately complicated the task. He regularly improved upon fact, as if it were his aesthetic duty to do so. He embellished and indeed sometimes fabricated his adventures, and he revised his mots and paradoxes in frequent rehearsal. Both friends and enemies in turn furthered the legend by retailing misquotation and hearsay. Ellmann sifts through much "unreliable testimony" such as that of Frank Harris, "whose made-up speeches for Wilde rarely ring true" (p. 266). For his own part he proceeds with caution in attempting to recover the spoken words of the legendary wit. He draws, for example, on two contemporary newspaper reports of Wilde's impression of Niagara Falls as "the first disappointment in the married life of many Americans who spend their honeymoon there" (p. 195). In their entertaining account of the American tour, Lloyd Lewis and Henry Justin Smith quote the same opinion as Wilde polished it for a British lecture audience: Niagara Falls "must be one of the earliest, if not the keenest, disappointments in American married life" (*Oscar Wilde Discovers America,* p. 163). This second version is surely the more poised and incisive, though the first is nearer to the event and presumably to the original remark (if indeed the two journalists did not garble the witticism). Again, Lewis and Smith (p. 35)—this time without documentation—record Wilde's alleged reply to the New York customs officer who asked what he had to declare: "Nothing—nothing but my genius." Ellmann finds no solid evidence that this perfect riposte was ever delivered, but nonetheless concedes that it does seem highly characteristic: "He may well have said it, for after a day in the harbor he could see the importance of having an epigram at the ready" (p. 160). Here Ellmann's wit competes with Wilde's; still we may feel somewhat cheated to think that the epigram, if indeed it were spoken at all, was hardly the spontaneous response we hoped it must have been. All the same the biographer's willingness to question or blunt the repartee inspires confidence in his determination to conform the legend to the demonstrable facts of the life.

Aware of the difficulties of recovering actual speech, Ellmann turns to Wilde's letters as giving us an accurate notion of "the way he really talked" (p. 543n). But the letters, of course, may involve considerable artifice and calculation, and, if we do gather from them a strong suggestion of Wilde's manner of talking, we must often remain wary of the tone and content, especially when we seek to arrive through them at the true essence of the man. The longest and best known of the letters is the one addressed from prison to Lord Alfred Douglas, eventually published as *De Profundis*. Whether or not this is, as Ellmann claims, "one of the greatest" love letters ever written (p. 515), it is certainly Wilde's only sustained attempt at a review and assessment of his own life. Recent criticism has contended that every autobiography is necessarily to some degree a fiction, a patterned selection from imperfectly remembered experience. More than most examples of the autobiographical genre, *De Profundis* engages fictional strategies—in its invention of a self and roles for the self to play, its characterization (especially the acid portrayal of Douglas), its calculated pathos and irony, and its furthering of the protagonist's legend. We may accordingly compare it—and perhaps Ellmann's biography, too—with a recent treatment of the same subject presented overtly as a work of fiction.

The Last Testament of Oscar Wilde (1983) by Peter Ackroyd purports to be a journal of Wilde's last three-and-a-half months in Paris, alternating brief diary entries with longer passages of autobiography, reminiscences of Dublin, London, and America, anecdotes, and parables. Ackroyd so adroitly reproduces Wilde's style, or his several styles, that the *Testament* reads like an authentic supplement to *De Profundis*. We readily yield to that illusion, though the jacket of the book assures us that "not a word here is Wilde's." Since the novel is in effect an extended dramatic monologue, we must assume that any errors of fact or misrepresentations are the self-justifying fantasies of the speaker. But we are inevitably concerned with the relation of the fiction to discernible truth. Did the real Wilde believe himself, as Ackroyd's narrator does, to be Speranza's son but not Sir William Wilde's? Could the real Wilde ever have met Flaubert, whose work, we know, he greatly admired? Ellmann reports neither the meeting nor the suspicion of illegitimacy. Ackroyd offers us a remarkable impression of a character and sensibility he has shrewdly appraised and brilliantly reconceived, and we are convinced that Wilde must have been very like his fictional portrait. But since we know that Ackroyd's imagination, whatever liberties he has allowed it, is working from a considerable body of actual fact, we may not improperly wish to measure the success of his tour de force against the verifiable data of a nonfictional biography.

Yet we should ask whether any full biography, even one as fine as Ellmann's, can, or indeed should be, completely "nonfictional." For whenever it aspires to present something more than a bald curriculum vitae, a good biography necessarily involves a reading of character and action and an assessment of its subject's achievement and significance, issues engaging the biographer's personal taste and judgment. More disinterested perhaps than an autobiography, it is less threatened by the possibilities of self-delusion (as in *De Profundis*) arising in the process of self-depiction. But it must, nonetheless, strive to evoke the image of a man or woman at least as credible, as "true to life," as one we expect to find presented in a competent novel. And if it is to serve as an example of biographical *art*, it must shape its materials aesthetically and impose a likely perspective on the scattered evidences of the life under scrutiny.

Richard Ellmann was an assured master of that art. His *Wilde* should remain for years to come the definitive source for reliable information about Wilde's career. But it is more than a repository of useful data; it is a studied interpretation of perplexing motives and responses, the rounded portrait of an elusive personality, a surprisingly serious and rather sober reading, which compels our regard and occasionally prompts our dissent. An introductory judgment announces the pattern of the whole: "In the smashup of his fortunes rather than in their apogee his cast of mind fully appeared" (p. xvi), and the narrative moves with tragic inevitability toward the revealing collapse. Wilde is seen as perpetually ambivalent, cultivating "half-choice" (p. 59), with "oscillation"—between the sacred and the profane, the social and the anti-social, between an affection for women and an irresistible attraction to young men—the "cardinal principle" (p. 360) of both his conduct and his writing. He is naive in his trustfulness, lavishly generous, more "earnest" than his public imagined, arch but "not so arrogant as he pretended" (p. 395). English "Victorianism" (never clearly defined) appears as a monstrous hypocrisy "ready to pounce" (p. 431) upon him (though the level of tolerance for his reputed delinquency seems to have been scarcely higher in France or America [cf. p. 458]). His fairweather friends become bitter antagonists; he is quite unable to deal with the "cruel" vindictive Whistler, "because cruelty was not in his own nature" (p. 134), and he is helplessly victimized by the "importunate, . . . infinitely resentful" Douglas, bent on a merciless squandering of Wilde's "time and money" (pp. 512–13). "Bosie" indeed, no doubt accurately rendered, is as unpleasant as any fictional villain, and his destructive, fitful love affair with Oscar, though thoroughly documented, is as paced and plotted as any novelistic intrigue.

Viewing Wilde's worst mistakes with charitable pity, Ellmann describes most of his work with a respect, sometimes muted, occasionally hyperbolic. He strains a little to praise *Lady Windermere's Fan*: "It has held the stage since, just as *Dorian Gray* has kept its public, because it is better than it seems to be. A kind of poetical glamour pervades it" (p. 367). He calls "The Ballad of Reading Gaol" "an almost great poem. Once read, it is never forgotten" (p. 534). He affirms the excellence of the critical essays and dialogues, especially "The Decay of Lying," where Wilde "gave his theories a voice" and "his paradoxes danced, his wit gleamed" (p. 304). And he describes the effect of *Dorian Gray* as "prodigious. No novel had commanded so much attention for years" (p. 323). More generally, he declares Wilde to have been "a moralist, in a school where Blake, Nietzsche, and even Freud were his fellows" (p. 100).

We need not accept these estimates without some question or demur. Yet each should lead us as readers back to the primary sources—which themselves remain immensely readable. And we should in any case grant the biographer a certain enthusiasm, the right of emphasis and some overstatement, and even the privilege of a little special pleading, if these are, as I believe, the natural and necessary concomitants of a vigorously sympathetic narrative. Ellmann's *Oscar Wilde,* the product of painstaking research and long consideration, is animated by a shaping energy and a humane but unsentimental concern for his half-legendary subject.

The Collapse of a Critical Model: Or, Was There a Rise of the Novel?

Maximillian E. Novak

Geoffrey Day. *From Fiction to the Novel.* London: Routledge and Kegan Paul, 1987. i–viii, 223 pp.

Michael McKeon. *The Origins of the English Novel, 1600–1740.* Baltimore: Johns Hopkins University Press, 1987. i–xiii, 529 pp.

Paul Salzman. *English Prose Fiction 1558–1700: A Critical History.* Oxford: Clarendon Press, 1985. i–xiv, 391 pp.

Shortly after the publication of Ian Watt's *The Rise of the Novel* in 1957, I had a conversation about the book with a colleague who specialized in the area of eighteenth-century fiction. Not only did he express his approval of Watt's work, but he felt that Watt had settled the question of the novel's origins for all time. This was the period of the New Criticism and of F. R. Leavis. Leavis had argued that time should not be wasted on inferior works and moved with assurance into a "great tradition" in the English novel that excluded Defoe, Richardson, Fielding, Smollett, Scott, Dickens, and Thackeray. The Brontes were good but not truly part of the tradition. Austen was acceptable but not representative of the most serious, moral, and mature work that could be done in the novel. The New Critics in that English Department also believed in making decisive critical judgments and were in the habit of saying, "The definitive article on this or that novel has not yet been written." Ian Watt's work had affinities with both of these movements, but he had little of their narrowness. He drew upon sociology, anthropology, history, psychology, and philosophy in making his judgments. And when he stopped to analyze given passages, he showed an ability to explicate that satisfied even the most doctrinaire New Critic.

When I look back over Watt's achievement, I wonder why I was so outraged by his book when I first read it. He revealed aspects of Defoe and Richardson that no one had thought were there, and he did it in a way that made them accessible to contemporary criticism. Alan McKillop had written a perceptive study, *The Early Masters of English Fiction* (1956), just one year before Watt's book appeared, but McKillop was essentially a literary historian, and his work attracted far less attention than Watt's more critically oriented study. To heap laurels on the more cautious and scholarly McKillop to the detriment of Watt would be a mistake, for while McKillop was far from being an unsophisticated critic, his arguments did not extend beyond specialists in early fiction. On the other hand, after Watt's book appeared, there was a surge of general interest in the progenitors of the novel, particularly Defoe and Richardson.

I was at the end of two years of research on Defoe's fiction, when *The Rise of the Novel* appeared, and although I recognized the brilliance of some of Watt's formulations—particularly his treatment of character and identity and his sociological reading of Defoe and Richardson—I considered his criticism of Defoe's occasional inaccuracies and inconsistencies as so much nitpicking. I did not think the New Criticism was an adequate system for treating fiction, and Watt, like everyone else at the time, had adopted ideas from that prevailing literary school. For example, he placed a high priority on unity in a work of art, and in commenting upon irony, he tended to accept the value-oriented sense of that word as used by Cleanth Brooks rather than the neutral rhetorical sense that was common in the eighteenth century. Although Defoe was considered a master of irony by his contemporaries, Watt had to argue against any irony in Defoe's writing. By this he did not mean that Defoe did not employ the rhetoric of irony; he was suggesting that Defoe lacked the complexity and unity that the New Critics understood by that term. Hence the long debate over irony in Defoe was actually about the nature of irony itself. But despite disagreements over these critical matters and over his treatment of Defoe's economic ideas, I admired his approach to the novel through realism. This was the legacy of Erich Auerbach's *Mimesis,* but Watt's formulation

The Collapse of a Critical Model

turned the encounter between the novelist and the world he portrayed into a philosophic exploration of reality. It was also the aspect of his criticism which raised the most objections from the start.

Of the three books under review here, only Paul Salzman is explicit about writing a literary history of early fiction in which realism is *not* the basis for judgment and about his objection to Watt's formulation, but all three set out to explore questions about early fiction with the implication that Watt's book is essentially irrelevant. That irrelevance springs, in part, from the defiance of realism in post-modern fiction. Italo Calvino's *If on a Dark and Stormy Night*, for example, refuses to allow the reader any comfort in complex characterization or realistic surface, and critics such as Catherine Belsey have attacked all novels that encourage the reader to slip into another world as examples of bourgeois corruption. The reader of the post-modern novel should not be passive. He or she should be kept constantly alert to the fictional situation and to choices that are being made. If Watt demonstrated that Defoe and Richardson created realistic worlds, so much the worse for those authors.

Fielding, whom Watt faulted for his lack of realism, appears better suited to survive this onslaught as a creator of self-conscious fiction, but among the eighteenth-century novelists, only Sterne is unanimously accepted. In recent years, Bakhtin has replaced Watt as a source of wisdom on the "novel," and for him, the novel form is essentially self-questioning and parodic. He allows for another line of fiction that he identifies as the "adventure story," but he has little to say about these works. The novel genre, which he sees as a developing form that may be analyzed and charted, belongs much more to the line developed by Sterne. And in recent years, when praising Defoe and Richardson, critics have tended to point to their imaginative worlds rather than to their realism. Anyone attempting to treat early fiction has to deal with a critical situation different from that faced by Watt some thirty years ago, and the three writers under consideration here are aware of this.

Geoffrey Day's *From Fiction to the Novel* is the least challenging of these studies, the least learned, the least thorough, the least thoughtful, but it is not without interest. It is actually less a study of fiction than of eighteenth-century criticism of fiction. Large portions are devoted to extensive quotations from the criticism. Twenty-four pages of a relatively short book are taken up with quoting a selection from James Beattie's essay, "On Fable and Romance," a work available in any research library, and at times, Day's book seems more like a selective anthology of criticism with brief comments by the editor than an organized discussion of attitudes toward fiction. I include it in this review because it demonstrates one important point and because it offers an original theory about the origin of the novel in England.

The important point has to do with the word *novel*. Day insists that there was no agreement on the existence of such a genre throughout the eighteenth century. He instances a collection, *Cooke's Edition of Select Novels*, published in 1800, as still containing anecdotes and miscellaneous material. In this, Day is absolutely correct. There were only three years during the eighteenth century when the number of works of fiction describing themselves as novels constituted a majority. Terms such as "History" or "A Tale" were far more common. This is important because Michael McKeon's book insists that Fielding and Richardson established the word "novel" as *the* descriptive term for works of fiction. Day is correct; McKeon is wrong. And since McKeon's argument depends, in part, on the novel as a new form that was recognized by all as an innovation, Day's evidence is worth considering.

Day's second major point is not worth considering. He argues that the novel did not really begin until the 1790s with Fanny Burney, Maria Edgeworth, and Jane Austen. Why? Day argues that they were truly novelists because they did not apologize for writing novels. He finds a critical justification in Laetitia Barbauld's essay, "Of the Origins and Progress of Novel-Writing" (1810), in which she makes pleasure the true basis for judging a novelist and defends her choice:

> To measure the dignity of a writer by the pleasure he affords his readers is not perhaps using an accurate criterion, but the invention of a story, the choice of proper incidents, the ordonnance of the plan,

The Collapse of a Critical Model 63

occasional beauties of description, and above all, the power exercised over the reader's heart by filling it with the successive emotions of love, pity, joy, anguish, transport or indignation, together with the grave impressive moral resulting from the whole, imply talents of the highest order, and ought to be appreciated accordingly. [p. 194]

Mrs. Barbauld certainly defends the pleasure of fiction, but Day skates over her mention of "the grave impressive moral" which, of course, she takes for granted. Day's argument has no weight whatsoever. In the "Advertisement" to *Belinda,* Maria Edgeworth stated that she was offering her work as a "Moral Tale" rather than as a novel, because most novels were so trivial and immoral. He provides almost no support for this conclusion, and if this is the result of what would appear to be a steadfast refusal to consult or at least to name more than a few secondary sources, he would have done better to have trusted less to his originality.

Day has a few good discussions. His treatment of typography in *Tristram Shandy* is excellent, and his examination of what Richardson meant by "Historical Faith" opens up some intriguing possibilities. But the work is dominated by a kind of literal-mindedness that is dazzling. He takes all of the remarks about adhering to truth and morality in the prefaces to fiction at their face value, and he seems to believe that because the authors do not, for the most part, stress the pleasure that the reader would have from the work of fiction, they thought of their fictions as moral treatises. He also seems to believe that they could not write fiction properly because they could not formulate a proper theory of fiction. If he had read Paul Salzman's study of fiction between 1558 and 1700, he might have realized that there was a great deal of fiction around and that the professions of telling a true story were part of the conventions of almost every work of fiction written during the seventeenth century. Missing this guide that is hardly new to anyone who has read seventeenth-century fiction, Day blunders into the next century's fiction and comes to the conclusion that almost all of the "novels" were merely disguised sermons. Now if a reader wanted to examine a work of fiction that was written *simply* for the pleasure of the fiction, there were ample translations from the French without much moral commentary. But most eighteenth-century readers in Britain believed that literature lacking some kind of moral commitment was not worthy of attention, and despite the tendency of much post-modern fiction to depict an amoral world, there are still many readers who continue to prefer something a little less trivial.

Day's attempt at examining the critical pronouncements on eighteenth-century fiction by the writers and contemporary critics is undertaken with little sophistication, and there is no certainty that he has actually considered his methodology very carefully. The same is not true of Paul Salzman, who concludes his work with a section titled "Writing Literary History." There he quotes from an essay by Jacques Derrida on genre, an essay in which Derrida is at his paradoxical best. "A text cannot belong to no genre," writes Derrida, "it cannot be without or less a genre. Every text participates in one or several genres, there is no genreless text: there is always a genre and genres, yet such participation never amounts to belonging" (p. 347). Salzman seeks to explain the bewildering mixture of genres which he, as literary historian, as "cartographer," has brought before his reader. He notes that the relatively neutral term, "prose fiction," in his title would have seemed odd to those Renaissance writers on whom he comments, since those writers were oriented toward particular genres. He then goes on to speak of the ways in which some works become defamiliarized over time and have an inspirational influence on authors who may be in revolt against the fiction of the previous generation. A literary historian, he argues, must be aware of these "grandfather" effects as he maps a course.

This final statement comes as something of a surprise, and while it says something for Salzman's openness to innovations in criticism, I am not certain that these are indeed the guiding principles of Salzman's work. What appears more central to his approach is a rejection of what he would consider an anachronistic approach to early fiction, the imposition of modern concepts of the novel upon older fiction. He also rejects what he sees as an evolutionary approach in Watt's work. McKeon is not entirely certain that Watt is guilty of employing a methodology which was normative in literary history from the second half of the nineteenth century up to the Second World War, but Salzman is right in sensing its presence. Although Watt does not spell it out, almost all of the literature treated in Salzman's book, prose fiction from 1558 until 1700, is treated by Watt as representative of primitive forms that were to be rejected in the struggle for literary survival. Hence Salzman rejects Watt's "realism" as irrelevant for the literature of the time. To praise works of the seventeenth century for showing flashes of the type of realism that Defoe mastered would be to continue the anachronistic game of the old literary history.

Having put realism, as a relatively unimportant device, behind, Salzman can revel in the spectacular defiance of realism in Sidney's *Arcadia* and even find something good to say for the chaotic narrative method of John Dunton's *Voyage Round the World*. Armed with the nice distinctions of Gerard Genette, he breaks down the narrative structure of the seventeenth-century French romance. And he is not concerned to find the psychological depth in character that we have come to expect of the novel. He points out how the romances moved toward analysis of character with the "portrait," and how the prose character enabled some writers to expand upon character types, but he wants us to understand why contemporary readers might have liked such devices. Salzman is constantly on guard against committing the kind of error made by critics of the romantic period when they speak of the eighteenth-century poet, Collins, as someone who just failed to achieve the true greatness of the romantics. He goes as far as to suggest that Sterne may have been influenced by Dunton, but he proposes that we enjoy Dunton for his free play of imagination and for his original narrative technique.

Salzman's overall method is somewhat reminiscent of Robert Hume's study, *The Development of Drama in the Late Seventeenth Century*. Both books proceed on the premise that new information and new critical ideas have made the older literary histories obsolete. Both are concerned with establishing particular genres within a format that is essentially chronological. But Salzman's methodology is better in a number of ways. He is more skeptical of some of the modern critical studies that he examines and more cautious about offering revisions of past ideas. He treats foreign texts as part of the flow of literature. The quixotic, the exemplary novel, and the picaresque from Spain and the romances and novels from France were rapidly translated or read in the original. To attempt to ignore these works in the name of a purely "English" prose fiction suggested by the title would have been to repeat the error made by Watt and others. Salzman justifies his practice partly on the grounds that many of the translations were closer to adaptations. Names were changed and sometimes the plot itself. But Salzman's real reason is that the fiction of this period was an international form. To consider Roger Boyle's *Parthenissa* without a discussion of the *roman de longue haleine* of Mlle de Scudéry and La Calprenède makes no sense at all. Hume certainly pointed out foreign influences upon English drama, but Salzman's method is surely more sophisticated.

Equally praiseworthy is the way Salzman treats the concept of audience. He informs us of the price of books and who would be likely to afford to buy them. He traces the ways in which some texts were abridged. Works like the popular romance, *Valentine and Orson* appeared in elaborately illustrated editions and in chapbooks of twelve to sixteen pages with crude woodcuts. Some form of fiction was available to all. One area that Salzman does not cover is the secondhand book. With a continually reprinted work such as Sidney's *Arcadia*, old and battered copies must have been available for very little. Where Salzman is strong, however, is in his refusal to succumb to generalizations about middle-class audiences for some books and upper-class audiences for others. He shows us Dorothy Osborne and William Temple discussing the latest French romance and speculating on the character and action. The salon society that spawned these works had its parallel in England. Doubtless the copies in French that reached England were read mainly by the aristocracy and gentry, but once they were translated and in circulation, they were probably read by as many people as could afford a copy. Salzman is willing to make certain divisions, but he is never doctrinaire on a difficult subject.

The book has for its subtitle "A Critical History," and Salzman notes his willingness to offer his own critical judgment and analysis. He shows this side of his work to better advantage in the seventeenth-century section than in the earlier section. He has more secondary criticism to deal with in the early section, and there are some pages that read like reprints from *The Year's Work in English Studies,* that valuable but often tedious attempt to transform a bibliography into a running critical commentary. The passages on Sidney's *Arcadia* suffer from this, and while Salzman mediates between the various theories he presents, he might have done better to have lumped the critics into more manageable camps and dealt with them rapidly. But there is a bibliographical side to this book. Salzman is careful to distinguish between various editions of individual works and provides a list of all the fiction written during his time period with the seventeenth-century works broken down according to genre. He includes foreign works in translation and however much one might quarrel with the various genres, the list should prove useful to everyone working in the field.

Although Salzman is an excellent scholar, his discussions are not always even. The sections on the imaginary voyage and utopia are particularly weak. One would hardly know that this was the great period for these genres. McKeon sees Bacon's ideas as central to the fictional tradition. Salzman hardly mentions Bacon's *New Atlantis.* Cyrano de Bergerac, Gabriel de Foigny, and Denis Vairasse appear in the bibliography at the end but are not mentioned in the text itself, and the chapter on these genres is dominated by two peripheral figures—Margaret Cavendish, Duchess of Newcastle, and John Dunton. Instead of an exploration of ideas and satirical fictions, Salzman gives us a discussion of two of the most scatterbrained writers ever produced in England. I am probably one of the few appreciative readers of Cavendish's *The Blazing World,* but it should be seen in terms of other imaginary voyages dealing with science. Salzman prefers to treat it as imaginative fiction, suggesting, perhaps, a parallel with some experimental modern fiction. Certainly the way in which Cavendish splits her character in two has a certain fascination but then so do some of her ideas. Salzman might have compared it with the allegorical voyage in Gracián's *The Critick,* but he has that classified as didactic fiction. Salzman would probably have no objection to crossing genres for such a comparison, but we might wonder if the grouping in the bibliography is as helpful as it might be.

Also somewhat uneven is his treatment of the picaresque. He gives a scholarly presentation of the development of *The English Rogue*, but he feels that audience reaction to the behavior of Meriton Latroon and his companions must have been ambiguous. I doubt it. English society during the Restoration involved a mixture of extraordinary freedom and severe restraint. A synonym for rogue was the word *extravagant*, a word which contained a sense of wandering and outrageous actions. There is one scene in *The English Rogue* that has a character performing an act of comic revenge by defecating in the middle of a floor in a public place. If this does not appear terribly funny to us, it is because, as Bakhtin has suggested, we have lost some of the comic sense of the body and its functions. I would guess that every social order in the Restoration would have found that scene amusing and that the anarchic activities of the rogue would have seemed as comic to them as the Marx Brothers appear to us. Because he does not see the humor in *The English Rogue*, Salzman worries unnecessarily about the morality of the work. We might as well worry about the tragic implications of the war in *Duck Soup*.

But these are relatively minor objections. Salzman had demonstrated just how much fiction was available for readers and how various it was. In his *English Common Reader*, Richard Altick presented a public in 1740 waiting in a mood close to desperation for a novel such as Richardson's *Pamela*. If this mythical public was waiting for anything, it was for someone to convince the members of this public that fiction could be respectable and moral. Once that point had been made, readers could choose from a vast number of earlier works if they wished. Salzman makes that case convincingly through literary history that is usually quite traditional. His book is unquestionably less impressive than Michael McKeon's more theoretical work, but it has the virtue of containing a great deal of information and thought that will stand up under any change in critical fashion. Michael McKeon's book, on the other hand, is as much a study of intellectual attitudes during the seventeenth and eighteenth centuries as

The Collapse of a Critical Model 69

of the fiction of the time; or rather it argues that there is no separating the writing of fiction from developments in the surrounding culture. This would be basic to any Marxist approach to the novel, but McKeon is after something else—after establishing a "dialectical method in literary history," as he calls it in his introduction. That method, though it has the virtue of a certain clarity, consistency, and precision, does not strike me as the book's real strength, and in so far as it tends to render it often dull and sometimes difficult, it may have the effect of continuing to leave the field to Watt's eminently readable study.

What McKeon attempts is a reduction of the early novel to a struggle between a dedication to morality on the one hand and an exploration of truth on the other. The dialectical synthesis of these two eighteenth-century attitudes produces the novel. Whereas Salzman struggles to separate and distinguish between various genres, McKeon dismisses such an effort as futile. In his opening sentence of a chapter on the "Destabilization of Generic Categories," McKeon remarks, "Modern studies of seventeenth-century prose fiction used to suffer from a particularly virulent form of taxonomic disease." The attempt to distinguish between forms became an end in itself. He continues, "Typologies of fiction, romance, history, and novel are posited, take root, sprout subcategories, and quickly send out feelers that intersect with one another to create strange, hybrid forms whose very existence finally must vitiate the discriminatory function of the original taxonomy." If McKeon had read Salzman's book, he could not have delivered a more deadly critique. Salzman had said that he wanted to provide a map through a jungle of genres. McKeon is saying that what we need is not a map including every significant work from every genre but a simplified explanatory model.

The problem for McKeon, as for any critic attempting to offer something akin to a scientific explanation of the working power of a literary work, is that while the reader may admire how well his system operates, he or she may wonder what it has to do with literature. For example, Salzman devotes some ten pages to Aphra Behn in the context of the "Restoration novel." He relates her accomplishments, discusses the way contemporaries regarded her use of detail to create a convincing reality, examines her plots, and concludes with an examination of Congreve's *Incognita* as a work representative of a more skillful narrative method—a method involving a clever play between the self-conscious creation of fiction and observations about the reality of things. McKeon, on the other hand, is involved in connecting everything to his system. Comparing Congreve's work with Behn's fiction, he remarks, "The comparison with a highly self-conscious antiromance like *Incognita* is instructive, for Behn shares with Congreve the energizing antiromance impulse and the will to pursue questions of truth into the plot itself; yet the pursuit stops short of extreme skepticism even though the logic of that movement into self-parody feels at times quite implacable" (p. 112). And writing specifically of Behn's *Oroonoko*, he concludes, "Behn may perhaps be assured that our simple and receptive faith is rewarded not by imposture but by the truth of what really happened. The hope is that antiromance, the negation of the negation, will thus fulfill itself as the true history of travel narrative. The risk is that for skeptical readers it will simply seem the "new romance" (p. 113).

It should be clear from these statements that, for McKeon, writing fiction is allied to a period's intellectual history, and indeed these comments follow a brilliant discussion of attitudes toward truth in the period, demonstrating how contemporary thought moved toward a model dependent upon verifiable truth. He shows how this was equally true of scientific investigation as of religion and theologians who believed they could demonstrate the truth of biblical miracles by treating them as convincing history. I think this has something to do with the move to realistic narrative in Defoe, but I am not at all sure that McKeon's formulation is right. As Salzman points out, the most outrageous fantasies would begin with an attack upon romances and an assurance to the reader that he was reading the truth. The process was so conventional that the reader of fiction in the seventeenth and eighteenth centuries might have been disappointed by its absence. And that brings up the possibility that some works of fiction are better explained by other fictions than by an analysis of the contemporary relationship between science and theology.

McKeon is on better ground with his approach to the social developments leading up to the novel. Here he can point to the

The Collapse of a Critical Model

decline in concepts of honor and to social change as dynamic forces in the creation of a literature that focussed on the lives of those in the middle ranks. McKeon insists that he is not forcing an ideological concept upon his materials but that if he sees a dialectical play of forces in the eighteenth century, it is because history itself is dialectical. Not everyone will agree, but few periods lend themselves so well to such a reading. What McKeon calls "aristocratic ideology" was indeed in a constant struggle with "progressive ideology" at this time, and relating such attitudes to romance and moralizing fictions makes a great deal of sense. McKeon makes this part of his case carefully, with ample references to historical developments, and no one is going to complain about insufficient learning or a lack of sophistication in handling historical data. And as might be expected, his discussion of Deloney's tales of industrious craftsmen far surpasses Salzman's quite able handling of that writer. McKeon is usually sensitive to what constitutes the political and social element in a work of fiction, but his failure to read the picaresque as a progressive rather than a conservative form strikes me as odd. Quevedo always struck me as a sport among writers of picaresque fiction in allowing his rogue no moments of real pleasure in his freedom. McKeon's explanation of why the picaresque is a conservative form is certainly ingenious, but I find it unconvincing, particularly for works such as *The English Rogue, The French Rogue,* and some of the late adaptations of Alemán's *Spanish Rogue*. The libertine nature of such works leads to other questions. Is libertinism, as it appears in narrative, an aristocratic or a progressive ideology? And what happens to the system if some parts are dead wrong?

I have concentrated on the early sections of McKeon's book because he states his ideological positions most systematically here. The third section is a study of "The Dialectical Constitution of the Novel" through an analysis of major writers: Cervantes, Bunyan, Defoe, Swift, Richardson, and Fielding. The premise behind this study of fictional developments is that there is a particular form we know as the novel and that it grew out of the debate between the adherents of Richardson and Fielding. Now, as I have mentioned previously, Day does not believe this debate was conclusive and challenges the notion that a form known as the "novel" emerged from it. Day has the better of the argument not only because McKeon was wrong in concluding that the term "novel" did become the dominant descriptive term but because, in any given year of the eighteenth and early nineteenth century, there continued to be published imaginary voyages, utopias, romances, satiric fictions, fictional memoirs, and picaresque adventures. McKeon presents us with a literary history of the novel in the style of Foucault—one with an abrupt change. The difficulty is that such a history has little to do with reality. Unlike Salzman, McKeon says little about translations, chapbooks and abridgments, and publication of older works of fiction. Certainly some forms died, but even the long French romances had enough of a readership in England at midcentury to make Charlotte Lennox's *Female Quixote* intelligible to its readers. After the publication of *Tristram Shandy* (1759–1767), anything from a collection of anecdotes to personal essays might identify themselves as novels.

What is probably most disappointing about McKeon's book is that the third section does not represent anything like a major breakthrough in the reading of individual works. He is very good on Richardson, but he has little to tell us about Defoe and Fielding that we have not heard before. Although this would not appear surprising in a critic of less learning and insight, it seems a loss in so perceptive a reader and thinker as McKeon. His major categories—questions of truth and questions of virtue—are so broad and so uninteresting that they leave him with little of real importance to say. They resemble the structural categories of Svetan Todorov; their presence is undeniable but of little importance for locating the real excellence of a work. I have to admit that I would have preferred a study of early fiction from McKeon which was less restricted. Day has almost no method at all; McKeon too much. At the end of his periodical, the *Review*, Defoe remarked, "Trade was the Whore I doated on." Of McKeon it may be said, "System and theory were the whores *he* doted on," and like the ladies of the night, system and theory may lead their lovers astray. He has written an excellent book on the history of the novel, but with all his knowledge and acumen, he might have written a better one.

Realism, Naturalism, and the New American Literary History

William E. Cain

Walter Benn Michaels. *The Gold Standard and the Logic of Naturalism*. Berkeley: University of California Press, 1987. ix, 248 pp.

In this bold and brilliant book, Walter Benn Michaels demonstrates a compelling new approach to American literary and cultural history. *The Gold Standard and the Logic of Naturalism* is a complex, difficult study, and its challenges are intensified by the demanding, indeed uncompromising, mode of address that it takes towards its readers. But this is, clearly, a significant, highly original piece of work that deals incisively with many literary, philosophical, economic, and psychological texts—some of which are well known, others of which Michaels has rescued from oblivion—written during the late nineteenth and early twentieth centuries. *The Gold Standard and the Logic of Naturalism* is a book from which literary critics and theorists will learn much and with which those who hold contrary views of this crucial period in American history will certainly have to reckon.

The Gold Standard and the Logic of Naturalism begins with an introduction keyed to Charlotte Perkins Gilman's moving short story "The Yellow Paper." Here Michaels explores Gilman's complicated rendering of "writing as work." He uses his analysis of this text to exemplify his strategy in the book as a whole—the "investigation of the position" of certain literary texts within "a system of representation" produced by capitalism. Seven chapters—all except the last one have been published previously—follow: "*Sister Carrie*'s Popular Economy," a formidable critique of both Dreiser's novel and Howells's *The Rise of Silas Lapham*; "Dreiser's *Financier*: The Man of Business as a Man of Letters," which aligns Dreiser with Ida Tarbell and John D. Rockefeller in order to dramatize the crisis and conflict of "value" at the turn of the century; "Romance and Real Estate," a shrewdly managed interpretation of the meanings of "property" in Hawthorne's *The House of the Seven Gables*, William Goodell's *The American Slave Code*, and Stowe's *Uncle Tom's Cabin*; "The Phenomenology of Contract" and "The Gold Standard and the Logic of Naturalism," both of which illuminatingly employ Norris's *McTeague* as a means through which to examine affiliations between gold, money, value, and contract; "Corporate Fiction," which fastens on the problematic identity of the "corporation" through a careful inspection of Norris's *The Octopus*; and, finally, "Action and Accident: Photography and Writing," an adroit treatment of speculation, accident, and gambling that concludes with a brisk and lively reading of Wharton's *The House of Mirth*.

The Gold Standard and the Logic of Naturalism has many strengths. It is, first of all, an adventurously interdisciplinary book. As my brief report on the chapters indicates, Michaels does have much to say about familiar realist and naturalist novels. Yet he also ranges widely, lingering attentively, for example, on James's *Principles of Psychology*, S. Weir Mitchell's writings on nervous disorders, Josiah Royce's philosophical and literary texts, the progressive political economist Richard T. Ely's massive *Property and Contract in Their Relations to the Distribution of Wealth*, and Joseph Pennell's and Alfred Stieglitz's essays on photography. He also invokes Adam Smith, Karl Marx, and congressional reports, and, in one of his chapters on Norris, spices his inquiry into Trina McTeague's suffering at the hands of her brutal husband by scrutinizing Krafft-Ebbing's observations on female masochism.

Michaels reads these various texts effectively, but it's important to note that while he often comments valuably upon them— his section on Ames's role in *Sister Carrie* is a case in point—he is not primarily interested in proposing new readings of specific books and essays. Rather, he is engaged in reading the culture, in describing general structures that characterize the texts of American capitalism. He seeks to locate a logic or dynamic that figures in, and accounts for the kinship among, a broad span of texts.

Testily opposed to "literary formalism," Michaels does not regard himself to be about the business of interpreting a particular novel by Dreiser or Norris and mustering ancillary texts designed give his close reading a new angle. The flaw in this procedure, Michaels avers, is that it hews to the customary path of literary history: it places the individual author or text at the center and, in the process, marginalizes the "structures whose coherence, interest, and effect may be greater than that of either author or text" (p. 175).

By highlighting authors and texts rather than organizing structures and systems, literary historians have, in Michaels's judgment, tended to identify literature as somehow "outside" or "beyond" culture. Authors and texts are indubitably *within* the culture of capitalism, Michaels claims. A writer like Dreiser does not do something "to" or "with" capitalism, as though he were in some fashion separate from it, ready, willing, and equipped to look at it critically from a distance. Instead Dreiser's novels, in line with other texts of the period, exemplify and illustrate the workings of capitalism and its forms of representation. The culture itself provides the conditions within which a novelist writes; he cannot write, and does not in fact exist as a self and subject, outside them.

From this vantage point, Dreiser counts in literary and cultural history not because he possesses a critical attitude toward consumer culture, but, rather, because he is so profoundly part of that culture and does not (i.e., could not) ever transcend it. Some might reply that this argument portrays Dreiser as a less imposing and urgently relevant figure for resolute critics of capitalism. But Michaels insists that it is unproductive, if not wholly unsound theoretically, to talk about writers taking critical attitudes, or adopting critical stances, toward capitalism. They are in it; they embody and bear witness to it.

Michaels does not say so explicitly himself, but he would likely add that while he may furnish us with a different, less critical Dreiser, he also provides us with a more interesting Frank Norris. Frequently indicted for his stylistic excesses and ideological confusions, Norris counts in Michaels's book in a large way. Even *Vandover and the Brute*, from which many of Norris's devotees often shrink, receives serious attention in *The Gold Standard and the Logic of Naturalism*. Norris's novels possibly fail to display "literary value" in the older sense of the term; but, seen within the signifying patterns of turn-of-the-century capitalism, they manifestly exhibit the very concerns which the new literary historian will wish to register. With Norris as with other writers, Michaels is thus not seeking to demonstrate literary merit; his aim is to assemble, and, in some instances, to recover and recuperate texts that will enable him to foreground the "logic" of naturalism and express that logic cogently. Michaels balks at interpreting texts in strictly formal or stylistic terms, for such an approach would once more intimate a false separation between literature and the conditions within which it is defined and given its life.

One key dimension of *The Gold Standard and the Logic of Naturalism* is, then, its revisionary understanding of authors, texts, and the writing of literary and cultural history. Another lies, I think, in its appraisal of the relation between literature and the economic base of society. Michaels emphasizes that economic conditions do *not* simply produce or generate literary texts. Such texts do not mirror, reflect, or spring from the culture, but, in words which Michaels yet again favors, more generally illustrate and exemplify it. Literature and the economy participate in the same system of representation, partaking of, and testifying to, a common field of force. If I follow Michaels correctly, he appears to be stating that the texts of a culture display a certain shared logic even as he also affirms that there is no necessary relation between the special interests of capitalism and literary texts. Such texts exist within the system of capitalism—which is different from saying that they minister to, and serve the needs of, a capitalist cause and class. We cannot comfortably discuss a writer as a critic of capitalism, as though he were skeptically "outside" it. Nor can we label him a servant of capitalism, as though he were "outside" it in a different sense, somehow writing and laboring on its behalf and taking his cues from higher powers.

As this summary suggests, *The Gold Standard and the Logic of Naturalism* is an extremely provocative book, rigorously conducted and relentless in its argumentative demands. Michaels pointedly alters the framework for criticism, expands the range of texts to be considered, and redefines the reasons for reading them. He charts new directions for critics and historians to pursue while also sharply disputing kinds of literary approaches and political judgments with which critics have regularly aligned themselves. Many readers, and I number myself among them, will find Michaels's book to be extraordinarily stimulating; other readers—not altogether unfairly—will judge it to be too extreme, too radical, and, hence, alarming and angering. *The Gold Standard and the Logic of Naturalism* is not a scholarly work one can be neutral about; it intends not to "add" to our knowledge of the period, but, more fundamentally, to reorient and dramatically change our ways of making knowledge and writing history.

Like any high-risk critical venture, *The Gold Standard and the Logic of Naturalism* has its troubling limits and shortcomings. Occasionally, Michaels allows the spiraling nature of his insights to get the better of his prose, as in the following sentence from his analysis of what it means to "personify" the economy: "The desire to personify the economy is the desire to bridge the gap between our actions and the consequences of our actions by imagining a person who does not do what we do but who does do what what we do does" (p. 179). Sometimes, too, Michaels's readings seem forced and unpersuasive, as when, in his chapter on *The Octopus*, he claims about the starving Mrs. Hooven that "it is almost as if starving to death represents somehow a failure to be hungry enough and hence as if Mrs. Hooven's final experience of her body is in some sense comparable to the satisfaction experienced by the Gerards and their guests" (p. 183). Norris's text doesn't really support this view, and Michaels's own hedging of his point ("almost," "as if," "as if," "in some sense") reveals that he is not entirely convinced that it does either.

Especially in his chapters on Norris, Michaels also slights the exorbitancy and downright strangeness of so much naturalist language. One recalls, for instance, Norris's verbally intoxicated description of the harvester in *The Octopus*, a description that offers, by the way, grandiose opportunities for commentary on hunger and satiation:

It was the feeding of some prodigious monster, insatiable, with iron teeth, gnashing and threshing into the fields of standing wheat; devouring always, never glutted, never satiated, swallowing an entire harvest, snarling and slobbering in a welter of warm vapour, acrid smoke, and blinding, pungent clouds of chaff. It moved belly-deep in the standing grain, a hippopotamus, half-mired in river ooze, gorging rushes, snorting, sweating; a dinosaur wallowing through thick, hot grasses, floundering there, crouching, grovelling there as its vast jaws crushed and tore, and its enormous gullet swallowed, incessant, ravenous, and inordinate.[1]

In reading Norris, it's often hard to avoid feeling that his language "is" the story, for it so egregiously calls attention to itself and revels in its own energy and exaggeration. Norris loves packed pages and overpopulated sentences and paragraphs: he enjoys indulging in, and parodying, his own verbal prowess, and constantly plays metaphorical changes on the object of his stylistic interest. Here, the harvester is less Norris's referent than his writerly opportunity, something to be seized upon and blown up into huge cartoons. Because Norris inveterately writes like this—his prose is typically as "inordinate" as the harvester he boisterously depicts—his characteristic forms of extremist language would seem to mandate analysis. To be sure, Michaels does cite and interpret passages from *The Octopus* and Norris's other novels, but he does so in order to further his search for the naturalist logic they exhibit. Though certainly appropriate, this procedure risks being too narrowly focused, too negligent of the self-evident surface of Norris's prose.

More generally, and intriguingly, there are signs in *The Gold Standard and the Logic of Naturalism*, a purportedly historical study, of Michaels's own hesitancy about prosecuting a historical argument. For example, though he attends fleetingly to Richard Chase and Donald Pizer, he basically shuns engagement with the many scholars who have written about the literature produced at the turn of the century. He makes no mention, for example, of estimable books by Alfred Kazin, Leo Marx, Larzer Ziff, Harold Kaplan, Edwin Cady, Warner Berthoff, Gordon O. Taylor, and Charles Walcutt. These books constitute prior ways of examining realism and naturalism, and it would appear necessary for any new book—necessarily existing within a field others have shaped—to acknowledge this historical fact and outline what it means.

The chapter on Hawthorne, which does not fit historically with the rest of the book, is also perplexing. True, Michaels does deal here with property, real estate, money, and other issues related to those he tackles elsewhere. Yet one wonders just how closely Michaels can tie Hawthorne and writers of the 1850s to Norris, Dreiser, and others who were active in the 1890s and early 1900s. Michaels succeeds in providing thematic links between the two periods and groups of writers, but this is not the same as demonstrating their historical relatedness. If his argument in the Hawthorne chapter were primarily a historical one, he might have enlarged his discussion of slavery to include Frederick Douglass as well as Stowe and Goodell. Along with his fellow abolitionists, Douglass pondered the disturbing ambiguities of the slave as the "property" of his master; according to Southern law, when the slave ran away, he was a thief, because in stealing himself, he was stealing what did not belong to him—he belonged to his master and therefore held no title to his own body. From one perspective, I am inclined to say that Michaels should have done this: he should have introduced Douglass's and other blacks' writings on these issues to supply a richer historical context for his chapter. But, of course, if he had done so, he would have found his Hawthorne chapter growing all the more historically particularized and, consequently, detached from the main focus of his book. As it stands, the Hawthorne chapter does arguably make sense in *The Gold Standard and the Logic of Naturalism*, but it's a kind of sense that is essentially thematic rather than historical.[2]

Michaels's avoidance of previous scholars' work and his somewhat puzzling inclusion of a chapter on Hawthorne expose, I think, his own desire to do what he claims cannot be done—transcend, that is get beyond or outside, the conditions within which one writes. He does not want to be caught within past scholarly debate, nor does he wish to be confined to the period he chose for the subject of his monograph. Michaels himself regularly professes not to believe that we can step to the side of historical conditions and reflect upon them; they inform and, indeed, "are" our consciousness, and it is folly to imagine we can dwell somewhere else. Similarly, in his and Steven Knapp's vigorous essays on (or, rather, "against") literary theory, Michaels submits that we cannot articulate a "theory" of and for practice, since such a theoretical enterprise assumes we can move outside our practice in order to frame and formulate its conditions.[3] It is this tenet that likely accounts not only for the assumptions about the writing of cultural history which Michaels holds, but also for his refusal to develop and elaborate them in detail. The introduction to this book contains some reference to the assumptions that operate in and empower *The Gold Standard and the Logic of Naturalism*, but these are deliberately sketchy, asserted rather than argued for. Revealingly, too, the book has no formal conclusion. Where another critic might have spelled out the theoretical and methodological implications of his study, Michaels is silent.

While desirable for readers, an explicit introduction and conclusion would contradict Michaels's motivating belief—that what counts is the mapping of a system of representation, not the theoretical justification for the act or any attitude one might take toward the system itself. But, as I have suggested, contradictions nevertheless do already figure in the form and argument of Michaels's book. I would propose that these are inevitable, however much Michaels might want to escape or outflank them. It is inevitable that one will theorize about practice, reflect on the act of writing cultural history, and articulate and debate attitudes toward capitalist structures.[4]

The central section of Michaels's introduction bears importantly on the points I am making. "I use the term *naturalism*," Michaels states,

> rather than the more general term *realism* not to help breathe new life into the old debate over what naturalism is and how exactly it differs from realism; indeed, I hope to avoid that debate entirely and, if possible, some of the fundamental assumptions that govern it. Insofar as naturalism has been continually (and plausibly) defined as a variant of realism, it has been caught up in endless theorizing about the nature and very possibility of realistic representation: do texts refer to social reality? If they do, do they merely reflect it or do they criticize it? and if they do not, do they try to escape it, or do they imagine utopian alternatives to it? Like the question of whether Dreiser liked or disliked

capitalism, these questions seem to me to posit a space outside the culture in order then to interrogate the relations between that space (here defined as literary) and the culture. But the spaces I have tried to explore are all very much within the culture, and so the project of interrogation makes no sense; the only relation literature as such has to culture as such is that it is part of it. [pp. 26–27]

Historically minded as he is, why does Michaels seek to avoid the "history" written by his critical predecessors? Indeed, why does he assume he *can* avoid it? Throughout *The Gold Standard and the Logic of Naturalism*, he stresses that writers are inevitably "in" culture and layered in history. Yet here Michaels himself strikingly shows how a writer can do, or at least desire to do, what he has contended cannot be done—surpass the conditions of writerly work. What we witness at this moment is not a commitment to history but the determination, exercised through sheer will, to move beyond it.

This same determination is evident in Michaels's handling of the question, did Dreiser like or dislike capitalism? Michaels judges that we cannot usefully deal with such a question, because it posits attitudes that exist outside the very system which gives them any meaning they might possess. He therefore dedicates himself to interpreting Dreiser's texts in ways that will disclose their place in the system, their site in the culture. We can no more profitably define Dreiser's attitude, Michaels implies, than we can, in the final analysis, summarize the "logic of naturalism" itself. Scanning texts engaged in cultural work, inspecting the logic of naturalism in action in particular instances—these tasks, for Michaels, comprise the agenda for criticism and literary history.

Here again, however, one wants to intervene in order to remark upon the warring tendencies within *The Gold Standard and the Logic of Naturalism* and the conflicted position Michaels has embraced. Whatever he wills or wishes, most readers who take up his book will be interested in discovering how it succeeds or fails in supplementing critical discourse about realism and naturalism. To imagine otherwise would be, precisely, to conceive of *The Gold Standard and the Logic of Naturalism* as existing outside a set of historical conditions. To imagine otherwise would violate the very belief that Michaels has expressed so fervently.

Furthermore, why must Michaels rule out the question whether Dreiser "likes" capitalism? Such a question may seem to lack sophistication, yet it has just the kind of starkness and crude honesty which Dreiser himself would have found compelling. What do I think about capitalism? How do I feel about it? These questions, too, have a historical dimension, and Dreiser, for one, asked and delved into such questions all the time. They inhabit the culture—they are cultural questions—and that is why it seems both restrictive and illogical to describe (and dismiss) them as Michaels does.

"If, then, I speak of the logic of naturalism," Michaels maintains as the passage from the introduction continues,

> it is not to identify a specific relation between literature and the real, or even a specific ideological function of literature in relation to the real. I want instead to map out the reality in which a certain literature finds its place and to identify a set of interests and activities that might be said to have as their common denominator a concern with the double identities that seem, in naturalism, to be required if there are to be any identities at all. And if "The Yellow Wallpaper" is for me an exemplary text, it is not because it criticizes or endorses the culture of consumption but precisely because, in a rigorous, not to say obsessive, way, it *exemplifies* that culture. [p. 27]

In his reading of "The Yellow Wallpaper," and in other readings presented in *The Gold Standard and the Logic of Naturalism*, Michaels indeed brilliantly delineates the manner in which texts exemplify their culture, but I remain unclear why this type of analysis excludes others. "Liking or disliking" capitalism, and "criticizing or endorsing" it, are formulations that are not at all separate from the contexts of capitalism. Michaels, it would appear, could provide an exemplary account of the workings of a text, could proceed—as part of the same inquiry—to consider the critical or uncritical attitudes toward capitalism which the text illustrates, and all the while could remain within the terms and conditions of culture. His unwillingness to take this route is the most curious feature of his important and immensely challenging book.

Notes

1. Frank Norris, *The Octopus*, ed. Kenneth Lynn (Boston: Houghton Mifflin, 1958), p. 423.

2. Surprisingly, Michaels does not analyze any writings by black authors. In part, this results from his central emphasis on well-known naturalist texts by Norris and Dreiser; it may be that he does not see Charles Chesnutt, Sutton Griggs, James Weldon Johnson, and other blacks to be situated in this tradition and manifestly implicated in its logic. But these novelists and short-story writers and, even more, such educators and polemicists as Booker T. Washington and W. E. B. Du Bois, would nevertheless seem highly relevant to the cultural history of the period. For obvious reasons, these men were very much absorbed in (and vexed about) the rise of American capitalism, the explosive growth of big business, the problems of personal and corporate identity, and the nature of representation.

3. See Walter Benn Michaels and Steven Knapp, "Against Theory," *Critical Inquiry*, 8 (Summer 1982), 723–42, and also the responses to this essay and Knapp and Michaels's reply to their critics, *Critical Inquiry*, 9 (June 1983), 725–800.

4. Commentators on Michaels's work sometimes describe him as having shifted from Derrida to Foucault, from deconstruction to new historicism, but this is, I think, a potentially misleading account. In one of his early essays, "*Walden*'s False Bottoms," *Glyph*, 1 (Baltimore: Johns Hopkins Univ. Press, 1977), pp. 132–49, Michaels does perform a deconstructionist reading; in this respect, one can perhaps accurately observe a significant adjustment in his current, openly historical procedure and in the types of non-literary, often out-of-the-way texts he is now regularly drawn to cite. But in his present research, as in his past, Michaels has been especially interested in the constitution of the self and subject. How do texts render the processes according to which selves are defined, formed, valued?—this has long been Michaels's dominant concern, and it looms larger than the question whether he has changed allegiances from one master-theorist to another. Cf. "The Interpreter's Self: Peirce on the Cartesian 'Subject'," *Georgia Review*, 31 (Summer 1977), 383–402, and "Writers Reading: James and Eliot," *Modern Language Notes*, 91 (October 1976), 827–49.

The Dreiser Surge

Philip L. Gerber

Richard Lingeman. *Theodore Dreiser: At the Gates of the City, 1871–1907.* New York: G. P. Putnam's Sons, 1986. 478 pp.

Thomas P. Riggio, ed. *Dreiser-Mencken Letters: The Correspondence of Theodore Dreiser and H. L. Mencken, 1907–1945.* Philadelphia: University of Pennsylvania Press, 1986. Two volumes. xxiii, 843 pp.

While the Second World War raged in Europe and Asia, Theodore Dreiser and his friend Henry Mencken—both now on the downslope from middle age—began giving serious consideration to the manner in which posterity might view them and their careers. More important, they took steps that would assure access to vital documents for scholars of the future. Our knowledge of this concerted action begins with Dreiser's word to Mencken that the University of Pennsylvania was "taking over all [his] stuff, lock, stock, & barrel" (p. 671). Every few days, a shipment of liquor boxes stuffed full of papers was leaving Hollywood for Philadelphia. Scattered among these informal archives were "a lot" of Mencken letters, and Dreiser was curious to know whether his old friend wanted him to continue sending what he found or perhaps wished the letters to be saved in a separate place.

As it turned out, Mencken himself had begun to collect copies of his letters as aids in the writing of his projected *Magazine Days* memoir and was delighted to discover that his correspondence with Dreiser, dating back to 1907, had not been tossed into the trashbin. His own archives contained hundreds of letters from Dreiser. Joined, would not these sets of letters by themselves make an interesting record? By early 1943 Mencken had obtained photostats of his letters and Dreiser's and arranged them in a sequence he thought loaded with "interesting stuff," a collection certain to "edify posterity" (p. 682). In fact, the complete Dreiser archives, of which the letter sequence was only a miniscule portion, could not help but become a fountainhead of future scholarship, thought Mencken, and he predicted, in the hyperbolic style he so often adopted with Dreiser, that it would not be long before a "couple of young Ph.D.'s" would tackle the Dreiser papers and produce a "series of studies so profound no one on earth will ever be able to read them" (p. 682).

So far as the value of the Dreiser archives is concerned, Mencken's forecast of a half-century ago has proved to be right on the nose. Both he and Dreiser have made steady progress into solidly recognized positions as the major influences upon an era which quite conceivably could come to be known in literary history as the Times of Dreiser and Mencken. Particularly where Dreiser is concerned, scholarly attention has not lagged. The past half-dozen years alone have brought a dazzling range of publications which both presume and confirm Dreiser's permanence as "the master and innovator" of the period which climaxes with the First World War, those years when the battle for literary realism in American was won.[1]

This recent outpouring might be said to have gotten underway with the publication of the Pennsylvania Edition of Dreiser's 1900 masterwork, *Sister Carrie*, produced under the general editorship of Neda M. Westlake, longtime curator of the Dreiser papers at Penn. That edition, accompanied by a full panoply of editorial apparatus, including the history of the book's composition, variant readings, revisions and emendations, maps and photographs, has proved to be only the first volume in an ambitious plan eventually to reissue all of Dreiser's works in authoritative editions. This means, often, the restoration of suppressed materials which show Dreiser to have been far in advance of his day in the frank delineation of reality. The unexpurgated *Carrie* appeared in 1981, and the following year the University of Pennsylvania Press issued a wholly new Dreiser book, *American Diaries, 1902–1926*, based upon hitherto unpublished manuscripts in the university's treasure trove. *American Diaries*, once again under the guidance of general editor Westlake, was edited impeccably by Thomas P. Riggio and James L. W. West III, who are to play major roles in the full Pennsylvania Edition as it evolves. The *Diaries* are most notable for an infusion of detail which fleshes out the otherwise somewhat skeletal record of Dreiser's daily life, recounting most memorably his relationships with the several women friends/editors who became his sleeping partners, though not necessarily in that sequence.

In the *Diaries* Dreiser also reveals a powerful tendency toward hypochondria and provides details of the depressive abyss into which he tumbled after the publishing debacle of *Sister Carrie* in 1900. How the novelist recovered from that neurasthenic plunge has been told in yet another autobiographical account, *An Amateur Laborer*, again from the University of Pennsylvania Press and edited from archival materials by Richard W. Dowell, since 1970 the capable editor of *The Dreiser Newsletter*, lately metamorphosed into *Dreiser Studies*. By the time this essay appears in print, these new works will have been joined by an extensive array of newspaper pieces written while Dreiser was a young reporter in St. Louis, now ferreted out and identified by Theodore Nostwich of Iowa State University and to be entitled *Theodore Dreiser's "Heard in the Corridor" Paragraphs and Related Articles*. Nostwich has also prepared a collection, for the Pennsylvania Dreiser Edition, of Dreiser's other apprentice newspaper work—this volume to be entitled *Journalism, Volume I*. In addition, Nostwich is working on the Pennsylvania Edition of Dreiser's autobiographical *Newspaper Days*, a book from whose first incarnation huge slabs of data were slashed in order both to condense an outsize text and to forestall a very real threat of censorship. These Nostwich editions will disclose a great deal that is new about the writing Dreiser did during the 1890s and will demonstrate that *Sister Carrie* was far from being an inexplicably lucky fluke by a would-be novelist. Rather, *Carrie* topped off a decade of steady composition and publication nearly on a daily basis.

In addition to the first-time publication of works left in manuscript by Dreiser, we have a continued parade of critical studies. Among them, Philip Fisher's *Hard Facts: Setting and Form in the American Novel* (1985) is of particular interest. As he argues the centrality in literature of three American settings, Fisher writes of the partially conquered wilderness and the problem of the Indian as exemplified by Cooper's *Deerslayer*; the independent, stable, family-sized homestead and the question of slavery, most memorably written of in Stowe's *Uncle Tom's Cabin*; and finally the half-built industrial city with its commerce and exchange patterns, for which Dreiser's *An American Tragedy* and *Sister Carrie* are the outstanding cases in point. But the true significance of Fisher's book for Dreiser scholars is the inclusion—sans apology or comment—of Dreiser on equal footing with earlier and less controversial members of the novelistic canon. He is perceived, not as an anomaly, but as a key figure in a natural historical progression. That has not always been so.

Something of the same is implied by publication of *The Small Canvas* (1985), Joseph Griffin's study of Dreiser's shorter fiction, its title borrowed from an interview in which Dreiser told Montrose J. Moses that he neded to work on a larger canvas than the short story typically provided. That the term "short story" was by definition incompatible with Dreiser's usual methodology soon became a cliché, even with critics kindly disposed toward him. Mr. Griffin recounts all this without being dissuaded from devoting a volume (appropriately a slim one) to the ostensible aim of proving precisely the opposite. It is notable, however, that after 144 pages of argument, Griffin arrives at the point where he began. Having considered a trio of outright Dreiser successes—"Free," "The Old Neighborhood," and "The Second Choice"; having given the nod to a handful of also-rans—"Convention," "Typhoon," "Sanctuary," and "Nigger Jeff"; having then stretched credulity more than a bit in order to include that staple of the genteel-era anthologists, "The Lost Phoebe," Griffin concludes that Dreiser wasn't really much of a short storyist after all, and that Charles Shapiro was on the mark in 1962 when he agreed with Ray B. West's judgment made a decade earlier that Dreiser's stories too often resemble novels which have undergone compression and dehydration. Were there any solid case for glorifying Dreiser as a short-story writer, it would have been made by now. All the same, it is arguably of value to have a volume devoted solely to the shorter works of fiction, for such a volume befits the serious treatment of a major author. The big writers should have all aspects of their careers examined, even if only to settle the dust for once and all. This is the virtue of *The Small Canvas,* which, once again, implicitly recognizes Dreiser's status. And there are other recent works which bear upon Dreiser in intriguing ways, but there is insufficient space here to do them justice.[2]

However, in the recent history of Dreiser studies, the appearance of Richard Lingeman's *Theodore Dreiser* is a genuine publishing event. The first full-blown biography since W. A. Swanberg's *Dreiser* (1965), it is clearly ambitious in scope, one proof being that this first volume requires well in excess of four hundred pages to arrive at the Dodge republication of *Sister Carrie* in 1907. Not only Swanberg but all of Lingeman's biographical predecessors have contributed significantly to the foundation upon which he has erected his own effigy of Dreiser, man and writer. The first of these, Dorothy Dudley, had the advantage of working directly with Dreiser during the years following his great, unexpected success with *An American Tragedy,* and much of what she wrote would be irrecoverable today had she not completed her quirky but useful *Forgotten Frontiers* (1932). Robert H. Elias also had the advantage of working directly with Dreiser, but during the novelist's twilight years. In addition, Elias was a scholar who took pains to verify his data before presenting it to the world. Combined with his collecting of new data through interviews and correspondence with many who knew Dreiser and were still among the living, Elias's scholarly approach makes his *Theodore Dreiser: Apostle of Nature* (1948) a reliable text today, even though it was first issued forty years ago.

Swanberg, relying even moreso than Elias upon letters and taped interviews with Dreiser contemporaries, was aided by the fact that, with Dreiser safely dead, many who knew him could now speak frankly. After reading the behemoth biography produced by Swanberg—614 pages closely packed with fascinating detail—one's impression was that here, without any doubt, must finally be gathered everything even half-worth-knowing about the novelist's life. Swanberg seemed to draw his motivation from the same source that inspired the reporter-hero of Dreiser's "Nigger Jeff" to promise himself: "I'll get it all in! I'll get it all in!" Recent readers of Swanberg have detected other motivations, of course. Among Dreiser scholars in particular there runs a strong current of suspicion that the biographer was propelled by an innate dislike for his subject. Others have located in Swanberg's subtext a pervasive image of Dreiser as a child who never grew up.[3]

If Lingeman's *Dreiser* proves anything, it is that the biographical record is never as complete as one might hope or believe it to be, for Lingeman incorporates a great deal that is new since Swanberg, based upon his own and on others' scholarship. One result of this labor places a new emphasis upon the novelist's father, John Paul Dreiser, correcting somewhat the biased view given by his jaundiced son. This is an important addition, for Dreiser's German father sailed to America from a non-English-speaking nation, and his resultant immigrant experience was that of the Outsider. The fact is crucial to understanding his son's stance vis-à-vis society and the development of a defensive attitude which is reflected accurately, although perhaps innocently, in Lingeman's subtitle, *At the Gates of the City*. In the years since Swanberg wrote, Dreiser's erotic courtship letters to his fiancée, Sara Osborne White, have been released from the tight restrictions that discouraged their use, and Lingeman has drawn upon them at considerable length to expand his portrait of Dreiser at that most critical juncture in his life: marriage. Lingeman is interested also in presenting the reader with an American context of historical, social, and economic details, taken more often than not from contemporary newspapers and within which the life proceeds. I find this a commendable aim, although at times the integration of context and life is not wholly successful. Ironically, it is in his contextual sidelights that Lingeman seems most likely to slip into inaccuracies that have the unfortunate effect of calling into question the reliability of his book as a whole. Examples here would be Lingeman's inclusion of William T. Stead's muckraking exposé *If Christ Came to Chicago* among the "popular novels" of the 1890s (p. 88). Even though on page 120 he appears to know otherwise, his date for Stead's book, 1895, is a year off the mark. It is careless to assert, as Lingeman does on page 93, that Charles T. Yerkes founded a newspaper, *The Inter-Ocean*, whereas in reality the newspaper was already a going concern in Chicago and was purchased precisely for that reason and in order to provide Yerkes with an organ possessed of some readymade reputation that might rub off on him and serve as an antidote to his nefarious schemes for ruling Chicago. It is careless also to confuse the electric fountain which Yerkes gave to the city, to enhance his image as a benefactor rather than as a buccaneer, with the later fountain designed for the White City of Chicago's World's Columbian Exposition (p. 120). To dwell upon such errors of fact, all of which occur in the space of thirty pages, might seem excessively nitpicking, and to say that Lingeman demonstrates something less than a complete awareness of Charles T. Yerkes and his Chicago activites might seem inconsequential were it not that Yerkes, who was to serve as Dreiser's model for *The Financier* (1912) and *The Titan* (1914) is certain to be pivotal in the second volume of the biography.

On a more positive note, I am moved to predict that in his second volume Lingeman will bring into sharper focus his already apparent thesis-in-the-making. If a single strand runs consistently through the first volume, wherever Dreiser's life and his writings are touched upon at once, it is that of an author at the mercy of his sexuality. This is quite respectably twentieth-century, of course. One might even depict it as *de rigueur*—the image demanded by the age. Lingeman insists upon the sex theme more consistently than any previous biographer, here following Swanberg, who was the first to heed Dreiser's erotic goings-on, even if somewhat voyeuristically. I see Lingeman on solid ground here. He says early on of Dreiser: "From the start, his creative drive was powered by erotic energy" (p. 126). That concept soon becomes the controlling device in his analysis of *Sister Carrie*, with its turnabout image of Carrie seducing her pair of lovers, Hurstwood and Drouet, from the stage of the theater in which they watch at she plays Laura in "Under the Gaslight." Lingeman's thesis surfaces occasionally throughout the book, never intrusively and only sometimes explicitly. "There is a strong undercurrent of eroticism in Dreiser's writing," he reminds us (p. 244–45), sometimes joining such a statement with examples. Or he may suggest that the fictional Carrie Meeber achieves reality sufficient to genuinely rival Dreiser's bride of two years, a girl not quite perceptive enough to notice that her husband was "borne along by an erotic subcurrent of desire for his heroine" (p. 251). Eroticism is seen as central to later works of fiction as well:

> Dreiser's sexual desires, which demanded variety, were thwarted by the constrictions of monogamy. . . . He saw Jug [Mrs. Dreiser] as an obstacle to his sexual fulfillment [and] in his desire to be free of [her] lay the beginnings of an understanding of Clyde Griffiths' feelings toward Roberta in *An American Tragedy*. . . . Dreiser's marriage provided the psychic key that would admit him to the forbidden place—the mind of a murderer. [p. 403]

Passages such as this heighten a reader's anticipation of volume two. In producing it, Lingeman will have as resource the private diaries—in particular the American diaries referred to earlier in this essay—which recount in mesmerizing detail the bedhopping that Dreiser indulged in after his marital break, years in which his varietism ran riot. This is strong stuff. It will be interesting to see whether Lingeman makes it work for him as effectively as it does in the first portion of his effort to chart the life of the complex man who was Theodore Dreiser, novelist.

Coincidentally, Thomas P. Riggio's edition of *Dreiser-Mencken Letters* picks up in 1907, almost precisely where Lingeman's first volume closes. *Letters* is one of these scholarly contributions from which only good things can flow. It comes to us in two handsome volumes and 800 entertaining pages which at last reveal firsthand the length, breadth, and depth of the bonds between the foremost American novelist and the most influential literary critic of the period 1910–25. Every biographer who has written at any length about either Dreiser or Mencken has necessarily dealt at some point with the connections between them. But the record of their complex and long-term involvement is a story by itself and deserves—nay, requires—the expanded treatment accorded it here.

As Riggio reminds us, the two men started writing to each other in 1907. Their friendship lasted until Dreiser's death nearly forty years later, and by far the best record of it is contained in the more than 1,200 letters they left behind. Riggio's claim that these letters constitute one of the major exchanges in American literature is quite true. And yet, that statement by itself provides only a meager view across the expanse of literary territory which these two giants traversed and only a suggestion of the influence they wielded over it.

In 1907 Dreiser was nearing forty and stood at the height of his editorial power, lording it over a fumed-oak office as he managed the Manhattan offices of Butterick Publications. Mencken, not yet out of his twenties, was collaborating with a Baltimore physician (on baby-care articles!) in hopes of being published in Butterick's million-circulation *Delineator*. Improbable as it might seem that the ponderous Dreiser and the dapper, quick-witted Mencken might hit it off, they seem to have taken to each other at once, thereby supplying proof for the attraction-of-opposites theory of human conduct. Whatever the case, they needed each other, at first in a purely business sense, Dreiser wanting popular articles to feed his magazine's voracious maw and Mencken seeking a national outlet for the products of his pen. But this basis of mutual needs soon moved to a higher plane, for Dreiser, on the verge of losing his prestigious and lucrative post, would return to fiction-writing and would require an influential critic to boost and defend his unconventional stories. Mencken himself was driven by literary ambition and already was the author of a book on George Bernard Shaw. But he was in need of a post which might be transformed into a tower of influence, and in achieving this Dreiser was happy to help by recommending his new friend to the *Smart Set* as book reviewer.

Events moved rapidly. Within a half-dozen years, Dreiser left Butterick's, published *Jennie Gerhardt*, *The Financier*, *The Titan*, and *The "Genius"*, and came under such savage fire from the Comstocks that he seriously considered quitting the fiction game flat. Now it was Mencken's turn to act. Having made himself into something of a voice to be reckoned with, he found in the suppression of *The "Genius"* an ideal target for his literary cannons. In springing to Dreiser's defense, he could boost this friend who, fortuitously, had turned out to be a first-rate writer, and at the same instant strike a demolishing blow at their mutual foe, the Purtitan Tradition.

But before that could happen, the First World War intervened, bringing to the surface the strong ethnic ties that bound together Dreiser and Mencken as closely as did their devotion to literary freedom in America. As soon as the outbreak of the war unleashed waves of bitter anti-German sentiment, it became obvious to both men that their interdependence rested as fully on their common Germanic origins as on a harmony of literary attitudes. Perhaps by happenstance, the suppression of Dreiser's books coincided with the peak of anti-German feeling, with the result that the years 1915–17 bring the correspondence to its first dramatic peak. The more prudent Mencken spelled everything out for the impulsive Dreiser, reminding him that the United States was really and truly under Purtian domination and that any attempt at victory through frontal attack under wartime circumstances was bound to prove futile. With the nation in a state of "moral mania," a wise man must be content "to stall off the moralists however he can and trust to the future for his release." Once free of present commitments, promised Mencken, his whole life would be "devoted to combatting Puritanism" (p. 246).

Never content to play the cautious man, Dreiser shot back a predictable reply: "I have a plan. Am perfectly willing to break the postal laws and go to jail myself. It will save me my living expenses this winter" (p. 246). So panicked was Mencken by receiving this news that he tried telephoning Dreiser long distance from Baltimore and, failing to connect, wrote him an urgent note concerning the present realities. In his hurried missive Mencken tried to make clear the odds to be faced by a German challenging the Moral Establishment in a New York court circa 1915. In contrast to Mencken, Dreiser appeared to have zero appreciation of the formidable obstacles created by the juncture of moralism with waves of virulent anti-German sentiment. Mencken was more immediately aware of the public pressures on school boards to drop the German language from their curricula, on libraries to withdraw German books from circulation, on individuals and businesses to Anglicize their Germanic names. Was Dreiser, for instance, at all aware of the campaign to collect fifteen miles of signatures on a petition to President Wilson calling for a ban on publication of newpapers and magazines and books in German? In a courtroom the moralists and patriots would make mincemeat of him:

You would not have one chance in a million against them. Immediately you put critics on the stand in your defense, they would get before the judges all the anti-German snorting that has been printed. And the result would be a mad glad time of it for the patriots.... Please don't get the notion that I am disinclined to tackle the moralists. The one thing I am against is tackling them with both hands tied. [pp. 248, 251]

The *Letters* carry Mencken and Dreiser splendidly through these critical years prior to 1920 when they fought happily in the literary trenches side by side, determined to make the ghosts of the Puritans gibber in the streets.

The *Letters* carry Mencken and Dreiser through sad years of later estrangement as well, and then of eventual reconciliation. But thin-skinned as both of them were, each in his own manner, they retained beneath it all a bottom-line appreciation one for another. In his most direct expression of this bond, Dreiser would write of his perception that he would never have made a dent with his novels had not Mencken fought for him valiantly, unstintingly, and even murderously:

I remember how, almost fatalistically, you arrived in my life when, from a literary point of view, I was down and out, and you proceeded to fight for me. Night and day apparently. Swack! Smack! Crack! Until finally you succeeded in chasing an entire nation of literary flies to cover. It was lovely! It was classic. [pp. 690–91]

And Mencken's side of the collaboration could be put even more succinctly: "You are the one man in America who can write novels fit for a civilized man to read" (p. 290). Whatever else changed, these attitudes endured.

A number of these Mencken-Dreiser letters have been published before, but always in collections devoted solely to the works of one man or the other. It is cause for rejoicing that we should now have both sides of the correspondence. Linked together as they are here, they carry the Mencken-Dreiser story from 1907 to 1945 in what amounts to a dual autobiography.

Notes

1. Maxwell Geismar, *American Moderns* (New York: Hill and Wang, 1966), p. 23.

2. As an instance of a comprehensive critical study, one would wish to cite Lawrence E. Hussman, Jr., *Dreiser and His Fiction* (Philadelphia: Univ. of Pennsylvania Press, 1983). Yoshinobu Hakutani's two-volume *Selected Magazine Articles of Theodore Dreiser* (Rutherford: Fairleigh Dickinson Univ. Press, 1985 and 1987) reflects the recent impulse to make hitherto uncollected writings more generally available. *A Sister Carrie Portfolio* (Charlottesville: Univ. Press of Virginia, 1985), by James L. W. West III, with its cache of period photographs, maps, and facsimiles of the Dreiser manuscript, is a valuable supplement to the novel itself and one which attests to *Carrie*'s status as a modern classic.

3. This is the view presented by Dennis W. Petrie in his *Ultimately Fiction* (West Lafayette: Purdue Univ. Press, 1981), where he cites other works, notably Vera Dreiser's *My Uncle Theodore*, as corroboration.

Samuel Johnson and the Printed Word

Walter J. Ong

Alvin Kernan. *Printing Technology, Letters and Samuel Johnson*. Princeton: Princeton University Press, 1987. xvi, 357 pp.

Robert DeMaria, Jr. *Johnson's* Dictionary *and the Language of Learning*. Chapel Hill: University of North Carolina Press, 1986. xiv, 303 pp.

Richard L. Harp, ed. *Dr. Johnson's Critical Vocabulary: A Selection from His* Dictionary. New York: University Press of America, 1986. xlv, 268 pp.

Literature and technology used to be considered two quite disparate phenomena. Recent comparative studies of oral, writing, and print cultures have made it apparent how closely the two are connected. The technology of writing transformed orally based thought and verbalization. Beginning largely with the work of Milman Parry on the Homeric poems, differences between oral tradition and literature in the sense of written composition have been worked out in great detail across much of the world, but only now are we beginning to assess in depth the effects of print in producing the world of "letters" that we know today—a world which is a much farther cry than is commonly thought from the scribal world of Horace or of Chaucer or even from the early print world of Shakespeare. In *The Printing Press as an Agent of Change* Elizabeth Eisentein has thoroughly documented many of the widespread intellectual, psychological, social, and other changes effected by print. But the changes took time. The full shift from oral-scribal society to a print society really occurred in the eighteenth century. Then it was, in the British Isles at least, that the press "began to affect the structure of social life at every level," as Alvin Kernan puts it in his *Printing Technology, Letters and Samuel Johnson* (p. 48).

Johnson was a product of the new age, in many ways its most typical as well as its most distinguished product: a person who devoted his life to writing in order to have his works printed, and thereby to make his living. By the early eighteenth century, print had become "the basic, inescapable fact of letters," as it continued to be until our present electronic revolution. Print was the medium in which writing must exist if it was to have its major effect, and indeed the medium on which even writing that never made its way into print was most often modeled. Professor Kernan's book studies Johnson's own development as a focal point in the new era that was emerging and that would change the sense of "letters" and the feeling for literature from Johnson's age on. Kernan's work is deeply informed and thoughtful, not reductionist but relationist. He does not pretend that print was the direct cause of all the changes he discusses, but shows rather how many or most of the changes relate in one way or another to print, are interwined with it.

Print ended the world of courtly or "polite" letters, where the writer was presumed to be a gentleman and man of means or at least to enjoy the patronage of courtly or gentlemanly persons who somehow had a say over written composition. In *The Dunciad* Pope bemoaned the shift to the mechanical, democratic, and capitalistic world of print. But Pope also understood the publishing business as a fact of life, rejected overt patronage, and made his living, as Johnson was to do, out of having his writing printed, including his letters, in which, as George Sherborn's edition of the *Correspondence* showed, Pope even shifted around paragraphs from one letter to another for publishing purposes.

Kernan's introduction shows that, as Johnson himself was aware, the new form of "letters" replacing the older courtly or polite letters, indeed depended on printers but was ruled not so much by printers as by readers. In other words, in the world of "letters" a producer economy had been replaced by a consumer economy. Kernan's interpretations—and indeed many of Johnson's own insights—dovetail into much present theorizing, such as that concerned with reader-response criticism and with theories connecting the forms and uses of literature with economics.

A meeting between King George III and Samuel Johnson in 1767 in the King's Library showed how forces were realigning themselves. In a deft analysis, comparing Boswell's account of the meeting with what was probably Johnson's own account (pp. 35–47), Kernan shows how Boswell's account, though shaped by "numerous and tangled, and probably ultimately undecipherable" motives, brings out realistically the King's de facto subservience to Johnson and Johnson's "barely concealed refusal to write at the King's gracious command" (p. 40). Johnson felt that he was writing for a print-created reading public and not for the court. Johnson's feeling was to be borne out soon enough when the King's Library, with its "courtly letters" assumptions, was replaced by the national library at the British Museum (now the British Library), geared rather to the service of readers.

Print made authors authors much more than manuscript culture ever had. Even in the post-print Renaissance, anonymity often shrouded published works, and Swift still played games with anonymity during Johnson's lifetime. But print inexorably made new authors' names commercially marketable items, like trade-mark labels for manufactured products, as authors' names had not been in a manuscript culture, where texts were copied rather than manufactured. Inevitably, copyright laws would come into being, tying works more securely to their authors. But being simply marketable, while it may make one a living, is not an encouraging human experience of itself, and Kernan calls attention to the ensuing efforts of commercially powered authors to create "an acceptable, a livable, poetic role for themselves" (p. 87). The later romantic mystique of the author as an utterly special person, some sort of seer, as Mallarmé was later to proclaim, seems to have some deep roots in print technology. Boswell, as Kernan shows in detail, made Johnson as man-of-letters into a culture hero, "the image of the writer needed to authenticate letters and the life of writing in the age of print" (p. 117). In actuality, however, Johnson was less a simple and triumphant culture hero than Boswell made him out to be. Recent work on

Johnson has shown how complex he was, skeptical, doubtful both of himself and often of social values he defended.

While scribes could turn out an average of two complete manuscripts per year, Kernan estimates that about fifty-five million books were produced in eighteenth-century England. These multiple, cheap copies of books of all sorts, made possible by print and satirized by Swift in *The Battle of the Books*, obscured the idealized classics and brought into being systematic theoretical criticism, such as that of Boileau, Dryden, Pope, and many others who undertook to evaluate and create order in the new flood of reading materials. We can now see how romantic literature managed to provide printed works with a new aura (p. 152 ff.). This it did in complex ways, but one of the factors at work was the "print logic" Kernan discusses (pp. 48–57), the "concept of a single accurate text" (p. 165), always exactly the same in every copy and presumably the same as a fixed text in the author's mind. Johnson was aware of the ability of this print logic to confer authority on texts of a different order than that of texts in a manuscript culture. Print has a "platonizing power," as Kernan observes (p. 165): the "single accurate text" is like a concatenation of Platonic ideas.

Johnson, it appears, had actually made print logic a part of himself, in the sense that he could produce with great speed first drafts of written texts printable without revision. Johnson could even speak in the same lapidary way. Citing W. K. Wimsatt on Johnson's style, Kernan calls attention to Johnson's constant parallelism, antitheses, and the like. These of course were ways of stabilizing discourse long before print or even before writing. They are some of the techniques essential to the organization of thought and expression in primary oral cultures—cultures antecedent to any writing.[1] Such techniques could be fine-tooled by persons who knew writing, and were from the time of the ancient Greek sophists on. Paradoxically, in producing his print-style discourse, Johnson was falling back on some of the techniques that had given stability to preprint utterance.

The prime exhibit for the relationship of Johnson to print technology is of course Johnson's most famous work, *A Dictionary of the English Language* (1755), about which more will be said below in discussing Professor DeMaria's book. Kernan points out that the *Dictionary*, like most of Johnson's books, started with the publishers. It was needed by the printing industry because of print's "inbuilt tendency toward systematic regularity," which is to say because of its mass-production technological base. This inbuilt tendency affected printers most directly—a dictionary is "the essential book of print" (p. 184), but it also affected writers who wrote for print and indeed all writers, who more and more wrote as though they were writing for print, even when they were not. (The "English" taught today in schools is for the most part essentially "edited English," not spoken English.) Although he started with somewhat different assumptions, Johnson came to understand, in Kernan's words, that a dictionary is a "print-derived rationalistic system imposed amid and upon a chaotic scene of actual living, speaking and writing" (p. 185). Of course, the popular view is otherwise; a dictionary is a kind of thing, a repository of the hard-core, "real" meanings of real words (real words being the words in printed dictionaries).

Johnson's views of language were not innovative or original, but neither were they naive. They were of course not so thoroughly thought through as Kernan's or others' views today. One finds in Johnson traces of an "Adamic" view of language: each word has an "original" or "proper" meaning which was initially quite clear and from which other meanings deviate. But in the last analysis Johnson in effect repudiates this view, for he finds that ultimately language is entangled in human history, where words seldom have clear-cut origins. Language originates and evolves through chance and mutation and casual interests. It is essentially limited. Experience is larger than language, and many ideas, feelings, and perceptions, as Johnson states, words are insufficient to explain. To put it another way, words begin less as labels than as heuristic devices. Johnson's views here are not unlike those of F. H. Bradley (1846–1924), on whom T. S. Eliot was to write his Harvard doctoral thesis, never to be defended but ultimately to be printed as *Knowledge and Experience in the Philosophy of F. H. Bradley* (1964).

Johnson was of course not fully consistent, for he worked on the principle of earlier lexicographers that a particular meaning of any word was legitimate only if it could reasonably be derived from a passage in a printed book. No matter how widespread, oral usage alone did not count as "real" English. (This principle, long rejected by linguistic scholars, was not repudiated by dictionary-makers until the latter half of the present century.) And not all printed books would do as authorities for Johnson, as DeMaria's work well shows.

Kernan discusses many other developments attendant on Johnson's relationship to print. Print altered the relationship of reading and talking, ultimately downgrading oratory in favor of conversation (pp. 204–9). Johnson, great reader and great conversationalist, collected books, but as articles for use that print had made books to be, rather than as sacred objects. Johnson read mostly by skimming. With easy print access, knowledge was in a way moving from "wisdom" to "information" (p. 218). With the author and original context even more evidently missing in print than in writing, the printed text is "marked by absences, gaps, silences and opacity" (p. 221), and Johnson was well aware of this fact. Books, Johnson knew, were always flawed in their very conception, always contrived and never complete. Deconstruction is anticipated in Johnson's awareness here. A context of other texts had to be established to make up somewhat—never completely—for the full context of the original talking world, where speaker and hearer could fully engage one another. The dictionary implemented the needed intertextuality.

Readers became central to Johnson's concern with meaning, and it is likely enough that the term "common reader" was coined by Johnson himself. With the implied institutional authentication of courtly or polite letters no longer operative, it is the mythical common reader who confers on texts their worth and their measure of truth. He or she (and women readers became much more numerous with print) brought in those absolutes of nature and the "common sense" (pp. 236–37) which now formed the touchstones of truth. But Johnson was not naive here either, and at times shows awareness of the precariousness of the "common reader's" full grasp of articulated truth, although he credits the common reader nevertheless with an existential knowledge that is in the reality more decisive than mere articulated learning. Long before the deconstructionists, Johnson was aware that words can never be fully and consistently made clear by other words—that is to say, that no purely verbal construction is ever self-sufficient. Human words simply as words self-destruct. For as words they depend on the nonverbal existential situation in which they happen to be embedded.

Library catalogues, encyclopedias, and various knowledge trees (such as one finds in the opening foldout of Diderot's and d'Alembert's *Encyclopédie*) were other ways of coping with the chaos that the print-supported growth of knowledge threatened. As Robert Darnton has pointed out, "Pigeon-holing is . . . an exercise in power" (p. 257). It guards borders which, unprotected, might collapse. Print's tendency to fixity encouraged pigeon-holing and classificatory schemata more than ever before and eventually gave rise to "the new print-based conception of 'literature' in the sense of belles letters" (p. 259). Earlier, "literature" or "letters" had referred more generally to anything treated in writing. In this way, the concern with aesthetics in Kant and subsequent philosophers can be seen as interest in a print-generated pigeon-hole.

Johnson's *Lives of the Poets* was another attempt to order the chaos that print was exposing and promulgating. History is a strategy for establishing order, and an order which Johnson felt to be much more real than that of any philosophical organization. Kernan's discussion here (pp. 264–82) is particularly rich and suggestive, though one feels that his allowance for the threat of chaos, here and elsewhere, is rather more assertive than Johnson's would have been. Johnson was no fool, but he had a faith in the inner order of the world, sensed existentially by his "common reader," which shored him up and kept his darker moments from being as dark as those of many persons today. Again, Kernan rightly brings his exposition around to print. Whatever his earlier vague thoughts about the project may have been, Johnson set to work on the *Lives of the Poets* themselves, as commonly in the case of his other books, at the instance of three old friends and publishers, Tom Davies, William Strahan, and Thomas Cadell.

Johnson's concern with the common reader should not obscure the fact that in his mind the writer, although subject to the judgment of the common reader, was "the basic fact of letters" in the print age. This position of the writer, Kernan points out, to some degree anticipates romantic visionary poetics, but Johnson's writer lives with limited powers in "a historical scene of complex social change" not yet in the romantic's beneficent nature or transcendental truth (p. 273). For Johnson, Pope's poetry, polished, perfected, well-edged, urbane in every sense, was the height of poetic accomplishment. Johnson did not sense that a new age, the romantic age, was well in process of formation during his own lifetime. He did, however, sense literature as being formed and as existing within history, "written, read, and responded to vigorously by real people with particular interests like himself" (p. 282).

Romanticism moved away from Johnson's world of the city to the world of nature, transcendencies, and the depths of the unconscious self. Whereas Johnson's style was geared to stating social meaning, Wordsworth's romantic metaphysics produces poems which are felt as "verbal forms of natural being" (p. 291). But print had made possible romanticism, too. Locking vast amounts of knowledge firmly and reassuringly in place, it freed the mind for the cult of the remote, mysterious, inaccessible.

Kernan's book is rich and rewarding, although it works from a hermeneutic of suspicion greater than any Johnson would have consciously allowed. The "common reader" and "common sense," despite their weaknesses on close examination, did provide real support for Johnson when all else failed. But there was a dark side to Johnson's awarenesses that frequently shows, and Kernan—with the assistance of the many other recent authors he cites—has rightly brought it to our attention. What Kernan has chiefly contributed is the demonstration that the presumed clarity that print seems to call into existence was one of the things at the root of the darkness, because print only *seems* to call clarity into existence. History is not part of print; print is part of history.

Kernan concludes: "All literary history is inevitably revisionary history reinterpreting past events to support present theories, and neither the history nor the theory offered in this book can be exempt from the judgment of whether it contributes positively to the cultural function of letters" (p. 321). In fact Kernan's work does so conspicuously and rewardingly.

Samuel Johnson's *Dictionary* was essentially a *book*. Robert DeMaria begins by making this fact clear. A few years ago, a distinguished professor at a distinguished university recounted to me how a student with whom he had been discussing the use of a word, not entirely to the student's satisfaction, returned to him the next day with the definition of the word copied out—as I recall, from *Webster's Third New International Dictionary*. "Sir," the student said, "did you know that this is the definition of the word we were discussing?" "Yes," the professor responded, "I wrote the definition." The student's jaw fell. It had never occurred to him that words did not come equipped with definitions, that when he "looked up" a word in a dictionary, he was reading something that an individual or individuals had to compose in writing for print. A dictionary was only another book. A dictionary is always a book, although most people seldom think of it this way today.

Professor DeMaria shows that as late as the nineteenth century some readers—Coleridge among them—still could readily think of dictionaires as books. Johnson referred to his dictionary as "my Book" and saw the dictionary as a general encyclopedia, a book providing a basic survey of all knowledge, as well as a lexicographical work in a class of its own. As a book, Johnson's *Dictionary* relates to a great many other books, and it is its relationship to other books with which DeMaria chiefly concerns himself. He is interested not merely in Johnson's definitions but also in the works Johnson chooses and the illustrative quotations he cites from these works as well as the editorial remarks he makes in the process of constructing his definitions. DeMaria's book, based on a computerized index of some 23,000 records, is an account of how Johnson treats his subjects—which means also how the "standard," accepted authors he cites treat them.

DeMaria examines Johnson's *Dictionary* as a specialized vision of language and of the world, "different from the vision in, say, Charles Richardson's *Dictionary* or *Webster's III*" (p. x). The difference is not merely a matter of the new words included by Richardson in 1839 or *Webster's III* in 1961. It is a difference of outlook. Johnson's dictionary represents Johnson's view of language and of the world, as later dictionaries also represent their compilers' views—more complexly than Johnson's, for Johnson's *Dictionary* was essentially Johnson's own one-man work. (He used amanuenses, but they were only that. The book is his own.)

Books also have readers, and DeMaria, more briefly, writes about them, too. Johnson thought of his readers largely as learners, among them "the common workman." The book was not merely for the use of "criticks but for popular use" as well (p. 12). Johnson's purpose is educational and therefore, in his view, quite conspicuously moral in a tradition continuous with the previous history of Continental lexicography. But the central purpose of Johnson's *Dictionary* was philological and linguistic, for all that.

There are a great many studies of Johnson's *Dictionary* and specialized studies of its contents, but DeMaria's computer-based accumulation and alignment of material is new and invaluable. DeMaria has been able to identify what he calls a "central cluster of concerns" in the *Dictionary*. These show up in his chapter headings as knowledge, ignorance, truth, mind, education, language, the arts of reading and writing and speaking, the arts and sciences, fundamentals (that is, of religion), and happiness. A dictionary is also an encyclopedia, DeMaria is careful to note, providing a basic overview of knowledge for its readers, and Johnson's *Dictionary* shows how this round of subjects has been treated by the authors Johnson cites, who are mostly "standard" English authors and who thus illustrate how these subjects have been treated by a significant segment of English culture (from 1580 to 1660, the period Johnson's *Dictionary* chiefly covers). Certain subjects DeMaria omits, as he explains, for specific reasons: politics, he feels, requires separate treatment because the background is so diversified and vast, and natural science, history, and technology in Johnson's book have already been treated thoroughly in William K. Wimsatt's *Philosophic Words*. Because of the dictionary format, Johnson's treatment of his materials is necessarily discontinuous and is not always completely consistent, and DeMaria has undertaken to synthesize material where this does not deform Johnson's thought.

The *Dictionary*'s most important immediate ancestor was Ephraim Chambers's *Cyclopaedia or Universal Dictionary* (1728), and Johnson's chief amanuensis, Alexander MacBean, had in fact worked for Chambers. Johnson shares Chambers's somewhat mixed feelings about the worth and dignity of the lexicographer. Yet Johnson's famous satirical definition of the lexicographer as "a harmless drudge" has to be set against his much more serious evaluation of the importance of lexicographical work, as DeMaria makes clear. Although DeMaria's chapter headings make it evident that Johnson's *Dictionary* was, inevitably, ideological, it is equally clear that Johnson's overall approach was empirical and historical. The *Dictionary* was distinguished from its English forerunners and related to Continental dictionaries by its extensive use of quotations—116,000 of them—to back Johnson's definitions. Johnson's aims were educational and by the same token moral, as Kernan's treatment noted above also makes clear. But the aims were not simplistic or naive. Although DeMaria on the whole presents Johnson as more openly motivated and programmed than does Kernan—for the latter is concerned much more with the total intricacies of cultural history—DeMaria has no illusions that Johnson was a simple soul: "The 'man' one finds in the *Dictionary*, or indeed in all of Johnson's works, is a public presentation circumscribed by the larger, less regular, and finally unknowable person who created it" (p. 19).

What does DeMaria's careful inventory of the topics on which so much of Johnson's *Dictionary* hinges say about the nature of the *Dictionary* and of its age? Only a few sample observations about Johnson's views presented by DeMaria are possible here. Not every one of these is a new discovery of DeMaria's, but the total assemblage found in his book provides a more complete view of the ideology of the *Dictionary* than we have ever had before.

Epistemological questions frame Johnson's world. Johnson maintains confidence in immediate experience rather than hypothetical systems as the basis of all knowledge, together with the sense that knowledge is best manageable in "small, compact pieces" (pp. 48, 39). Experience is nevertheless a source of error and needs to be monitored. Learning and sense experience serve to correct one another (p. 49). Following Locke (Johnson's guiding philosopher), the *Dictionary* mostly rejects innate ideas (p. 51). However vain human learning, a desire for knowledge is a foundation for "surmise" regarding religion. Johnson cites Hooker at length to make the meaning of "surmise" here clear. For God is true knowledge (p. 55). Knowledge deals ideally with the "general" and thus at its best is likened to wisdom. In epistemological thinking, Johnson defers to the "general": the shift in emphasis to particulars was to come toward the end of Johnson's age (p. 60).

Johnson's *Dictionary* is replete with confessions of ignorance—not only in treating knowledge in general but also in regard to the universe, both macrocosmic and microcosmic, to philosophy, and to the mysteries of religion. Our ignorance is a reminder of our reliance on God. Pseudodoxia or false beliefs, treated in Sir Thomas Browne's well-known *Pseudodoxia Epidemica*, command Johnson's attention often, and among them the errors of idolatry.

The writers Johnson cites in the *Dictionary* treat of truth in terms of logic or philosophy less than Locke does: DeMaria finds that Johnson thinks of truth as "solid, tangible, independent, inflexible" (p. 78). (One recalls his famous refutation of Berkeley by kicking a stone.) DeMaria in fact calls attention to the fact that even Locke frequently adverts to truth as "substance." Probability and opinion of course receive their own share of treatment, with abundant quotations. DeMaria points out that probability and opinion are in effect Johnson's own special territory: his distrust of philosophical systems that provide total consistency and his pragmatic philosophy produced "an essentially classical mind . . . that does not flow in a continuous stream" but batters its way by indirection to "the obstinate, enclosed truth" (p. 91). Putting it another way, one might say that Johnson's intellectual disposition was rhetorical, not systematically logical.

Most of Johnson's authors commonly equate the "mind" with the "soul." Cogitation or thought is evidence of the existence of our incorporeal and immortal souls. Johnson's alignment of quotations charts the language of mind in a progression from spiritual to logical language. Memory, in the *Dictionary*, "has the place of honor that romantic theorists like Coleridge reserve for the imagination" (p. 100)—a fact that shows Johnson's and his authors' connection with the ancient Augustinian heritage. In Johnson's examples of usage, fancy and imagination are rarely praised except in some quotations from Dryden. "It is impossible to say what the *Dictionary* asserts about mind or any other subject," DeMaria concludes. The *Dictionary* records less clear-cut, separate meanings than zones of meaning (p. 105).

Education is discussed in various ways in the *Dictionary*, and is indeed "the subject of the whole book" (p. 106). Virtue is more important than learning in education. Classical study obtrudes throughout the *Dictionary*, and classical examples are constantly used for illustration, as when "dialect" is instanced as "Attic, Doric, Ionic, Aeolic" (p. 113). Grammar, rhetoric, logic, and philosophy are treated with a seriousness which is at time mixed with some amusement (pp. 120–27). Both uses and abuses of learning come in for attention. Teachers come off somewhat better than pupils (pp. 136–46). Education is not all purely academic, but can involve, for example, travel. In the last analysis, Johnson's treatment of teaching centers on moral and religious teaching. Being essentially concerned with language, the *Dictionary* tends to refer all other subjects in various ways to language. It is much concerned with what Johnson regards as linguistic abuse, and in ways which are not purely historical, especially when Johnson is thinking of the use of language to present meaning, particularly religious meaning.

Writing, reading, and speech are other special foci of

Johnson's book. Johnson thinks of writing chiefly as a matter of diction. By comparison with J. A. H. Murray and the editors of the *OED*, Johnson's ideal of diction leans toward the "scientific" and "technical" and rather away from the "literary" and the "colloquial." Johnson cites as an instance of the use of the term "decency" the lines of Roscommon, "Immodest words admit of no defence; / For want of *decency* is want of sense" (p. 178). Morality applies in the case of diction, too. Moreover, language that draws no attention to itself best serves its purpose.

In his "Plan" for the *Dictionary* Johnson proposes his illustrative quotations as coming from a kind of Great Books program, from the books it would be well for his readers themselves to read. The Bible (King James version) is the book among books, and Johnson uses some 5,000 quotations from it as illustrations from which to construct his definitions. But the *Dictionary* is occasionally satirical and skeptical about reading. What one does with one's reading is what counts, as Locke had maintained. Although he realized that the origins of language are oral, Johnson opposes what he calls "the corruptions of oral utterance." (He is a good example of the chirographical and typographic squint that writing and, even more, print generated.) He is ambiguous about rhetoric, but in general rather suspicious of it, as leading to inaccuracy. Deceit is, of course, bad.

Johnson attends to poetry and poets, to music, painting and architecture, and the "professions of the gown," medicine, divinity, and law (pp. 207–27). But the *Dictionary* "does not advance the science of criticism beyond the point to which Aristotle brought it" (p. 204). He gives a great deal of attention to the fundamentals of religion: faith, hope, charity, freedom, and death and judgment. Happiness he considers the proper goal of human life, and relates it to human life itself, to human wishes, and to work. Johnson's *Dictionary*, DeMaria finally observes, "is very nearly his life," not only "in spiritual terms, but . . . also in a somewhat more mundane way" (p. 265). He found the work of producing the *Dictionary* "a useful, morally beneficial, and financially sustaining form in which to embody" the powerful desire for "perpetuating existence in perpetual expression" that shows up in his own day in Christopher's Smart's *Jubilate Agno* and in our own century in *Finnegans Wake* (p. 266).

Kernan's and DeMaria's books complement one another. DeMaria does not spread his canvas as wide, but he covers it well with relevant detail. He does not advert so explicitly as Kernan does to the dictionary as a product of print—indeed, in many ways, as has been seen, the most typical product of print. Interestingly enough, DeMaria's own book is the product of the next, our current, age: it would have been virtually impossible to work out with only writing and print, for it is largely the product of computerized lists, sensitively analyzed.

Both Kernan and DeMaria interpret Johnson in terms of twentieth-century concerns, linguistic, critical, historical, and other. What other ways would be genuinely available for interpreting him? In doing so, they both reveal a person who fits surprisingly well into our world, not a naive "harmless drudge" but a complex and in the last analysis mysterious person. The *Dictionary* does not explicitly reveal all about everything it contains nor about its makers. Nor do Johnson's other works and his world reveal everything about themselves or about him. The age of reason in which Johnson lived was not, to Johnson any more than to ourselves, fully reasonable, totally explicable.

The deconstructionist message that you cannot ever make language come out even, that it conceals as well as reveals, and does so by its very design, that in this sense it always deconstructs itself, would have been no surprise to Samuel Johnson. It was part of his way of understanding language and life. He relied on "common sense" or the "common reader" to make language work—as it did make language work existentially—even though language alone, especially printed language, did not come out even in its own economy of operation. But Johnson was also aware that "common sense" and the "common reader" were not very tidy concepts. The visual tidiness which print introduces does not make intrinsic meaning clearer, although it makes many persons think that it ought to be and mostly is completely clear.

The computer age has made compilations easy and efficient (if not always cheap). One of the many recent useful works is *Dr. Johnson's Critical Vocabulary: A Selection from His* Dictionary, edited by Richard L. Harp. The *Dictionary* is particularly helpful in the assessment of the history of criticism, and Harp's work serves a useful purpose in illustrating one man's use of critical terms as against the several dictionaries we now have of more general usages. It gives Johnson's citations of usage as well as his definitions, and thus fits in with and complements DeMaria's work.

Note

1. See my *Orality and Literacy: The Technologizing of the Word* (London and New York: Methuen, 1982), pp. 33–42.

The Riot of Gorgeousness: The Poetry and Prose of Marianne Moore

Sidney Burris

Marianne Moore. *The Complete Prose of Marianne Moore*. Ed. Patricia C. Willis. New York: Viking Press, 1986. ix, 723 pp.

Taffy Martin. *Marianne Moore: Subversive Modernist*. Austin: University of Texas Press, 1986. xv, 151 pp.

Grace Schulman. *Marianne Moore: The Poetry of Engagement*. Urbana and Chicago: University of Illinois Press, 1986. 136 pp.

John M. Slatin. *The Savage's Romance: The Poetry of Marianne Moore*. University Park and London: The Pennsylvania State University Press, 1986. viii, 282 pp.

Modernism, like one of Marianne Moore's sentences, does not parse easily. Although the major writers of the period plume themselves with the notion that their work represents a radical departure from the literary tradition of the nineteenth century, their departures often appear destined for inhospitably different stations. Alfred Prufrock and Hugh Mauberley, given an afternoon together, might recognize in one another a shared disaffection, but Prufrock would find Mauberley overbearing in his confident condemnations, and Mauberley would diagnose Prufrock's diffidence as a symptom of the cultural maladies that he condemns. Eliot's decision to employ the first-person monologue and Pound's decision to use the third-person narrative reflect their different concerns: as Prufrock's voice falters, paraphrases, and proceeds spasmodically, the authority of the poet's voice decays and fades to a whisper; yet as Mauberley's presence in the poem weakens, the indicting voice of the narrator strengthens and replaces Mauberley's misconceptions with the narrator's vigorous desires to correct them. The theme of disaffection, viewed from the different perspectives of the first and third person, appears in Eliot's poem without the hope of a future consolation, in Pound's poem, without the narcotic despair that attends a crippling self-consciousness.

But disaffection from the received literary traditions also instigated extensive reconstructions, elaborate attempts to concoct canons that often seemed idiosyncratic in their various nominations. Distracted by the brazen sloganeering of much modernist doctrine, critics often forget that amidst the clamor for reform several of the major modernist poets were engaged in traditional literary history, and this essentially conservative enterprise is an important, often overlooked, obsession of the period. Yeats's *A Vision*, which was first published in 1937, originated in 1917 when his wife began the automatic writing that would eventually provide him with an elaborate system of metaphors. As his gyres organized cycles of history, so the twenty-eight incarnations of his wheel revealed his literary values. Phase fifteen, the phase "of complete beauty," the phase when "Christ . . . mourned over the length of time and the unworthiness of man's lot to man," is bounded at the fourteenth phase by Keats and at the sixteenth phase by Blake.[1] Yeats edited an edition of Blake, and Blake's mythopoeic work provides in several ways the proper nineteenth-century analogy for Yeats's *A Vision*, so he surprises no one by placing the English poet next to "complete beauty." The American myth-maker, Walt Whitman, appears at phase six, where he "makes catalogues of all that has moved him, or amused his eye, that he may grow more poetical."[2] Such indiscriminate sensibilities are consigned by Yeats to the bestial phases where the subjective mind has not fully emerged.

More obviously, but no less intently than Yeats, Eliot reconstructed the canon that would most facilitate his own development, and several of his essays have become classics of the genre.

In 1921, Eliot reviewed Grierson's anthology of seventeenth-century verse and helped to restore the Metaphysical poets to their position of eminence; fifteen years later, he accused Milton of "having done damage to the English language from which it has not wholly recovered."³ Tom Paulin, a contemporary Irish poet and critic, has taken issue with Eliot's monarchist revisions of the canon, and although he finds much to admire in Eliot's poetry, he insists that the Republican province of English letters, the province of Milton's sovereignty, still represents the most vigorous tradition of the literature. Admiration for Eliot's verse "ought not," he argues, "to make us collude with Eliot's displacement of the major tradition of English political verse and we must be alert to the Burkean High Anglican conspiracy which has so distorted literary history."⁴ Eliot's literary essays, like Yeats's wheel, reveal his allegiances, his own designs, methods, and conspiracies, and these in turn have elucidated his poetry by exposing its revisionary intentions. And Pound wrote the *A B C of Reading*. Yeats, Eliot, and Pound were arduous historians of the literature, charting their literary future by reshuffling their literary past.

Marianne Moore, although generally assigned to the amorphous group of American modernists, never attempted to explain her verse by renovating a literary tradition. She was a prolific essayist and reviewer, but her work has continually suffered charges of eccentricity and obscurity partly because Moore refused to participate in the sorts of poetic excavations that occupied Yeats, Eliot, and Pound in their prose. Deprived of these interpretive essays and confronted with a difficult body of work, her critics have often found her verse attractive, but, like a hothouse orchid, incapable of weathering persistent scrutiny. Perhaps she cultivated this aura of rarity and aloofness, but her illustrious peers, including Eliot, Pound, Williams, and Stevens, accepted her work warmly, with a sincere, if occasionally befuddled, appreciation. The early modernists offered radically different accounts of their origins, and they often shared little in the way of stylistic experimentation, but they clearly considered Moore's poems to be a vital entry to their crusading canon.

Moore's published prose extends over a period of sixty-one

years, and the reader who wishes to investigate her literary preferences, hoping to locate the implicit judgments that would link her to a tradition, will find the task greatly simplified by Patricia C. Willis's handsome edition of *The Complete Prose*. The volume—containing over 700 pages—not only collects the work that occupied Moore during her editorship of the *Dial*, but also gathers the youthful pieces written as an undergraduate at Bryn Mawr and includes, in chronological sequence, the reviews done for *Poetry*, the occasional pieces done for the more generalized publications, and the jacket blurbs that often return to haunt the generous literary celebrity who agrees to produce them. Everything is here, and Willis's unobtrusive introduction, informative but not interpretive, tacitly recognizes that the serious evaluation of Moore's contribution to American letters is just beginning and that it is best to avoid hasty assessments in a volume that will figure prominently in those evaluations.

Thom Gunn, reviewing the volume for the *Times Literary Supplement*, labeled it a "good bedside book, where it might last you for years."[5] Moore's style encourages the brief, concentrated reading session, and although familiarity with her prose breeds fluency with her prose, her argumentative techniques do not lend themselves to the extended developments needed for a sustained analysis. Her offensive sentences never offend for lack of talent; most often they read as if they are failed experiments in English prose style. Describing an exhibition of engravings at the New York Public Library, she writes: "Among the engravings the well-known but to genealogists of Dutch New York, never hackneyed 1717 William Burgis map of the south prospect of New York commends itself—depicting cattle and cattle-pen, the French Church, the English Church, the Dutch Church, the Fort, the Chappel in the fort, 'Collonel Morris' Fancy turning to windward with a sloop of common mould,' under the not entirely it would seem characteristically American legend, *Arte non Impero*" (p. 175). The passage profits by several readings, but, appearing in the "Comment" section of the *Dial*, it should not require several readings. Much of her best work, however, lies in this monthly column, an informal essay that ranged from two to three pages and addressed the varied subjects of her roving attention. Moore abandoned the composition of poetry during the five years of her editorship at the *Dial*, and as Willis suggests in her introduction, these pieces often read as if they were well-intentioned substitutes for the poems.

Moore's serious criticism, which appeared largely in the form of reviews, often relies on the startling juxtapositions that characterize her poems, and her habit of continual quotation shapes her prose pieces as much as it does her verse. The inserted snippets often interrupt the argument, and the train of thought is abandoned, preparing for the next quotation. Moore was certainly aware of her methods from the beginning—"peculiar style must precede peculiar expression" reads the quotation that begins one of the "Comment" essays of 1926—and by 1958, in the *Christian Science Monitor*, she was acknowledging the criticism her methods had received: "Of poetry, I once said, 'I, too, dislike it'; and say it again of anything mannered, dictatorial, disparaging, or calculated to reduce to the ranks what offends one. I have been accused of substituting appreciation for criticism, and justly, since there is nothing I dislike more than the exposé or any kind of revenge" (p. 504). Moore's reputation as a bright—even brilliant—but playful critic remains untarnished. High seriousness never claimed her, and she never wrote the essay of central importance, like Eliot's "Tradition and the Individual Talent," or Stevens's "The Noble Rider and the Sound of Words." Her requirements for excellence in literature were never as clearly enunciated and incisively applied as those that distinguished Louise Bogan's writing. But seriousness is not always to be taken seriously; Moore decided early on to adopt the dancing rhythms of the "masters of slang" and surprise us with her gravity rather than assume the solemn cadences of the high style and interrupt them with her irrepressible word play. "One's humor," as she writes in her review for the *Dial* of Stevens's *Harmonium*, "is based upon the most serious part of one's nature" (p. 93).

Acutely perceptive, Moore was consistently excited by the most exciting writers—she read and ardently reviewed the verse of Eliot, Pound, Williams, and Stevens long before their Olympian reputations were made. Good taste, the silent, unfathomable partner of a reviewer's opinions, came to Moore in abundance, but she reserved special admiration for the unfolding development of Stevens's verse. And a closer look at her assessments reveals that she understood the complexities of his verse with the kind of critical sophistication that has only been granted his work in the last two decades. Seven years before the publication of *Harmonium* (1923), Moore cited one of his poems in *Poetry* as exhibiting the "naturalistic effects" in rhyme, "so rare . . . as almost not to exist" (p. 34). And when *Harmonium* appeared, Moore cherished Stevens's "riot of gorgeousness"—an inspired description—and commended his "achieved remoteness" where the "imagination precludes banality and order prevails" (pp. 91–92). Moore has the emphasis just right. One of Stevens's early and enduring concerns was epistemological in nature, pitting the exotic authority of the imagination against the insistent "pressure"—to use Stevens's term—of reality. And although she never deploys the term *Romantic* to describe this fundamental division, her initial insights jibe nicely with the current consensus.

Yet Moore was well aware of the dangers of an imaginative hedonism. In 1925, two years after the publication of *Harmonium*, she characterized Stevens's "plumage" as "morosely ecstatic," which she correctly attributes to the French influence (p. 149). Eleven years later she reviewed *Ideas of Order* for the *Criterion* and labeled Stevens's "exact portrayal . . . intoxicating," a description she reinforced during the following year in a similar review that appeared in the February issue of *Poetry*. There she called Stevens "America's chief conjurer," the poet whose imaginative vigor is exercised by his need for the illusions of his craft. But the illusion-making imagination has traditionally exacted a profound sense of alienation when it proves—as all imaginations must—ultimately unequal to its task. Discussing *The Auroras of Autumn*, Moore arrived at such conclusions long before Stevens's other critics had begun to formulate their own ideas concerning his relation to the Romantic tradition in English letters: "Sensibility imposes silence which the imagination transmutes into eloquence, and then, for the spiritual mariner, however northern, stranded, or chilled, there is society in solitude" (p. 430). The pieces dealing with Stevens's verse reveal an undeniably impressive critical sophistication, even clairvoyance. If part of the reason for Moore's obscurity lies in her refusal to guide her critics, as Eliot did, through a maze of poetic influences, then part of the critic's burden must now be to give these essays the attention they deserve. Moore once described Stevens's verse as "an opulence of jungle beauty, arctic beauty, marine beauty, hothouse beauty, and natural beauty" (p. 583). The exotic aspect of Stevens's verse—and of Moore's depiction—recalls Pater's famous definition of Romanticism as the "addition of strangeness to beauty." Add to this Pater's further suggestion that "it is the addition of curiosity to this desire for beauty, that constitutes the romantic temper," and Moore's own strange and curious verse comes to mind. Her keen insights into the complexities of the latter-day Romanticism that structures Stevens's verse would seem to indicate a sympathy with the tradition. It is not surprising, therefore, to find in John Slatin's fine book, *The Savage's Romance*, perceptive discussions of Keats, who was perhaps Stevens's greatest influence. Slatin does not attempt to read Moore as a Romantic poet of the Stevensian persuasion. But by comparing several of her poems to "Ode on a Grecian Urn," "Ode to a Nightingale," and "Ode to Psyche," by showing how her poems accept and revise several of the concerns central to Keats's odes, he has begun the process of demystifying her verse, and done so with an admirable authority. Although Moore's poetic style is "radically innovative," Slatin argues, "it combines both conservative and radical aesthetics without aligning itself (or Moore) fully with either" (p. 5). The statement might easily stand as a motto for his entire project—without disregarding Moore's genuine originality, he situates her verse in its literary tradition.

The spirit of Romantic visionary literature found its congenial, if austere, soulmate in Emerson's writing in America, and Slatin takes advantage of the well-known influences that moved westward to these shores from England. His fifth chapter offers a reading of Moore's "An Octopus" that regards the poem as expanding "the Emersonian tradition by bringing it into conjunction with its English parent-tradition," and Slatin's performance here represents some of the finest criticism that Moore has yet received. Distinctions between American and English literary values often fall short of their goal, but Slatin shrewdly combines Emerson's vision of America's "ample geography" with the myth of Paradise and reads the various, often confusing, perspectives of Mount Rainier that constitute the poem as a series of attempts to describe the world through our fallen vision:

> The perspective here is not just aerial; it is also *fallen*. Our vision is bound up in illusion from the outset because—though we have no way of knowing it at first—the poet has already lost the power of naming. We must be reminded, moreover, that we have lost that power as well; and so the poet resorts to the 'much needed' faculty of 'invention' . . . to find the series of rapidly 'shifting' analogies and metaphors whose radical incompatibility with one another makes it virtually impossible for us to bring the image confronting us to a satisfactory resolution. [pp. 169–70]

Moore uses the vast rush of images—so typically American—to construct both her own native version of the Fall and the necessary reconstruction of Paradise. Slatin has placed Moore in an old tradition and found those radically incompatible elements of her style indispensable to her new interpretation of that tradition. The nature of the myth demanded the style of the verse—that is the implication of his argument. In Slatin, Moore's verse has found one of its ablest critics.

Although the critical work done on Moore is scant and uneven, and although much of what has been produced seems more impressionistic than incisive, her writing has already attracted the likes of R. P. Blackmur, Kenneth Burke, Marie Boroff, and Helen Vendler. And then there are the major poets of her age. In *Marianne Moore: The Poetry of Engagement*, Grace Schulman begins with the conviction that Moore's work concerns "the individual in the modern age" (p. 1); and she cites Blackmur as the first "to show the life-apprehending effects resulting from the poet's juxtapositions of the explicit and the strange" (p. 4). Again, the Paterian resonances of the word "strange" recall the Romantic ideal of beauty, and although most good verse of the century ultimately concerns the individual in the modern age, Schulman subscribes to the notion—generally conceded—that Moore's verse depends upon a "dichotomy . . . between imagination and fact, emotion and intellect, [and] ornament and understatement" (p. 4). Her model for the individual, then, is fundamentally Romantic in its epistemological division. But she starts with an essential observation that neatly presses biography into the service of critical insight:

> Of the five major figures born in the years 1883 to 1888 (William Carlos Williams, 1883; Ezra Pound, 1885; Hilda Doolittle, 1886; Marianne Moore, 1887; T. S. Eliot, 1888), Pound, Eliot, and H. D. were established residents of London by the end of World War I, and Williams had studied abroad. Marianne Moore, on the other hand, visited Europe only once during the early years, in the summer of 1911, with her mother. [p. 11]

A pound of torpid interpretation for an ounce of inspired fact—that is always a judicious trade, and here it leads Schulman to a comparison of Moore's "Dock Rats" and Whitman's "Crossing Brooklyn Bridge." Both poets, she claims, "are poets of place, creating wonder in the landscape and things of America, in this case, lower New York Harbor" (p. 14). As in Slatin's reading of "An Octopus," Schulman's treatment of "Dock Rats" emphasizes the multiplicity of the American experience and the need to describe the given scene from several angles. The dichotomy between the observer and the observed remains intact, but the external world, in the American version, is always bustling and assuming such rapidly shifting guises that New York Harbor, for example, represents a visual seduction unknown to traditional Romanticism.

Schulman recognizes that in Moore's poetry, "the passion for discovery of real things leads to a tension between the desire to amass factual material and, on the other hand, a 'reverence for the great mystery'" (p. 43). Her third chapter—in many ways, the most important—grapples with the "process of seeing, or obtaining knowledge by sight," a concern that dominates most of Moore's verse (p. 43). Schulman sees the methods of visualization developed in the poems as a manner of argumentation, of inner debate, and "we find," she claims, "in her poetry, as we do in the structures of Donne and Herbert, the unification of a rhetorical pattern by the attempt at close analysis and elaboration of the thing seen" (pp. 48–49). But the religious metaphor, the divine gambit, distinguishes much of Donne's and Herbert's poetry, and this is difficult to find with a corresponding regularity in Moore's verse. Eliot's high estimation of the Metaphysical poets justifies Schulman's insight—his estimations quickly became cultural influences—but Eliot responded with a preternatural sympathy to the seventeenth century's spiritual quandary, and this sympathy often orders his poems. Moore's "inner dialectic," as the chapter title has it, records secularized meditations depending upon the syntactical arrangements that once propelled the metaphysical poem through its elaborate schemes. Schulman finds order everywhere in the poems that she discusses, and her notion of the metaphysical allows her to include in her scheme, as Slatin did in his, Moore's emphasis on perception, on the art of seeing.

Critics of Moore's writing have an enormous amount of material to confront—aside from the massive volume of prose, Moore also left to the Rosenbach Museum and Library in Philadelphia an archive superseding in size that of any other major American writer. Such diversity and magnitude of sources encourage a corresponding diversity in critical approaches, and Taffy Martin's *Marianne Moore: The Subversive Modernist* includes a fine discussion of "the *Dial* years," those five years in which Moore stood at the helm of the illustrious magazine, writing prose prolifically, managing the major talents of the time, and ignoring her own verse. Beginning with a critical commonplace—life in the twentieth century has witnessed its own disassociation of sensibility—Martin finds that Moore routinely arranged the order of the poems, essays, and sketches to reflect the disparate array of themes and images that characterized her decade: "In yet another instance of this deliberately humorous but unspoken ironic reflexivism, Moore followed her arrangement of Pound's elaborate Guido Cavalcanti translation, complete with esoteric commentary, with two drawings of American rodeo scenes and William Carlos Williams's prose sketch, 'The Venus,' which begins, innocently enough, with the question 'What then is it like, America?'" (p. 49). Even skeptics will admit that Moore could not have been blind to the quiet deviousness that Martin discovers in this arrangement, and the more we learn about her practice of keeping meticulously indexed reading journals and diaries, the more such purposeful attention to the ordering of the *Dial* material seems credible. Willis, in her introduction to *The Complete Prose*, suggests that the "Comment" essays provided Moore with a substitute for her poems. Martin has found the same aesthetic concerns that order Moore's poems ordering the layout of the magazine, an insight that if applied parsimoniously and with precision reflects Moore's developing aesthetic.

Concerning the poetry, Martin is less original, but her general idea that Moore anticipates the post-Modernist emphasis on the "carefully fractured and interrupted compositions" reserves for the poet the aesthetic clairvoyance that all major writers possess (p. xii). Pessimism often attended the modernist attempt to obliterate through organization these fractures and interruptions, but Martin recognizes in Moore's verse a simple but essential element: "While she opposed complacency or blind denial of our faults, she also opposed those who responded to the inevitable truth with pessimism" (p. 55). Perhaps Moore's poems, with their practice of relentless quotation, appear to shore up fragments against her ruins, but she never used such desperate language to describe her poetic practice. As Schulman recognized, Whitman occasionally intrudes in her poetry, and he has left there that singular ecstasy of observation that finds its consummation in the diversity of the American landscape.

Martin sees in Moore's verse what she finds in Moore's prose: a good measure of willed chaos. Discontinuity, when the poems do not add up, is the point. Although the essays move by fits and starts, their overall development nonetheless—as in the case of the Stevens essays—does reveal a coherent and unified critical perspective. And although Martin's sensibilities are finely honed to catch Moore's subversive intentions—she begins Part II by characterizing the poetry as "negatively capable," an insight that implicates Keats in the design—she roams far afield in search of exotic theories to support her ideas. Jacques Lacan's theory of "the mirror stage of development," that time when at six months of age the child's self-concept is forged by gazing into the mirror, accounts for the difference in the way that Scofield Thayer, the previous editor of the *Dial*, and Moore envisioned the monthly "Commentary" essay (p. 47). Psychological theories of development, because they claim universality, are often unhelpful in understanding the specificities of an artist's work.

Moore's poetry does present carefully ordered but purposefully unresolved images, and Martin's insight should be acknowledged. Moore's reputation is passing through an important critical phase now when most studies will be called "ground-breaking," and when the old illusions about this elusive poetry and poet will be clarified. Clarification, after all, is the watchword of most critical evaluations that come to resurrect an author. The poems have been with us all along, in varying capacities, but as these three books admirably reveal, the poems, when held to the light, reveal facets that we had neither seen nor expected.

Notes

1. W. B. Yeats, *A Vision*, (New York: Macmillan, 1937), pp. 135–36.
2. *A Vision*, p. 114.
3. T. S. Eliot, "Milton," *The Selected Prose of T. S. Eliot*, ed. Frank Kermode (London: Faber, 1975), p. 264.
4. Tom Paulin, "Introduction," *The Faber Book of Political Verse*, ed. Tom Paulin (London: Faber, 1986), p. 28.
5. Thom Gunn, "Observation of the Octopus-mountain," *Times Literary Supplement*, 6 February 1987, pp. 127–28.

The Attenuated Self and Meta-Memoir

Panthea Reid Broughton

Virginia Woolf. *Moments of Being: Revised and Enlarged Edition.* Edited with an introduction and notes by Jeanne Schulkind. London: The Hogarth Press, 1985. 230 pp.

Writing autobiography was traditional in the Stephen family. Virginia Woolf's great-grandfather wrote the *Memoirs of James Stephen Written by Himself for the Use of His Children;* her grandfather, Sir James Stephen, wrote an introspective diary; her father Sir Leslie Stephen published an account of his beginnings entitled *Some Early Impressions;* he also constructed a private account of his grief over his wife's death (his children dubbed it the *Mausoleum Book*); Virginia's aunt Caroline Emelia Stephen explained her conversion to the Society of Friends in *Quaker Strongholds*.[1] Other ancestors completed their earthly travail (as the more religious of them might have put it) by writing the stories of their lives. These autobiographies were both edifying and self-justifying. Their authors created selves from which moral and pragmatic lessons could be drawn.

While Virginia Woolf continued the family habit of writing autobiography, she radically altered the tradition. Rather than attempt to affect others, she examined others' effects upon her. With her, autobiography entertained rather than taught. With her, autobiography sought to recover the past rather than justify the self. With her, autobiography entailed biography. With her, memoirs overcame absence and recreated presence. And, with her, at least in her last work, method as well as memory became the subject of autobiography. Consequently, Virginia Woolf's autobiographical writings are among the most delightful, most experimental, and (almost inadvertently) most revealing in the language.

In 1972 Quentin Bell published his masterful biography of his aunt Virginia Woolf.[2] Among the many strengths of his book, probably the most exciting was his sparing use of Virginia Woolf's then unpublished autobiographical writings. (These must have been last-minute, hold-the-press additions to the biography since, according to information in the University of Sussex archives, neither he nor his sister had seen the most revealing of these writings before 16 June 1972). Bell's tantalizingly brief quotations from and summaries of these documents hinted at missing explanations for such personal matters as Woolf's fear of male sexuality, her bouts with mental illness, her ambivalence about her eminent parents, and her dependence upon her sister Vanessa Bell. Bell's excerpts also provided evidence of how closely linked Woolf's fiction was with her life. Bell's quotations aroused curiosity about the complete documents. Though not completely revised and perhaps not written for publication, these autobiographical writings were too significant to remain unpublished.

The orginial autobiographical documents had been left by Leonard Woolf to the University of Sussex. Jeanne Schulkind, a doctoral student there, edited them for publication. Under the title *Moments of Being: Unpublished Autobiographical Writings,* they were issued in 1976 by the University of Sussex Press and subsequently by the Hogarth Press. The collection included the 1907 "Reminiscences," written ostensibly about the childhood of Virginia's sister Vanessa Bell and addressed to the child Vanessa was then carrying. The volume bundled together three talks Woolf presented before the "Memoir Club," a Bloomsbury group which met in the 1920s and, less frequently, the 1930s and on into the 1950s, to entertain with amusing and absolutely frank (though usually exaggerated) reminiscences. Woolf's titles for these talks are: "22 Hyde Park Gate," "Old Bloomsbury," and "Am I a Snob?" The volume also included the 100-page "A Sketch of the Past." Written in the last eighteen months of Woolf's life, the "Sketch" represents Woolf's most mature and sophisticated analysis of her past.

If autobiography offers, to use James Olney's term, a "metaphor" of the self, these writings create an odd metaphor because all of them except the sixteen-page "Am I a Snob?" deal with Virginia Woolf's very deep past.[3] Of course, she considered these writings memoirs, not autobiography; nevertheless, the metaphor their extreme pastness suggests is an attenuated self: the present-self is more and more present as writer/reflector, subject/self, but the past-self is more and more present as object/self. Georges Gusdorf says that autobiography offers a "second reading of experience, and it is truer than the first because it adds to experience itself consciousness of it."[4] "Reminiscences," "22 Hyde Park Gate," and "A Sketch of the Past" all deal with the pre-1904 period of her life. Thus Woolf offered not only a second, but a third and, finally, in the "Sketch," a fourth truest reading, of a single crucial unit of experience. Her various returns to that same period (in her fiction as well as her autobiographical writings) suggest a self in which girlhood eclipsed womanhood.[5]

Since their 1976 publication these writings, especially "A Sketch of the Past," have generated a series of biographical and psychobiographical interpretations of Virginia Woolf. Articles have been devoted to Woolf's memories of sitting on her mother's lap, or fighting with her brother Thoby, or discovering that the flower and the earth are one whole, or hearing the waves at St. Ives break on the shore. Books have been written based upon her recollections of her Duckworth half-brothers' sexual improprieties or upon her imagining she saw a strange man sitting on her mother's death bed and finding herself unable to grieve. Woolf explored such psychically revelatory details almost exclusively in "A Sketch of the Past," this last "reading" of early experience, whose history requires retracing here.

Woolf included, within the text of the complicated "Sketch," the dates of composition. These dates affirm the intrusion of the present into the past and also provide insight into Woolf's mature working methods. From April of 1938 she worked on the biography *Roger Fry* and the novel *Pointz Hall* (later *Between the Acts*) almost in tandem. She finished the first draft of the Fry biography on 10 March 1939, and almost immediately began the rewriting that occupied the next year. On 18 April 1939 she added a third item to the constellation of projects; she called it "A Sketch of the Past." She gave several reasons for writing it: "Nessa [her sister Vanessa Bell] said that if I did not start writing my memoirs I should soon be too old. I should be eighty-five, and should have forgotten. . . . As it happens that I am sick of writing Roger's life, perhaps I will spend two or three mornings making a sketch" (p. 64). Woolf saw difficulties because of "the enormous number of things I can remember" and because of "the number of different ways in which memoirs can be written" (p. 64). Rather than delay while choosing a method, she says she determined simply to begin. Her proclaimed uncertainty about method actually was a pose for developing a unique autobiographical method. We might call this method "meta-memoir." By bringing the present (both the problems she faced as memoir-writer and the threats England faced as Germany's foe) into her recollections of the late-Victorian past, Woolf repeatedly made memoir-writing part of the subject of her "Sketch of the Past."

Woolf worked on the sketch, incorporating the dates into her text, on 2 May, 15 May, 28 May, 20 June, and 19 July 1939. Her typescript of this first portion of the "Sketch," now MH/A5a at the University of Sussex Library, bears manuscript corrections by both Virginia and Leonard Woolf. (These materials may be examined without traveling to Sussex, for the entire Sussex collection of Virginia Woolf manuscripts, along with parts of the Leonard Woolf collection, is now available on microfilm through Harvester.) Woolf seems to have thrown away manuscript sheets as she retyped them, but a four-page sequence (MH/A5b) dated 20 June 1939 survived, as did twenty-one handwritten pages dated 19 July 1939 (MH/A5c). These fragments confirm that, when Woolf retyped the narrative, she retained the date of composition.[6] The longer fragment allows us to infer something of her principles of revision. In the context of discussing her mother's and Stella's deaths, the manuscript refers to Woolf's first "breakdown." It goes on to treat various distant cousins and members of her extended family. In revising, Woolf deleted both the too-personal references to her breakdown and the too-impersonal references to her relatives.

Woolf dropped memoir-writing for nearly a year, with the

Virginia Woolf and Autobiography

exception of a fragment dated 28 January 1940, now in the Berg Collection, which considers the tea table as the "center of Victorian Life." At the University of Sussex there is a sixty-four-page handwritten continuation (MH/A5d) of the sixty-nine-page typescript (MH/A5a). The first date on this manuscript is 8 June 1940. The typescript (MH/A5a) ends with a rewriting of the first ten pages of this manuscript. When Schulkind printed the 1976 "Sketch" she used the *a* typescript and then the remaining fifty-four pages, written and emended in Woolf's rather difficult hand, of the *d* manuscript. Based on an apparently finished typescript and an unfinished manuscript, the 1976 text exhibited different levels of polish. As we have seen, however, the comparative roughness of the latter part of the text has not deterred readers from making innumerable close and telling readings of "A Sketch of the Past."

What Schulkind did not know in 1976 was that there was another typescript, a rewriting and extension of MH/A5d. This typescript, purchased by the British Library from Sotheby's in 1981, begins with Woolf's note: "to follow after p. 69." A revision and replacement of the earlier manuscript MH/A5d, this typescript was Woolf's final continuation (as far as we know) of the 69-page typescript MH/A5a. The British Library typescript (BL Add. 61973) is not, however, just a more polished version of MH/A5d. It is also a major expansion. It includes an extensive section (pages 107–24 in the published text) for which there was no antecedent in MH/A5d. This new material was written on 19 June and in late July and possibly August of 1940. It offers significantly revised perspectives on Woolf's relationships with her parents. The remainder of the BL typescript (dated 19 August 1940, 22 September 1940, 11 October 1940 and 15 November 1940) is an extensive revision of MH/A5d and of the brief tea-table fragment. For roughly two years, the only readers at the British Library to examine this typescript were Lord Noel Annan (who was rewriting his biography of Leslie Stephen) and Jeanne Schulkind (who was preparing a second edition of *Moments of Being*). The British Library and the copyright holders have since made the typescript available to other readers. In 1985 the Hogarth Press published this second edition of *Moments of Being,* based on the Sussex *a* typescript and its continuation in the British Library typescript.

Because the only substantive changes between the first and second editions of *Moments of Being* reflect the discovery of the new typescript of "A Sketch," my comments will focus upon those changes. The revisions illustrate Woolf's careful sense of craft. Awkward sentences in the MH/A5d manuscript used for the 1976 *Moments of Being* are now clear; concrete details fill out a picture. "Innumerable cats" becomes "innumerable cats with their fishbones in their mouths" (p. 128). "I 'broomed her round the garden,' the grown ups laughing and approving" becomes (still with no clear sense of remorse) "I 'broomed her round the garden.' I remember scuffling her like a drift of dead leaves in front of me" (p. 129). "It was a sight that made father gloomy" becomes "The waiting pilchard boats . . . made father pish and pshaw at table" (p. 131). In the early version the Victorian socializing machine "brought innumerable teeth into play." In the revision it "bit into us with innumerable sharp teeth" (p. 152). Most catalogues are expanded and made more interesting and sensory.

Woolf's writing is more confident. She speaks of herself as a "professional" and, to confirm her assertion, asks, "Have I not conveyed Roger from one end of life to the other?" (p. 136). Woolf judges her father in a more objective tone: "Roger Fry said that civilisation means awareness; he [Leslie Stephen] was uncivilised in his extreme unawareness" (p. 146). Woolf rewrote the final paragraph, so that the entire memoir ends climactically:

> Greatness still seems to me a positive possession; booming; eccentric; set apart; something to which I am led up dutifully by my parents. It is a bodily presence; it has nothing to do with anything said. It exists in certain people. But it never exists now. I cannot remember ever to have felt greatness since I was a child. [p. 158]

Here I think Schulkind's usually excellent editorial judgment failed her, for she prints the anticlimactic paragraph with which MH/A5d ended in brackets *after* this paragraph on the grounds that "it is unusual for VW to omit entire paragraphs from the manuscript version in the typescript" (p. 158n).[7] Schulkind could have justified placing the final paragraph from the *d* manuscript *before* this final paragraph or including it in a footnote, but she diminishes the force of what Woolf clearly intended to be her final paragraph by following it with the weaker (and I think rejected) paragraph from the earlier manuscript.

My sense of the appropriateness of ending the "Sketch" with the final paragraph from the British Library typescript is both textual and thematic. It is this text which is the final known version and which Schulkind has been following (pp. 107–59). Also in this final typescript Woolf treated greatness or "the 'genius' legend" (p. 145) as themes that unify the revised memoir. She even aligned herself modestly with nineteenth-century greatness by adding to this version the recollection: "Thoby told Nessa, who told me, that he thought I might be a bit of a genius" (pp. 130–31). Aesthetically and thematically Woolf moves from a discussion of both the limitations and the grandeurs of the past to a final concession: "I cannot remember to have felt greatness since I was a child" (p. 158). Schulkind fails to see the appropriateness of leaving Woolf's ending as it is.

These few examples suggest how firm Woolf's control of her craft was just months before her death. The new section she added to the memoir in the summer of 1940 suggests not only technical but psychological mastery as well. Woolf exhibits a willingness to present both her father and her mother in fresh lights. After an introductory paragraph about the current condition of Mecklenburgh Square (where she was writing) and France (where dictators were conquering), Woolf writes: "My father now falls to be described, because it was during the seven years between Stella's death in 1897 and his death in 1904 that Nessa and I were fully exposed without protection to the full blast of that strange character" (p. 107). Readers familiar with Woolf's biography might expect another exposé of Leslie Stephen as domestic tyrant. We get some of that perspective and of the young Virginia's rage at him, but she also tells us that "in me, though not in [Vanessa], rage alternated with love" (p. 108). Woolf goes on to contrast her father with the prototypical "steel engraving" of a Cambridge intellectual which "lacks picturesqueness, oddity, romance" (p. 109). Her father lacked none of those qualities. His temper made him picturesque and it even carried a certain poignancy, for the Victorians believed "that men of genius were naturally uncontrolled" (p. 109). Thus Leslie Stephen "took it for granted . . . that he was exempt, because of his genius, from the laws of good society. But was he a man of genius? No; that was not alas quite the case" (p. 110). Therefore, Leslie Stephen's "frustrated desire to be a man of genius" (p. 110) provoked him to indulge his temper as if the effect (irrational behavior) confirmed the existence of the cause (genius).

Woolf spends several pages presenting an aspect of her father's character that she had never acknowledged before: the attractive, social, and sexual Leslie Stephen. Her determination to present this side of Stephen is suggested by an emendation Schulkind notes: Woolf wrote, "He must have been a man of distinction," but then she crossed out the last four words and substituted "an attractive man at fifty" (pp. 113–14). She tells that "he was so struck, so normally and masculinely affected by Mrs. Langtry's beauty, that he actually went to the play to see her. Otherwise he never went to a play . . . " (p. 114). As Woolf's father becomes softer, more sociable, her mother in these pages becomes generally harder, less kind. Woolf does present a charming picture of her mother as an "omnibus expert" (p. 121), but she also discloses her mother's cold and hypocritical disregard for the servants' living conditions. She tells of her mother's hostility toward women's suffrage; Julia Stephen held that "women had enough to do in their own homes without a vote" (p. 120).

Woolf characterizes the Stephen home at 22 Hyde Park Gate as a "cage." She describes the house in ways that help explain her own work. Her own living quarters were divided into a "living half" and a "sleeping side." Woolf uses this room arrangement to emblematize the mind/body dichotomy within her. Of the two sides, she says, "How they fought each other" (p. 123). Writing, apparently, in late July of 1940, Woolf made an oblique reference to her mental breakdown: "And it was from that room Gerald fetched me when father died. There I first heard those horrible voices. . . . " [her ellipses] (p. 123). Woolf ends the new section with a poignant paragraph about the effect upon her of

Virginia Woolf and Autobiography

her step-sister Stella's death. These excerpts suggest that Woolf was at last willing, in this 1940 rereading of her past, to face the pain of 1897:

> My mother's death had been a latent sorrow—at thirteen one could not master it, envisage it, deal with it. But Stella's death two years later fell on a different substance; a mind stuff and being stuff that was extraordinarily unprotected, unformed, unshielded, apprehensive, receptive, anticipatory. . . . The blow, the second blow of death, struck on me; tremulous, filmy eyed as I was, with my wings still creased, sitting there on the edge of my broken chrysalis. [p. 124]

This new section must be digested by all biographical critics of Woolf, for it alters significantly what we have thought about her past, especially her relationship with her parents. For example, studying the 1976 text of the "Sketch," Virginia Hyman writes that Woolf contrasts "the unworldly and ascetic Stephen with the worldly and sexual George Duckworth." Hyman feels that by 1939–1940, when Woolf wrote the "Sketch," the "pattern which was to dominate her life had coalesced; the preference for intellect over convention, for asceticism over sexuality, for the world of the Stephens over the world of the Duckworths."[8] This 1985 edition, which insists upon the social and sexual side of Leslie Stephen, calls for a revision of Hyman's thesis.

I find one minor factual error in Schulkind's notes. She writes that John Lehmann "eventually became a partner of the Hogarth Press" (p. 107n); she should have written that he had been (in 1940) a partner for two years. Her editing is usually scrupulous and careful, but I wish that she had made two changes. The British Library typescript shows a number of emendations in Woolf's hand. For example, after remarking that her mother died at forty-nine and her father found it "very difficult, so healthy was he, to die of cancer at the age of seventy-two," Woolf orginally wrote, "But, though I slip in" and continued typing memories of St. Ives. Later, above the typed line she added the handwritten phrase after "slip in": "Still venting an old grievance, that parenthesis" (p. 133). That emendation evidences considerable self-awareness. That it was an afterthought tells us a good bit about Woolf's habits of revision. Schulkind could have given at least the most significant of such alterations. One can learn much about Woolf's methods from studying the microfilm of the Sussex Collection, but one must travel to the British Library to see these methods at work in the new typescript of "A Sketch of the Past." Schulkind's perspective is that recording "textual revisions and variations . . . would have greatly impaired the enjoyment of most readers" (p. 7). My sense is that such recording, done unobtrusively, can enhance the enjoyment of all readers.

My other quarrel with both editions of *Moments of Being* is that Schulkind orders the collection chronologically according to the period of Woolf's life under consideration, a rather odd arrangement since, as we have seen, both long memoirs deal with the pre-1904 period, as does one short one; another short one deals with the 1904–1910 period; and the final one is set in the 1930s. Obviously, no one would read *Moments of Being* through to learn Woolf's life story. But we could read it straight through to gain a sense of Woolf's technical and psychic development. Had the collection been ordered chronologically by time of composition, readers could better sense the differences between, say, the Julia and Leslie Stephen of the 1908 "Reminiscences" and of the 1939–40 "Sketch"; or could compare the defensiveness of "Reminiscences" with that of "Am I a Snob?"; or could contrast the cavalier tone of the Memoir Club papers with the final forgiving tone of the "Sketch"; or could distinguish between the early 1920s account in "22 Hyde Park Gate" of George Duckworth's emotional and sentimental excesses and the 1939 account in the "Sketch" of Gerald Duckworth's sexual impropriety. Reading such accounts in the order they were written would heighten readers' sense of the tension between early reticence and late frankness in Woolf's life and of the development of Woolf's mature understanding of herself and her past.

I find Woolf's wisdom only twice flawed in "A Sketch of the Past." Woolf sees "sudden shocks" as "a revelation of some order; it is a token of some real thing behind appearances," and yet she adamantly insists that "certainly and emphatically there is no God" (p. 72). These statements sound contradictory. They suggest that the Virginia Woolf who achieved an open mind about her parents and herself simply closed her mind to the possibility that that "some real thing" might be divine.

The other flawed explanation in the "Sketch" is more intimate. Woolf reveals the story that, when she was quite small, Gerald Duckworth felt under her dress until he reached her "private parts." The vivid revulsion which she still felt over the experience provoked her to conclude:

> This seems to show that a feeling about certain parts of the body; how they must not be touched; how it is wrong to allow them to be touched; must be instinctive. It proves that Virginia Stephen was not born on the 25th January 1882, but was born many thousands of years ago; and had from the very first to encounter instincts already acquired by thousands of ancestresses in the past. [p. 69]

Woolf might have connected this experience with the depression she felt when she realized "why hurt another person?" Recognizing the senselessness of human cruelty, she felt, "It was as if I became aware of something terrible; and of my own powerlessness" (p. 71). She might have more healthily interpreted her revulsion over Gerald Duckworth's behavior as proof of an innate moral code that insists, not that parts of the body should not be touched, but that powerless children should not be sexually abused.

These two examples suggest that there were topics about which Virginia Woolf's mind (and body) could be closed, but in that she is hardly alone. Woolf admired her father for "his courage, his simplicity, for his strength and nonchalance, and neglect of appearances" (p. 116), but she saw the limitations of his mind:

> I find not a subtle mind; not an imaginative mind; not a suggestive mind. But a strong mind; a healthy out of door, moor striding mind; an impatient, limited mind; a conventional mind entirely accepting his own standard of what is honest, what is moral, without a shadow of doubt accepting this is a good man; that is a good woman. . . . That shows a very simply constructed view of the world; and the world was, I suppose, more simple then. It was a black and white world compared with ours; obvious things to be destroyed—headed humbug, obvious things to be preserved—headed domestic virtues. [p. 115]

In Woolf's time, as in ours, it was certainly still possible to see the world in black and white or conventional terms. What is remarkable about Woolf's fiction and non-fiction, witness "A Sketch of the Past," is that so very few personal, aesthetic, or moral assumptions went unchallenged. Memoir-writing in the Stephen family had been largely self-justifying. With Woolf's unconventional mind-set, it (at least in the "Sketch") became self-, past-, and memoir-exploring, meta-memoir. And so finally if the object-self in Woolf's autobiographical writings is attenuated, the subject- or writer-self is not.

Notes

1. For further discussion see Christopher C. Dahl, "Virginia Woolf's *Moments of Being* and the Autobiographical Tradition in the Stephen family," *Journal of Modern Literature*, 10 (June 1983), 175–96.

2. Quentin Bell deflected the Stephen tradition into biography, while his sister Angelica Bell Garnett has continued the autobiographical tradition with her *Deceived with Kindness: A Bloomsbury Childhood* (London: Chatto and Windus, 1984).

3. See Olney, *Metaphors of Self: The Meaning of Autobiography* (Princeton: Princeton Univ. Press, 1972).

4. Gusdorf, "Conditions and Limits of Autobiograpy," trans. James Olney, in *Autobiography: Essays Theoretical and Critical*, ed. James Olney (Princeton: Princeton Univ. Press, 1980), p. 38.

5. One might argue that "eclipsed" is too strong a word, for in her diaries Woolf expressed considerable interest in her present-self and, had she lived longer, might have continued her memoirs to include the entire course of her life. Nevertheless, since Woolf spent her lifetime trying to come to terms with her deep past, the metaphor of the attenuated or eclipsed self seems justified to me.

6. One odd exception is that the manuscript section dated November 17, 1940, is dated in the typed revision November 15, 1940. I presume that Woolf misdated the first version and corrected the date on the revision.

7. Woolf omitted another whole paragraph (this one about Jack Hills, the man who married Virginia's half-sister Stella). Schulkind does not reintroduce that paragraph.

8. Hyman, "Reflections in the Looking-Glass: Leslie Stephen and Virginia Woolf," *Journal of Modern Literature*, 10 (June 1983), 197–216.

Making Taliaferro Famus

Carl Ficken

Raymond C. Craig, ed. *The Humor of H. E. Taliaferro.* Knoxville: University of Tennessee Press, 1987. xii, 257 pp.

The Humor of H. E. Taliaferro, for one hundred and seventy-eight of its pages, presents the humorous writings of the North Carolina-born Baptist preacher and newspaperman who was a contemporary of the better-known Southwestern humorists Augustus Baldwin Longstreet, Johnson Jones Hooper, George Washington Harris, and Joseph G. Baldwin. Raymond C. Craig has taken these stories from Taliaferro's *Fisher's River (North Carolina) Scenes and Characters, by "Skitt," "Who Was Raised Thar"* (New York: Harper & Brothers 1859) and from the pieces Taliaferro submitted to *The Southern Literary Messenger* from 1860 to 1863. *Fisher's River* has not been reissued in the twentieth century; the *Messenger* stories were collected under the title *Carolina Humor* by David K. Jackson in 1938.[1] Though "Skitt" Taliaferro maintained his own narrative voice throughout the *Fisher's River* collection, he did yield frequently to a local character who then became the narrator of a particular tale. Because Craig draws a distinction between narratives by local storytellers and those told by Taliaferro himself, and because Craig feels that the "power" of the local narrators has been "dissipated" by the organization of *Fisher's River,* he chooses to group the stories by narrator and to omit most of Taliaferro's introductory and transitional material (pp. 42, 64). The result diminishes the contrast, usually associated with Southwestern humor, between the frontier yarn-spinner and the educated narrator; perhaps more seriously, the overall result is not a critical edition—as the jacket blurb announces—but a collection of stories with little textual integrity.

Craig has brought together here for the first time material published separately during Taliaferro's lifetime and has provided a biographical sketch and a discussion of the humor in the stories. Though Taliaferro's work appeared in anthologies and though he has been the subject of dissertations and articles, this volume marks the most serious published recognition, in book-length form, of his contribution to the tradition of Southwestern humor.[2] As such, scholars can be grateful for its appearance. The nature of Craig's treatment, however, raises questions about what scholars need today in the publication of nineteenth-century writing: might there not be some standards by which earlier literature can be made available to contemporary readers and still bear the integrity of the original version?

At the outset it can be said that Craig has given the modern scholar a clear and readable text of Taliaferro's stories which are, after all, an important, though minor, part of nineteenth-century American literature. Craig has sought to preserve the original spellings and punctuations: his deviations from that principle often seem more a matter of carelessness than intention. The book also benefits from the inclusion of the thirteen line drawings (why does Craig say "twelve"?) of the 1859 edition; these were done by John McLenan, who did illustrations for the American edition of *Great Expectations* and for *Vanity Fair,* the comic newspaper published in New York from 1859–1863 (p. 64).

In Part I of his volume, Craig presents a brief introduction to Taliaferro and his writing, a biographical sketch, and a discussion of Taliaferro's humor. While the purpose of the book is to make available the sketches themselves, this ancillary material has unmistakable value for the reader who wishes to learn something about a relatively unknown writer. One should not expect a full-blown biography or a definitive analysis. Still one might wish for a little more, in terms of accuracy, organization, and perception.

Inaccuracies breed suspicion. In the brief general introduction, Craig mentions Richard Walser's biographical research but places it in 1976 rather than the actual publication date of 1978. Further, he subsumes the most significant biography of Taliaferro—the 1983 dissertation of Heinrich Robert Bettich—under a footnote on page 4 which seems to list "recent work on Alabama Baptists and on early Baptist newspapers."[3] Then, in noting the appearance of Taliaferro's sketches in the Cohen and

Dillingham anthology, *Humor of the Old Southwest,* Craig uses the date of that volume's second edition, 1975; for a paragraph designed to trace the unfolding recognition of Taliaferro's work, mention of the first edition in 1964 would be more to the point.[4] To present a catalog of such errors in this background material would not be worthwhile, but one more should be pointed out because it suggests a carelessness about the research. Describing Taliaferro's early preaching in Alabama, Craig reports: "The rural churches where Taliaferro preached were often no more than wigwams, sometimes just a shady tree" (p. 12) and cites page 43 of Hosea Holcombe's history of Alabama Baptists.[5] Holcombe does discuss on his page 43 early worship conditions and does say that people often worshipped in structures somewhat like wigwams and under the trees, but he is talking about the time of first arrivals in Alabama, 1818, and he indicates that by the late 1820s the Baptists had better buildings. Taliaferro began his work there in 1835.

Given the limitation of the format, the biographical section offers an adequate recounting of Taliaferro's life. Craig has drawn on a great variety of sources and has paid special attention to the newspapers for which Taliaferro wrote. He has used both nineteenth-century and modern studies of Baptist history in Alabama to detail the movements of Taliaferro, his involvement with the church, and his family's circumstances. Inasmuch as Taliaferro's literary career seemed to cover only a short period of his life, Craig is justified in giving the bulk of this biography to a description of Taliaferro's work as a newspaperman and Baptist pastor. It would have been helpful, however, to have more careful delineation about the various types of Baptist theological positions; the definitions given are rather superficial. Consider the brief explanations of Arminianism and of the Hardshell Baptists (p. 15) and the reference, without explanation, to Campbellism (p. 35). The reader need not expect extended treatment of these viewpoints, but insofar as Taliaferro was engaged with such attitudes—either as advocate or enemy—some clarification would enable the reader more readily to understand Taliaferro's own attitudes and to have another resource for evaluating the stories.

The discussion of Taliaferro's humor, while it covers a number of basic issues, also has limitations. More comparison of Taliaferro's work with that of other Southwestern humorists would have been beneficial: passing reference to Simon Suggs and Sut Lovingood seems insufficient if a portion of the book's claim is that Taliaferro belongs to the tradition of such writers as Hooper and Harris. A paragraph and extended footnote hardly do justice to Taliaferro's use of folklore; the one-sentence footnote to Bettich's dissertation, which has a full chapter on the folk elements in Taliaferro's writings, does not atone for the minimal discussion in the text. Craig also seems to have missed Milton Rickel's 1981 essay on "Elements of Folk Humor in the Literature of the Old Southwest" and its frequent reference to Taliaferro's work: Rickels makes use of Mikhail Bakhtin's study of folk humor and thus engages the material at a level that is substantive, comparative, and analytical.[6] Nor does Craig indicate knowledge of Paula Anderson-Green's 1980 dissertation "Folklore and Fiction in Nineteenth Century North Carolina: Taliaferro's *Fisher's River* and Chesnutt's *The Conjure Woman.*"[7]

Perhaps a more basic difficulty of Craig's section on humor has to do with his tendency to dismiss Taliaferro's own literary contribution and focus on his journalistic skill in reporting the stories of the *Fisher's River* community. Since there is little evidence of Taliaferro's patterns of work—no surviving manuscripts, no commentary by Taliaferro about his development of these stories—one might well be cautious in making such observations. It is puzzling, therefore, that Craig can conclude: "The stories are not literary creations by Taliaferro but rather transcriptions, apparently touched up here and there by their recorder, of stories narrated by a circle of neighbors and relatives living in the mountains of North Carolina in the early nineteenth century" (p. 42). Other students of Taliaferro's work do not so easily dismiss Taliaferro's own creative powers; and, on the face of it, other evidence not being available and given frontier conditions, it is hard to imagine Taliaferro as only a recorder. Even if he transcribed the stories as he heard them in Surry County, North Carolina, and then returned to Alabama to write out the manuscript of *Fisher's River,* he must have been relying on his own memory of the narratives, his own choice of words and expression of dialect, his own decisions about which portions of a narrative should be included in a specific sketch. And by omitting Taliaferro's own introductory and transitional material from *Fisher's River*, Craig is minimizing Taliaferro's role in producing that collection. This reviewer would not claim that those sections of *Fisher's River* are great or profound literature, but they are a part of the text, and they belong to the man who gathered the stories, arranged them, and put them into a form that could be received by a literate audience. At the very least, Craig does not make a convincing case that the stories are "historical" rather than "fictional." Taliaferro does relate folk tales and tell stories he has heard; nonetheless, his is the literary consciousness that shapes and presents them.

Part II begins with an introduction which categorizes the narratives, explains editorial strategy, and then presents the collection of stories, some of them preceded by Craig's brief notes. In the introduction, Craig justifies his decision to group the stories according to narrator and to omit Taliaferro's own commentary on the storytellers; the editor claims to have been careful to retain Taliaferro's spellings and syntax, making only silent emendations of obvious punctuation and printing errors. Indeed, a comparison of the first three stories in Craig's edition with the *Fisher's River* text yields only six changes of punctuation (one replacing a semicolon with a comma, the others eliminating commas) and one adjustment from a lower case to a capital letter. Collation of Craig's text, the *Southern Literary Messenger* stories, and David Jackson's 1938 printing of those stories reveals more vigorous editing; in the sketch entitled "Tasting Religion," for example, there are fourteen variants, with Craig following Jackson even when Jackson is wrong. In the *Messenger* text, Dick Snobbs is described as "hard-hearted and stiff-necked"; he had become "hard-headed and stiff-necked" in Jackson's printing, through what was probably a copying error; that redundancy is repeated by Craig (p. 154). Similarly, Taliaferro used "loaning" and "loaner" in depicting the social exchange of property; Jackson changed the words to "lending" and "lender," and Craig followed his selections (p. 154). Both Jackson and Craig drop a "then," a perfectly appropriate "then," from a portion of Parson

Tempest's dialogue (p. 155). Such changes betray the scrupulous retention of language claimed by Craig (p. 64).

While Craig seems to have been more careful with the *Fisher's River* stories—and to be sure he had a better original copy there—he still manages to alter the narratives significantly by omissions. Not only does he drop Taliaferro's introductions and transitions, but he also leaves out several of the stories: "Uncle Frost Snow" (*FR*, 94–97); a lengthy portion of the "John Senter" story (*FR*, 165–73); "A Quarter-of-a-Dollar Fight" (*FR*, 202–4); Cooking, Big Eating, Etc." (*FR*, 217–21) and anecdotes about Dick Snow (FR, 98–116). By making the stories a consistent narration of the local storyteller, Craig also sometimes cuts out the descriptions which interrupt a character's opening sentence. Oliver Stanley's "The Escape From the Whale," for instance, begins this way in Craig's version: "On the shank ov one monstracious nice evenin' I toddled down to the seaboard" (p. 111). Skitt, the narrator of the *Fisher's River* text, adds details that contribute to the picture of Oliver Stanley: "'On the shank ov one monstracious evenin','" said the redoubtable Oliver, after spitting a stream of tobacco juice on a very decent floor, 'I toddled down to the seaboard'" (*FR*, 125). In his introductory notes, Craig does occasionally quote from one or another of these omitted passages; clearly, however, he has produced a work quite different from the original. In at least one story, four lines disappear from the end of the narrative without explanation (at the end of "The Tape-Worm," pp. 86–87; cf. *FR*, 88–91).

Two other irritants about the format of Craig's text must be noted. One is that Craig's brief introductions to the sketches do not clearly identify the original source. Usually the reader knows whether the story first appeared in *Fisher's River* or in the *Southern Literary Messenger,* but specific reference to the page numbers and, in the case of the *Messenger,* the date of the earlier publication would have been helpful. The second item is that Craig occasionally places the interpretation of an unusual word or spelling in brackets following the word, even though he has a glossary included in the volume. Part of the problem here is inconsistency. Sometimes he explains with bracketed material; sometimes he allows the word to stand, leaving the reader to turn to the glossary if clarification is needed; occasionally he seems to miss terms—expressions that might need illumination. The handling of Taliaferro's own explanations is also troubling. When Bob Snipes reports that the squire tied the "Gougin knot," Craig's text reads, "tied the Gougin [Gordian] knot" (p. 123); *Fisher's River* has, "'tied the Gougin knot' (the Gordian knot, I suppose Bob meant)" (*FR*, 183). Taliaferro sometimes placed an asterisk after a word or phrase he thought might be unclear and gave his explanation at the bottom of the page: in some instances, Craig puts Taliaferro's clarification in brackets in the texts; in others Craig drops the matter entirely.

The material at the end of this volume also requires brief commentary: a glossary, a list of abbreviations, a list of works cited, and an index. The glossary is preceded by the titles of reference works used in its preparation and is generally helpful, though students of Southwestern humor may find some of the entries unnecessary. The index is inadequate: with only thirty-three entries—and several of them incomplete in notation of page numbers—the index does not provide enough information to enable the scholar to find references within the text; in order to evaluate Craig's research. I had to make my own index of authors and works he had cited, and I found nearly forty additional entries which might have been included. It is the bibliographical section, however, which is most disturbing. Ten of the items in "Works Cited" (that is nearly a fifth of the entries) have some error, typographical or more serious, and a few have multiple errors (I was able to verify only about half of the entries: one-third of the items I checked had errors). The discovery of such inattention to these matters of detail makes one hesitant to rely on other material in the volume and on its overall conclusions.

In addition to the mistakes, the omission of several valuable resources contributes to a sense of weakness in the research. Some of the omissions have been noted earlier in this review; they include essays by Tristram P. Coffin, Paula Anderson-Green, Milton Rickels, and Richard Walser as well as the dissertation by Ms. Anderson-Green.[8] Some of this material appeared in the early 1980s, and that could explain why Craig does not seem to know about them; his own dissertation, however, was completed in 1983, and he does cite a 1984 Masters thesis and the Bettich dissertation of 1983. As disturbing as the omissions are, his failure to interact with Bettich's work is more unfortunate; perhaps the most charitable assumption is that Craig had nearly completed his preparation of *The Humor of H. E. Taliaferro* when he discovered Bettich's dissertation and so could give it only a passing notice. More than in the specific problems identified in these last two paragraphs, the list of works cited and Craig's general use of resources in the body of the book suggest that there was more homework to be done.

This review has been specifically critical of Craig's work, but the larger intention has been to raise questions about the appropriate treatment of the humorous literature of another century. After all, Craig made some decisions about how he would handle the material; he was faithful to those decisions; perhaps they can even be defended. Many of the errors in the text could be the fault of typesetters and proofreaders. The larger issue, however, centers on what readers and scholars today need in such a text. On the basis of my scrutiny of Craig's book and the related material about H. E. Taliaferro, I draw several conclusions:

1) It is valuable to have modern editions of the writings of nineteenth-century humorists. Taliaferro's contribution to that literature, his depiction of manners and customs, his reporting of folklore—all are much more readily available to a variety of scholars when those stories are currently in print and when readers do not have to work with either microfiche or crumbling early editions.

2) It is also valuable to have a writer's humorous works collected in one volume where that is possible, but the editor should not force judgments or parallels on the reader by rearranging or juxtaposing the sketches.

3) A photographic reproduction of the original text would have the advantage of giving scholars access to the earliest printing, but some early editions are flawed by poor editing or typesetting, and the exact copy of one text would not allow for comparison with subsequent editions. Craig indicates that his dissertation is a "formal facsimile edition" of Taliaferro's major work (p. 66); the abstract speaks of it as an "accurate copy text."[9]

4) What we might hope for would be a truly critical edition, one that preserves to the best degree possible the text closest to the author's own intentions, notes typographical errors and editorial changes, and compares the text to later editions. In one sense, Craig approaches this task: perhaps he does see this as a critical edition inasmuch as he follows the first printings and makes what he considers to be minor changes in the text. Nonetheless, the blending of material from two works, the omission of large portions of the original stories, and the absence of any textual apparatus prevent *The Humor of H. E. Taliaferro* from meeting the needs of contemporary scholars.

Craig and the University of Tennessee Press are to be commended for making a case for Taliaferro; unfortunately both the form and substance of the book finally blur the argument. Since Craig is more descriptive than analytical in his discussion of Taliaferro's humor, since he minimizes Taliaferro's own role as a creative artist and narrator, and since he does not pursue the relationship between Taliaferro and other nineteenth-century humorists, he does not finally advance a positive assessment of Taliaferro's work, nor does he make it easy for other scholars to do so. Many questions remain. How do Taliaferro's introductions, transitions, and conclusions affect the sketches? Does *Fisher's River* have narrative integrity or unity of its own? Can the reader sense an identity for Skitt Taliaferro, the narrator of these tales, as opposed to the identity of H. E. Taliaferro, Baptist preacher and newspaper editor? Craig may not find those questions significant; scholars must still go back to *Fisher's River* and the *Southern Literary Messenger* in order to make a judgment. To what degree is Taliaferro really a Southwestern humorist? To what degree did he see himself working in the manner of Augustus Baldwin Longstreet? He does seem to echo Longstreet's title, *Georgia Scenes, Characters, Etc.,* by putting his state before his *Scenes and Characters.* Might not the response to these questions affect the way one evaluates his narrative and his humor?[10]

The question of evaluation is a larger one than can be examined in this review. Craig's appreciation of Taliaferro seems to rest primarily on what Taliaferro has done as a recorder of language, folktales, frontier individuals and communities.

Speaking of Taliaferro's interest in and sympathy for those rural folk, Craig concludes, "It is his record of their language and their personalities that has given him a permanent place in early American humor" (p. 59). More substantive evaluation would attempt to deal with the issue of whether there is any depth at all in the tales, any probing of human nature, any sense of life's complexities. Mary Ann Wimsatt and Robert L. Phillips have judged that Taliaferro's stories do not deal with the "timeless conflict" of the human experience, the internal struggle of the heart or the battle with a hostile environment.[11] Craig would seem to agree with that evaluation, but it is significant that he does not raise such a point in his own study of the work.

A strong and accurate text establishes the foundation on which critics can build analysis and evaluation of the fiction. Relatively unknown writers of an earlier age must, it would appear, pass through a period wherein critics simply try to bring them out of obscurity and convince readers to sample the brew, much as Uncle Jimmy Smith finally gave in to thirst, drank the beer in which Hamp Hudson's dog Famus was reported to have drowned, and so freed others to drink as well, "Famus or no Famus" (p. 190–93). Much of the commentary about Taliaferro or his work to this point has seemed an attempt to say, "Here is a neglected minor writer who deserves better treatment"; and, in order to make him known, the critic must first tell the life story and give some summary of the work. Perhaps now, even with this collection of the stories, critics can move on to more thorough analysis and undertake a more careful evaluation of Taliaferro's contribution to our literature.

Notes

1. David K. Jackson, ed., *Carolina Humor: Sketches by Harden* [sic] *E. Taliaferro* (Richmond: Dietz Press, 1938).

2. See Craig's list of works cited, pp. 255–57, and Richard Walser, "Bibliobiography of Skitt Taliaferro," *North Carolina Historical Review*, 55 (1978), 375–92.

3. Heinrich Robert Bettich, "Hardin Edwards Taliaferro: Life, Literature, and Folklore," Diss. University of North Carolina, 1983.

4. Hennig Cohen and William B. Dillingham, eds., *Humor of the Old Southwest* (Boston: Houghton Mifflin, 1964).

5. Hosea Holcombe, *A History of the Rise and Progress of the Baptists in Alabama* (Philadelphia: King and Baird, 1840), p. 43.

6. Milton Rickels, "Elements of Folk Humor in the Literature of the Old Southwest," *Thalia*, 4 (1981), 5–9.

7. Paula Hathaway Anderson-Green, "Folklore and Fiction in Nineteenth-Century North Carolina: Taliaferro's *Fisher's River* and Chesnutt's *The Conjure Woman*," Diss. Georgia State University, 1980.

8. Coffin, "Harden [sic] E. Taliaferro and the Use of Folklore by American Literary Figures," *South Atlantic Quarterly*, 64 (Spring 1965), 241–46; Anderson-Green, "Folktales in the Literary Works of Harden [sic] E. Taliaferro: A View of Southern Appalachian Life in the Early Nineteenth Century," *North Carolina Folklore Journal*, 31 (Fall-Winter 1983), 65–75; Rickels, "Inexpressibles in Southwestern Humor," *American Humor*, 6 (1979), 76–83; Walser, "Skitt Taliaferro: Facts and Reappraisal," *American Humor*, 4 (Spring 1977), 7–10.

9. Raymond C. Craig, "An Edition of the Major Writings of H. E. Taliaferro," Diss. University of Illinois, 1983; Craig, "Major Writings," *DA*, 45 (1984), 182A.

10. James B. Meriwether asks whether Longstreet should be considered a Southwestern humorist and argues that placing him in such a category distorts evaluation of him as a writer. Taliaferro is not as gifted as a writer as Longstreet, but it may be that labeling him a Southwestern humorist prevents a comprehensive assessment of his work. See James B. Meriwether, "Augustus Baldwin Longstreet: Realist and Artist," *Mississippi Quarterly*, 35 (Fall 1982), 351–64.

11. Wimsatt and Phillips, "Antebellum Humor," in Louis D. Rubin, Jr., *The History of Southern Literature* (Baton Rouge: Louisiana State University Press, 1985), p. 153.

Documentary Editing: Critical, Noncritical, Uncritical

T. H. Howard-Hill

Mary-Jo Kline. *A Guide to Documentary Editing*. Prepared for the Association for Documentary Editing. Baltimore and London: Johns Hopkins University Press, 1987. xv, 228 pp.

A Guide to Documentary Editing was prepared by Mary-Jo Kline, the editor of *The Political Correspondence and Public Papers of Aaron Burr*, for the Association of Documentary Editing. Arthur Link relates in his foreword how the ADE appointed a committee to oversee the production of "an authoritative manual on documentary editing" and obtained seed money from the National Historical Publications and Records Commission and later, support from the National Endowment for the Humanities. The *Guide*, then, has reputable auspices. Yet ADE's Committee on the Manual quickly discovered "a strong consensus that the editing profession needed, not a *manual*, with a stern, single set of methods and standards, but a *guide* to historical and literary textual editing that would take into account alternative methods to deal with different—and sometimes widely different—bodies of documents" (p. xii). It is questionable whether the editing profession, already committed to this or the other editing methodology, could have been expected to hold any other view. A more appropriate consideration might have been the requirements of scholars proposing to embark upon documentary editorial projects and seeking an explicit statement of preferred methodology. In 1979 Link noted the absence of a manual for documentary editing. The *Guide* does not fill the deficiency; nevertheless, it makes a notable contribution to the continuing debate that may in time allow ADE to produce such a manual.

The history of the project, like the distinction between "guide" and "manual," is not irrelevant. Dr. Kline acknowledges the aid of "the men and women who have reviewed one or more versions of this manuscript" on behalf of ADE, and warns the reader of "four special idiosyncrasies of the guide" (p. xiv). The last is a disclaimer of ADE's responsibility for passages in which she describes "certain methods and editorial decisions in less than laudatory terms," thus violating her mandate (she writes) to prepare a descriptive rather than a prescriptive work on documentary editing. The impression given by this preliminary huffing and puffing—and confirmed by small details in the *Guide* itself—is that the work is the product of two competing influences: to contribute to the relatively sparse literature on the theory and practice of documentary editing, and to avoid advocating or criticizing editorial practices in a manner some members of ADE would take offense at. In some respects, I feel, the *Guide* would have been more useful had it *not* been written under official auspices; I intend that as a compliment to Dr. Kline's scholarship.

Editing, once one gets into it, is an intensely practical business, and the practical elements of managing editions of extensive documents and archives are thoroughly dealt with here in such chapters as "Initiating an Editorial Project," "Organising a Documentary Edition," "The Conventions of Textual Treatment," "The Practical Application of Editorial Conventions," "The Mechanics of Establishing a Text," "Preparing a Documentary Edition for the Printer," and "The Editor and the Publisher." These chapters comprise the bulk of the *Guide* and concentrate the experience of scores of editors. No one can read these pages without acquiring valuable insights into the arduous practicalities of translating original documents into scholarly forms. Inevitably, criticisms may be offered. It seemed to me that although the editorial use of computers was mentioned early (pp. 30–32) and quite frequently in the *Guide*, insufficient attention was given to the fundamental problem of character representation on computer keyboards, screens, and printers, and to the necessity for an editor to recognize that the use of computers obliges him to establish conventions for the representations of characters and symbols that (in turn) represent the characters and symbols of the original document. It is not a light consideration that the computer involves usually an additional transcription *and* coding stage. Ideally, the evolution of computer technology will make this less important. Nevertheless, the *Guide* does too little to prepare the tyro editor for the complexities he will encounter in using computers for large editorial projects (essential though their use is), and to inform him of the planning decisions computers imply initially. No doubt consideration of the sheer pace at which computers are evolving and the great range of editorial aids they can provide, as well as their ordinariness in modern life, inhibited more extensive treatment in the *Guide*, but one gets little sense of their importance or their complexity there.

There are issues even more important. The theoretical underpinnings of the *Guide* are stated concisely in the introduction and developed intermittently in subsequent chapters. "Documentary editing" is an expression of fairly recent currency though doubtless familiar to members of ADE. The index to the *Guide* claims that the term is defined on p. 1 where we read that "*documentary*, or noncritical, editing . . . can be distinguished from more traditional *textual*, or critical, editorial method." However, as G. Thomas Tanselle mentioned in his influential article "The Editing of Historical Documents" (*Studies in Bibliography*, 31 [1978], 1–56), frequently cited in the *Guide*, all the editing Dr. Kline, he, I, and the readers of this review are concerned with is documentary in so far as manuscripts and books alike are documents. The distinction between the schools of editing must be made on the other ground, that one is and the other is not "critical." Dr. Kline cites the scholarship of classical texts, for which originals have not survived, and the development of textual critical methods by editors of printed texts where scribes and compositors may have introduced corruptions during transmission, to explain "critical," and concludes that "the documentary editor's goal is not to *supply* the words or phrases of a vanished archetype but rather to *preserve* the nuances of a source that has survived the ravages of time" (p. 2). (She acknowledges that the transcription of the nuances of original documents invariably involves fine critical distinctions and judgments but—to my mind—without appropriate emphasis. The apposition of "critical" and "noncritical" in this context plays squarely into the hands of those who claim derogatively that editing is intellectually inferior to "criticism." Few readers will heed the distinction between "noncritical" and "uncritical" made much later in the book.)

However, the case for the adoption of noncritical methods (Dr. Kline's terminology, not mine) rests on the significance of the materials employed: documentary editors work from source materials which the *Guide* describes as "inscribed artifacts whose unique physical characteristics and original nature give them special evidentiary value." Their significance "demands that their editors provide editorial texts that themselves will communicate as much of the sources' evidentiary value as possible" (p. 2). These statements raise more questions than they answer.

The confusion an uninformed reader may experience is compounded when, after a survey of "Early American Documentary Editing," the *Guide* passes on to discuss "'Historical' Editing" with no statement of the relationship between the two. The reader must assume that the terms are synonymous, though why they should be—considering that historical editing is subsequently distinguished from and contrasted to "'Literary' Editing"—is hard to see. At different points, editing is defined according to the main interests of the editors, or according to the character of the documents which are edited. One would think therefore that the documentary editor's special province is writings of "unique physical characteristics and original nature" (p. 2), one-of-a-kind diaries, journals, letters, and suchlike personal documents. Literary editors are equally concerned with such materials and, by and large, deal with them in much the same ways as historical editors do. But historical editing involves public and official as well as personal and private documents. Consequently, it is difficult to see why documentary and historical editing should be equated unless historical editors claim that the methods appropriate to the class of documents that justifies the characteristic method of editing ("documentary") should nevertheless be applied also to a different category of documents

Documentary Editing 153

with radically dissimilar characteristics. If this is true, the theoretical underpinnings of documentary editing are shakier than they appear in the *Guide*.

I doubt whether any inadequacy I detect in distinctions made in the introductory chapter of the *Guide* should be laid to Dr. Kline's charge. She has, after all, provided a just, historical account of the fissures and imbalances that usually characterize vital fields of scholarship. (The establishment of ADE and its near-contemporary, the Society for Textual Scholarship, are clear manifestations of that vitality.) But it is unfortunate that much of the debate about editorial principles reminds one of the blind men who vehemently and variously identified a dead beast (an elephant, perhaps) on the basis of a limited, local exploration of its characteristics. The *Guide* makes appropriate acknowledgment of the fundamental truths that any text may be edited with any one of three principal objects: (1) It may be edited to define a text preserved in a single document, i.e., by removing the obscurities and ambiguities that result from handwriting or printing, the synchronic physical peculiarities of the medium, the elements of "documentariness" that are assumed not to bear significantly on the text. (The last clause suggests contentious issues that can be resolved ultimately only by redress to the original document itself: *all* editing, as Dr. Kline recognizes, is translation.) (2) The second object of editing is to produce a text in the form an author intended it, freed of any harmful accidents of transmission. (3) Lastly, an editor may aim to publish a text congenial to the needs of different groups of readers. However, editing is a single process involving text, meaning, and reader. All editors are readers, actively attentive to the meanings of the texts before them. A "documentary editor" who claims to edit the inscribed forms of a document without regard to their meaning deceives himself.

Further, it is inescapably true that all editions rest fundamentally on transcriptions of texts preserved in single exemplars. The obligation of the "documentary editor" to "translate handwritten, typescript, or printed source texts into a form that his reader can trust as an accurate representation of the specific original materials that they represent" (p. 114) is a recurrent theme in the *Guide*. (The advantage of making initial transcriptions of documents as literal as is practical is discussed on p. 168.) However, the basis for extending non-critical methods appropriate to original (autograph) or unique documents to printed editions (where the text was transmitted in intermediaries such as scribes or compositors) seems rooted in the assumed principle that documentary editions should provide the material for subsequent criticism rather than incorporate critical attentions which may be seen as violating the integrity of the historical artifacts. Dr. Kline writes in authoritarian terms: "The surviving copies of a given source must be evaluated to determine which is the best document, the one that is a unique [sic], authoritative source with evidentiary value. Once that source has been identified, it must be printed without being subject to emendation, conflation, or the other heavy artillery of textual editing" (p. 92).

There are occasional phrases in the *Guide* that invite critical attention (e.g., a surprising definition of *variorum edition*, p. 4; the association of Greg's copy-text theory and "*scientific* methodology" on p. 12; an unexplained distinction between copy-text and source text on p. 87), and there appears to be no mention of sublineation and its symbolic representation. Small matters. Dr. Kline has performed her task well. The *Guide* will be read avidly by editors of all persuasions, and by all profitably. The *Guide* was not intended to resolve contention amongst historical editors and may in fact provoke further debates on issues small and large. Notwithstanding, Dr. Kline's synthesis of the historical and literary methodologies is informative and useful; it would be surprising if the *Guide* does not help scholars produce even better editions of American documentary materials in the future.

The Figure in the Carpet Bombing: Pynchon's Patterns of Chaos

Dwight Eddins

Kathryn Hume. *Pynchon's Mythography: An Approach to* Gravity's Rainbow. Carbondale: Southern Illinois University Press, 1987. xxiv, 262 pp.

Thomas Moore. *The Style of Connectedness:* Gravity's Rainbow *and Thomas Pynchon*. Columbia: University of Missouri Press, 1987. viii, 312 pp.

David Seed. *The Fictional Labyrinths of Thomas Pynchon*. Iowa City: University of Iowa Press, 1988. x, 268 pp.

If there were any lingering doubts that *Gravity's Rainbow* has arrived, definitively and irrevocably, they were dispelled by its being chosen as the *pièce de résistance* for a recent reading marathon (forty hours, 887 pages) at Princeton University. One intrepid participant, perhaps swept away by an ecstatic identification with Pynchon's poor preterite masses, was said by the *New York Times* to have rolled around in a garbage can as he read his assigned eleven pages. It all suggests a postmodern version of the Great Awakening. The *Times* reporter himself, perhaps touched by the crowd's fervor for a text that is somehow both encyclopedic and discontinuous, was moved to proclaim that this novel "boasts more than 400 characters and several story lines with no clear connection between them."[1] With just such ease and certainty, journalistic élan soars above the sheer plod of pedants, the sort who would quibble about whether there is a direct ratio between numbers of characters and occasions for boasting, and about just what constitutes a "clear" connection.

The first question is easily dismissed as the result of a flawed faith in simple magnitude, rather like that of the Evelyn Waugh schoolmaster who offers his students a prize for the longest essay. The second, however, raises complex, subtle issues that lie at the heart of literary criticism—issues especially relevant to a book with the word "connectedness" in its title, to another that traces the network of connections inherent in a "mythography," and to yet another that finds these connections to constitute "labyrinths." For a start, it is obvious that both the clarity and multiplicity of connection that we discover—in a novel by Pynchon or any other writer—are going to depend upon what critical grid we apply to the work. And as to our choice of critical grid—well, the rub starts there and never stops. An incredible melange of factors involving temperament, training, and cultural conditioning goes into our decision about which approach—depth psychology, Marxism, deconstruction, etc.—is likely to produce the most "valid" connections and filter out the most "invalid" ones; and out of our particular choices come our particular wars (or alliances) with a given critical orthodoxy.

In this regard, Pynchon criticism has increasingly tended toward an orthodoxy of the unorthodox, i.e., of emphasis on poststructuralist discontinuities, particularly in *Gravity's Rainbow*. As Kathryn Hume puts it in the preface to *Pynchon's Mythography*, "Critics mostly register the reduction of structures, assumptions, and discourses to contradictions and absences" (pp. 1–2). What is salient and undeniable in Pynchon's fiction—epistemological ambiguities, disrupted narratives, inconsistently drawn characters, opaque or contradictory moral norms, chaotically proliferating parody—becomes the basis on which his critics elaborate theoretical structures that privilege multiple modes of undecidability and indeterminacy. The most cogent of these elaborators, perhaps, have been Thomas Schaub, Molly Hite, and Peter Cooper, who collectively occupy the de-centered center of Pynchon criticism—somewhere to the right of avid deconstructors, but decidedly to the left (as we shall see) of Hume and Moore.[2]

Hume attributes the prevailing emphasis on "postmodernist elements" in Pynchon's fiction to the shock of the new and draws (rightly, I think) a comparison with the original reception of

Ulysses. The first critics reacted most strongly, as she points out, to the "dissonant and disturbing elements" in Joyce's novel and "stressed its negative effects" (p. 32). Subsequent revisionists, however, have been able to recognize that book's more "positive elements"; and the time has come, in Hume's estimation, for a similar recognition in the case of *Gravity's Rainbow*. It is a process to which both she and Moore dedicate their considerable efforts. Seed, on the other hand, chooses to undertake his analysis more or less in the aura of what we might call the "ambiguitist" school of Hite, Schaub, and Cooper, continuing the delineation of Pynchon's impasses, inconsistencies, and paradoxes.

Hume is scrupulously careful to give this school its due, admitting the pervasive presence of the unresolvable and the indeterminate in Pynchon's fiction, and the propriety of poststructuralist critical techniques in dealing with this presence. But there are, she argues, three "devices" that "stand out as managing to escape the deconstruction applied to other unifying features: a principle of multiplicity, a group of psychoanalytical theories, and one kind of mythology" (p. 32). Concentrating on the last of these, she maps an elaborate web of mythic strands that does indeed amount to a structuralist (one is tempted to say, a pre-poststructuralist) x-ray of Pynchon's encyclopedic opus. This complex grid is set up as a "stabilizing" structure in a sort of symbiotic binarity with the "destabilizing" structures traced by critics who focus on *Gravity's Rainbow* as a stylistic embodiment of modern "disintegration and fragmentation" (p. 2). For Hume, it is not only permissible to read the novel in *both* modes—i.e., the constructive and deconstructive—but necessary if we are to grasp the totality of the complex experience it offers us. This prospect of an unresolvable critical dualism subsumed by a higher complementarity is both fascinating and problematic, and raises issues—to which I shall return later—that move beyond Pynchon's impasses to the present-day impasses of our profession.

When Hume progresses from her apologia for this dualism into her chosen mission of elucidating mythic structures, she acts with a sophisticated acuity and a surehandedness that make her book invaluable background for future Pynchon criticism. Careful at all points to keep her methodology and critical assumptions before us, she begins by examining the hermeneutical questions raised by the application of myth criticism to literature in general, and the particular relevance (or lack of it) to Pynchon of such practitioners as Claude Levi-Strauss, Eric Gould, Northrop Fry, Paul Ricoeur, and Mircea Eliade. Her own structuralist grid draws most heavily on the work of one of Levi-Strauss's disciples, Edmund Leach, who sets forth three analytical categories—oppositions, redundancies (i.e., repetitions of words and motifs), and mediations—whereby myths can be made to yield explicit meanings. Pointing out that the first two categories have long been standard equipment in literary analysis as well, Hume asserts that mediation—the use of a third term to "mediate" between two opposing terms—may also be useful in dealing with an author as mythically oriented as Pynchon. One of the examples she gives, the ideation of an afterlife as a way of mediating the "alive and not-alive" antinomy, would seem to have particular relevance to the natural/supernatural ambiguities of *Gravity's Rainbow* (p. 27).

Beginning her task of myth-mapping with Pynchon's cosmos, Hume decides that it is a "mythological cosmos" because "it is measured in human terms; it presents us with non-empirical realities; it is ultimately serious; and it relies on traditional archetypes" (p. 37). She justifies these criteria in a convincing array of allusions to Homer, the *Beowulf* poet, Dante, C. S. Lewis, and other crafters of cosmoi, and proceeds to apply the criteria to *Gravity's Rainbow* in the course of charting its symbolic physical geography, its symbolic non-physical geography (i.e., the Other Side), and the characters who inhabit both. The result is that we are left, as Hume intends, with a new sense of how Pynchon's landscapes, flora, and fauna (including the superhuman) cohere into a mythological whole, with a sharper delineation of the boundary between the natural and the supernatural, and with a fresh perspective on Pynchon as part of a distinguished "mythographical" succession.

But Hume as literary cartographer feels an obligation to go beyond the usual notion of a value-free map. Her schema includes investigations of how "positive and negative values" are distributed in Pynchon's cosmos, and of how "seriously" a given mythological datum is to be taken (p. 37). These inquiries inevitably lead her into the murkier waters of critical speculation. In Pynchon's cosmos, as she is forced to note, "An act, event, or person is almost always Janus-faced; from one perspective, it may seem bad, but from another, good or acceptable" (p. 76). This basic revelation marks, to my mind, a crucial juncture for any critic of Pynchon. At this point that critic may choose either to look behind this ethical duality in an attempt to understand the metaphysic that produces a Janus-faced cosmos; or, taking the duality as a *fait-accompli*, he/she may investigate its ramifications for a viable ethic and a practical course of behavior in the world determined by the novel's givens. Hume chooses, essentially, the latter path, giving us useful accountings of the ethical ambiguity, what we might call the good/bad ratio, attaching to various Pynchon symbols—music, the War, the serpent, etc.— and concluding that "the question is to find an optimum between control and freedom, closure and openness. At a guess, Pynchon does not favor others imposing controls on us but accepts the more generous limitations we are willing to place on ourselves, the kinds of limits and responsibilities we accept for love or friendship" (p. 78).

It is at this point that I have to wonder whether it is really true that the elephantine machinery of *Gravity's Rainbow* ultimately labors, in all its cosmic clangor and uproar, to bring forth a mouse of humanist moderation. There are certainly grounds for this more or less unexceptionable *via media* in the positive/ negative mathematics that Hume so scrupulously works out, and there are additional grounds in various moderating pronouncements of the novel's personae. Molly Hite, another astute critic of Pynchon's work, also locates his moral center in provisional "middles" between such extremes as freedom and control. The danger here, perhaps, lies in overemphasizing the desperate search for a workable norm *within* the novel's states of paranoid siege, and underemphasizing the larger metaphysical forcefields that produce (or mitigate) that state of siege. The practical "situation ethic" that emerges from a moral accounting on the novel's literal level seems somehow a poor and ineffectual thing compared to the vast dialectics of life-affirmation and life-negation that enshroud this level; and this discrepancy suggests that a more resonant and embracing ethic may lie behind Pynchon's proceedings. It won't do to make this most immoderate of contemporary authors too moderate a chap.

Along these same lines, Hume asserts that "the population [of the novel's 'Other Side']—angels, Titans, Qlippoth, guides, and astral influences—is not offered for literal acceptance as a new pantheon, given its heterogeneous nature and religious ancestry, but is a fairly playful embodiment of the argument that there are more ways of interpreting human experience than humans themselves see at any time" (p. 84). This argument typifies a widespread tendency in Pynchon criticism to demystify the author's supernatural references, to nudge the author himself closer to the rational, monistic perspectives espoused—one hazards—by the majority of his scientifically sophisticated readers. But it is precisely these perspectives that Pynchon targets in the freewheeling and fairly egalitarian ontology of *Gravity's Rainbow*. There are no textual indicators that the spectral visitations at the novel's seances, or even the dreadfully unplayful Qlippoth, are any less "real" than, say, Slothrop's youth in Massachusetts. Granted that Pynchon is not advocating some sort of literal Titan-worship, we owe him at least a suspension of disbelief, a margin of supernatural possibility, in keeping with his radical assault on prevailing ontological hierarchies.

As a whole, however, Hume's mythographical project enhances the cosmic resonance of Pynchon's novel, clarifying its status as a postmodern reflection of archetypal quests for order. Her chapter "Mythological Actions" convincingly weaves together, in its first part, four "histories"—those of Western culture, of Tyrone Slothrop, of the V-2, and of technology—into a composite "mythological history" that serves as a rationale of modern "immachination," the bizarre synthesis of mankind and its machines. The second part of the chapter is devoted to an application of Edmund Leach's analytical categories to various characters and themes of the novel. Hume demonstrates the usefulness of this methodology by tracing, for example, how such characters as Tchitcherine, Enzian, Gottfried, and numerous others "map on" to Slothrop and he to them in significant "redundancies" that serve to separate the novel's unifying myths from its encyclopedic potpourri. She is also able to locate an implicit "mediation" that resolves the "Pointsman-Mexico" dilemma, the disparity between the Pavlovian psychologist's espousal of an inflexible 0/1 binarity as a way of calibrating human behavior and the statistician's insistence on probability theory as a measure of what happens *between* the zero and the one.

Hume's next chapter, entitled "Mythology and the Individual," is perhaps her most imaginative. She takes Pynchon's protagonist Slothrop through the various embodiments of mythical heroes that Pynchon himself suggests, showing explicitly how he parallels or diverges from Faust, Tannhauser, Parsifal, and Orpheus, as well as a group of "juvenile heroes" ranging from Hansel and Gretel to Plasticman. It is, when its terms are juxtaposed, an amazing and enlightening series of incarnations, and Hume takes full advantage of the juxtapositions to demonstrate how Pynchon's versions systematically metamorphose the classical "hero monomyth"—the fable of the hero who saves his society and is entirely reconciled with it—into a "new pattern [that] shows the individual integrating with chaos and accepting it" (p. 182). It is a demonstration crucial to her larger argument—sustained overall, I think, with considerable eloquence—that "a mythology can interrelate with a complexly conceived uncertain universe" (p. 198).

Even though Thomas Moore shares with Hume the quest for continuities in a reputedly discontinuous novel, it is difficult to imagine a more striking antithesis in attitude and approach than that between *Mythography* and *The Style of Connectedness*. The former is a totally ordered exposition of a partial ordering, the latter a partially ordered exposition of a total ordering. While Hume, with meticulous logic and organization, builds the case for a unifying principle of "cosmos" that works to balance the novel's intractable postmodern "chaos," Moore outlines in three hundred loosely structured, rhapsodically allusive pages a principle of "pan-psychic connectedness" formulated to draw this chaos together into a "One" that can serve as an "alternative for belief, or for faith" (pp. 46–47). Faced with "the basic Pynchonian One/Zero problem," for instance, the "Pointsman/Mexico" dilemma that Hume undertakes to resolve through a complex equilibrium of binarity and probability, Moore applies a mystical Occam's razor to reach the conclusion that "at its heart the novel opts for the One" (p. 221). Similarly, disdaining Hume's elaborate accommodation with radical postmodernist views of the novel, Moore elects to take "only incidental issue with readers and critics who have found *Gravity's Rainbow* to be essentially nihilistic, ultimately downbeat in its view of the nature of human experience" (p. 2).

It would be a great mistake, however, to dismiss Moore as some naive and uninformed apostle of upbeat thinking. As his impressive range of historical, scientific, literary, and mythological reference shows, he is one of the most erudite critics Pynchon has had. Thus, when he opens his fifth chapter with the disarming admission that it is "long, preposterously ambitious in its synthetic attempts, nervous, amateuristic," he is somehow managing to be both candid and disingenuous (p. 149). These adjectives apply, in some degree, to Moore's entire book; but then they also apply—from a certain perspective—to *Gravity's Rainbow*. Perhaps the transgression Moore has committed here is the imitative fallacy, assembling a rambling, unalphabetized encyclopedia that both glosses and mimics Pynchon's, and manages along the way a roughly analogous combination of edification and entertainment. If so, it is ultimately—I think—a beneficent transgression. In his chapter entitled "Max Weber, the Spirit of Capitalism, and *Gravity's Rainbow*," for example, Moore explores a labyrinthine linkage between Weberian sociology, seventeenth-century Puritanism, modern capitalism, Marshall McLuhan's media theory, and the history of I. G. Farben. All of these subjects have been dealt with to some extent by previous Pynchon critics, but never with the depth and synthetic scope that Moore brings to the task. Calling upon a wealth of detailed historical evidence and a perceptive analysis of the relevant theoretical materials, he weaves a convincing picture of the socio-economic matrix that generates the world of the novel and incidentally identifies new possibilities of influences and sources in such books as J. S. Martin's *All Honorable Men,* an account of "clandestine corporate activities in the Zone," and C. Wright

Mills's *The Power Elite,* which studies the power mechanisms of mass societies (p. 143).

Like a number of critics before him, Moore is intrigued by the metaphor of *Gravity's Rainbow* as movie—a metaphor for which Pynchon himself provides warrant. But Moore develops this notion in a singularly comprehensive way. The individual frames of the film lead him to articulate the more general notion of *framing,* i.e., the cognitive acts of ordering and systemization that produce a patterned reality. The fluid motion that the camera breaks up into artificially individuated frames represents a mystical but fundamental unity that underlies all existence, and to which Moore refers by the use of such terms as "pan-psychic connectedness," "the Greater Life," and "the ontological plenum." He believes strongly that Pynchon exhibits a constant sense of this unity in *Gravity's Rainbow,* invoking it through a "style of connectedness, or of integration" that is "a continuous crackle of meaning-sparks leaping between charged points" (p. 52). Framing images, which represent "false arbitrations of an essentially holistic field," may be perversely oppressive as in the Hansel and Gretel "Oven" fantasy by which Blicero "frames" Gottfried and Katje, or liberating as in the archetypal Rainbow that restores us to a sense of the holistic field (p. 48). Even the irregularities of quantum physics, sometimes used as an analogue for postmodern discontinuities in Pynchon, are viewed by Moore as phenomena that can aid in this restoration—a view that he supports by quoting Werner Heisenberg on "approaching the 'one,'" and the quantum physicist Bernard d'Espagnat on the possibility that—at the quantum level—entities may "constitute an indivisible whole" (pp. 186–87).

Ultimately, it is the psychic integration of inner and outer offered by Jungian psychology that acts as the unifier of all unifiers for Moore. He settles in particular on Jung's concept of synchronicity, the "principle of an acausal but meaningful ordering of events within a 'psychic relativity of space and time'" (p. 277). This principle locates in seeming coincidences—both psychic and material—in time and space a mysterious "interdependence" that represents much more than mere chance. Applied to Pynchon's novel, it serves as a rationale for such seemingly irrational linkages as that between the filming of a propagandistic fantasy about black rocket troops and the actual appearance of the *Schwarzkommando* in Germany, or the one involving the map of Slothrop's amorous conquests and the map of V-2 strikes in London. On a more general level, synchronicity draws the wildly disparate images, plot fragments, and tonalities of the novel together into a grandiose panpsychic totality.

It is a scheme that aims for a sort of comprehensive positivity, and therein lies not only much of its appeal, but also its point of vulnerability. All organizing categories strip away the individuating elements of particular phenomena in the name of a common denominator; but when these phenomena are as ontologically diverse and as polarized between positive and negative, rational and irrational, as the events, characters, and symbolic entities of *Gravity's Rainbow*, they tend to prove refractory to this logical violence. And when the category in question is based on a massive psycho-mystical subversion of the subjective/objective polarity, the novel's urgent external conflicts and threatening external discontinuities—however fantastically realized—stubbornly resist dissolution into an archetypal soup. Moore's treatment of the V-2 rocket in terms of the "Mercurius" archetype provides a good example of this indissolubility. For Jung, Mercurius is a marriage of "incompatible opposites," a paradoxical combination of "hell-fire" and the fire of "divine love" (p. 248). Framed in this archetype, the rocket is the "ithyphallic tower, vertical channel, or *axis mundus* connecting primordial, subterranean energies with human systems of myth and belief 'above,'" its base a "sacred zone" in which the "Great Time" of the gods irrupts into "human time" (p. 251). It is certainly true that Pynchon connects the rocket with sacrality, but it is with a perverted religiosity, a sacrality gone wrong. Moore, to be fair, admits the danger of this "messenger in search of grace" burying us "Babel-wise someday in fallen rubble," but so sanguine is his approach, so bent on an affirmative integration of all the novel's givens, that this caveat is lost in a mythic epiphany that fails to account for the *supplement* of evil (p. 249). This objection registered—and I think it is an important one for the larger picture of Pynchon criticism—I must add that it is impossible to read Moore's account of the

Mercurius archetype or of any other symbolic plexus without significantly richer insights into the "deep structures" of Pynchon's fathomless novel. It is an important and commanding study, "amateurish" finally in that it is an erudite labor of love.

After the meticulous mythographical structurings of Kathryn Hume and the cavalierly ambitious "connectedness" of Moore, David Seed's *Fictional Labyrinths* presents something of a theoretical void. The minotaur in Seed's own labyrinth seems to be a relentless empiricism but little concerned with comprehensive interpretive schemes drawn from myth, religion, or depth psychology. This refusal includes not seeking to ground (as do, say, Molly Hite and Thomas Schaub) the postmodern Pynchon that he seems to espouse in some sort of postmodern theoretical construct. It is true that he suggests a larger framework for Pynchon's fiction by exploring parallels with such established influences as Henry Adams and Norbert Wiener, and with the work of such contemporaries as Tom Robbins, Peter Matthiessen, and M. F. Beal; but even in these cases he concentrates on specific comparisons to the neglect of establishing a broad ideological or aesthetic context.

What we have here, then, is an oddly moment-to-moment reading of Pynchon's entire fictional canon without systematic generalization and without as much cross-reference as one might expect between the discussions of individual works. Seed's introductory chapter is symptomatic in this regard; it discusses background and influences but never sets forth a methodology or a coherent group of organizing axia. It is only fair, on the other hand, to point out that some of the strands Seed will trace in Pynchon emerge in his discussions of Jack Kerouac and Marshall McLuhan, and that some sense of a theoretical context enters his study in his frequent debates with previous critics (like Hume and Moore, he has done his homework) and in the assumption of a postmodern Pynchon that runs throughout his study.

Unfortunately, the method that he uses to support this assumption is a variety of literal-minded reading that refuses to look beyond Pynchon's parodies and subtly engineered ambiguities for a larger symbolic resonance. For Seed, parody is parody, ambiguity is ambiguity; and their appearance at any point pretty well puts an end to possibilities of order, resolution, and continuity. I am reminded again of those early (and misguided) reactions to *Ulysses* that saw it as a pervasively nihilistic rejection of the modern world. One needs a certain aesthetic resilience and flexibility to read both Joyce and Pynchon, a capacity for seeing new, quite serious structures of connectedness (both positive and negative) in the middle of parody and of ostensible contradiction or incoherence.

This, I am afraid, Mr. Seed does not demonstrate. Faced with the surprise ending of the story "The Secret Integration," in which a black playmate of several white children is revealed to be an imaginary figure, Seed concludes that the issue of racial prejudice—the story's thematic focus—"evaporates into fancy" (p. 70). He misses entirely the highlighting of the parents' bigoted reality by the poignancy of the children's integrative imaginings.

Seed views this conflict between the claims of the imaginary and those of the real as inadvertent on Pynchon's part, a failure of craftsmanship; but he finds a similar confusion in *V.* to be planned, a more or less systematic subversion of quests for meaning through farce, irony, and contradiction. Herbert Stencil's quest for V., in particular, is singled out as an example of patent absurdity, principally because Stencil is often presented in a humorous light and because the dentist Eigenvalue mocks his notion of history as conspiracy. As Peter Cooper has pointed out, the dismissal of Stencil's historical reconstructions as possibilities amounts to the dismissal of the tension that animates the novel, reducing it to a monotonously extended debunking.[3] But this seems to be essentially what Seed thinks it is. V. herself, the enigmatic figure on whom the book centers, "not only has no power, but gradually collapses into total inanimateness and passivity" (p. 110). That V's power *lies* in inanimateness, that the coming of her entopic kingdom travesties traditional myth only to produce a new and terrifying myth, does not enter into Seed's equation of parody with devastating ridicule. Similarly, Hugh Godolphin's amazing discovery of a rainbow-hued monkey frozen in the ice of the South Pole is "a *negative* image which brings no insights" (p. 93). The possibility that the insight might be one into a perverse *celebration* of the "negative"—á la the bedizened vacuity of Vheissu, the monkey's home—never rises to temper Seed's absurdist vision of the novel. His final overview of *V.* suggests that, for the reader, a "clear overview [is] well nigh impossible" (p. 116). *Sic transit claritas Pynchonis.*

One is hardly surprised, then, to find this epistemological skepticism extending to *The Crying of Lot 49*, where—we learn— Oedipa Maas's inability to stabilize the text of a Jacobean play "mimes out the reader's difficulty in apprehending Pynchon's text" (p. 128). The difference between the reader's apprehension of a well-wrought confusion and the confused apprehension of the reader is not preserved in Seed's critique. Oedipa's quest for Tristero—upon which this novel's significance rests even more decisively than that of *V.* on Stencil's quest—is also revealed as a sham; Pynchon, it seems, uses "religious parody" to mock its "earnestness" (p. 132). Seed even invokes a species of literary mathematics to suggest that Oedipa's hope for spiritual enlightenment in this quest is misguided in that "the number of references to death far outweighs that of spiritual allusions" (p. 133). Ultimately, Seed believes, Pynchon gets himself into difficulties by excessive rhetoric that tends to validate the existence of Tristero, thus destroying the book's "carefully maintained ambiguity" (p. 150). To prevent this, the author must keep alive the possibility that Tristero "doesn't exist"; but this possibility "carries with it the corrolary [sic] that Oedipa's quest and the novel itself is [sic] WASTE." With such a judgment, Pynchon's novel would seem to suffer a corollary thrombosis of sorts, a clotting of its aesthetic viability.

When Seed abandons these foreclosing verdicts for the analysis of specific passages and specific parallels, he often has something to teach us. He is able, for instance, to throw new light on the symbolism of *The Crying of Lot 49* by discussions of Marshall McLuhan's theories and of Pynchon's own essay "A Journey into the Mind of Watts." And in his chapter on *Gravity's Rainbow*, he outlines a convincing thesis—not unrelated to Thomas Moore's—of how Pynchon "blurs the boundaries of character" into larger thematic concerns (p. 160). But these characters and themes, and the novel that contains them, eventually fall prey to the same destabilizing mechanism that claimed the textual integrity of the earlier novels. At the end of *Gravity's Rainbow*, says Seed, Pynchon finally "turns against his own fiction" as if he were "acting on the implications of his earlier implications that print is tainted by political oppression" (p. 219). The novel deconstructs before our very eyes, drawing our attention to the "technologies and media" out of which it grew. I am reminded of a freewheeling Freudian essay in which Eric Bentley suggests that Eugene O'Neill may have inserted soporific scenes and irritating character traits into his plays as bad drama in order to get even with his actor-father.[4] If Bentley and Seed are right, the purchasers of expensive New York theatre tickets can share with the readers of a mammoth novel the sadder-but-wiser edification of a prolonged artistic snipe hunt.

Moving toward an overview of the three critical works examined here, one might set up a quasi-serious analogy with a sequence from the history of philosophy. If Seed's epistemological skepticism vis-á-vis Pynchon's fictive structures can be roughly compared to David Hume's corrosive attack on the possibility of knowing orderings outside our own minds, then one may think of Kathryn Hume playing Kant to Seed's David Hume, i.e., validating a sense of structures that transcend the fiction's deconstructions, even while she admits the claims of the latter. Finally, Thomas Moore appears as Hegel to elaborate these structures into a Structure that embraces all contradiction and negation in its inexorable ordering processes. If one cannot fully accept either of the extremes represented, respectively, by Seed and Moore, it seems logical to return to Kathryn Hume's balance between the structural and the poststructural for a sense of some future direction in Pynchon criticism. I specify "direction" because I suspect that the balance itself—the framing of what I earlier termed "an unresolvable critical dualism"—is not one that can be maintained. The rage to order is, at our present juncture, in an unfriendly dialectic with the rage to demonstrate disorder, and subversion of the one by the other is more likely than a stable synthesis. An unabashed Derridean reading of *Gravity's Rainbow*, for instance, would aim first at destabilizing the very oppositions that Hume undertakes to place above the deconstructive ferment. If one cannot assent, however, to the *a priori* principles that produce this destabilization, then specific examples of disjuncture, disorder, and incongruity in the text become incentives to the quest for an ordering logos that will somehow comprehend them. It is, after all, impossible to prove that no such logos exists in the manner, say, that certain mathematical problems can be proved insoluble. And if it *can* exist, the categorical imperative of criticism demands an attempt to formulate it. The would-be formulator faces, of course, the difficult problem of identifying and embodying the parameters that generate the various modes of postmodern chaos without compromising—as Moore's scheme tends to do—the menacing illogic and disruptiveness of these modes. It is a metaphysically ambitious prescription, of precisely the sort that a metaphysically ambitious body of fiction calls for; and the analyses of Hume and Moore, at least, suggest that a response is well underway.

Notes

1. "A Marathon on Pynchon Stirs Readers," *New York Times,* 15 Nov. 1987, Sec. 1, p. 61.
2. Thomas Shaub, *Pynchon: The Voice of Ambiguity* (Urbana: Univ. of Illinois Press, 1981); Molly Hite, *Ideas of Order in the Novels of Thomas Pynchon* (Columbus: Ohio State Univ. Press, 1983); Peter Cooper, *Signs and Symptoms: Thomas Pynchon and the Contemporary World* (Berkeley and Los Angeles: Univ. of California Press, 1983).
3. Cooper, *Signs and Symptoms,* p. 160.
4. Bentley, "Eugene O'Neill," in *Major Writers of America* (New York: Harcourt, Brace, 1962), II, ed. Perry Miller, 567.

The Evasion of Consensus

Jeffrey M. Perl

Gerald Graff. *Professing Literature: An Institutional History.*
Chicago: University of Chicago Press, 1987. vii, 315 pp.

Gerald Graff's history of literature departments in America is not a book to judge, not even to review. It is an invitation for academic literary critics to discuss the future of their profession and is offered as the basis for an informed debate. Some books require, simply, thanks and a response.

Graff's book shows how academic battles are fought and then refought in different generations, in divergent social milieux, under a variety of names: ancients vs. moderns, rhetoricians vs. humanists, researchers vs. generalists, American studies vs. English studies, comparative literature vs. English and American literature, criticism vs. scholarship and history, criticism and scholarship and history vs. theory. Graff is careful not to make the Structuralist point, and underscores the significance of his variables to his structures; careful also to make his evidence inclusive. *Professing Literature* is a history of institutional arrangements, not of criticism (not of major figures). The attention given to forgotten figurines establishes a new context in which to read the histories of criticism left us by Olympians. The doctrines of New Criticism were not born full-blown from the brow of Cleanth Brooks but came, in Graff's retelling, piece by inconsistent piece, in response to adversaries often now unknown.

Thus Graff demonstrates as well a principle familiar from Thomas Kuhn's *The Structure of Scientific Revolutions* (1962), that institutional disputes resolve into arrangements that make them disappear. Graff differs, though, from Kuhn—or rather, the humanities from the sciences—in that for literature departments there seems no possibility of revolution. In the disputes

Graff traces there are no victors, no Kuhnian textbooks to erase beliefs and praxis of the defeated, because when the superannuated fade they reappear as avant-garde. In silence Graff lets pass details of the curriculum, and of the attitudes toward it, that were dominant in the nineteenth century—details that leave us wondering about what *future* means, and impressed with Graff's restraint. Vernacular modern languages and literatures were taken, one-hundred years ago, "as feminine preoccupations" (p. 37). Think of Carolyn Heilbrun's proposition that the "notable male bonding"among literature professors corresponds to their recognition that the majority of their students today are women.[1] Or think of E. D. Hirsch and his already famous List: compilations of facts-to-know, one-hundred years ago—of quotations to commit to memory and recite—were the rule in almost every college. There are no radicals and no conservatives in the Directory of the MLA, only varieties of reactionary, dreaming of once-thought-repressive pasts that each reactionary now conceives as progress. Revolutionaries qualify uniquely as exponents of the status quo: "The American university is itself something of a deconstructionist, proliferating a variety of disciplinary vocabularies that nobody can reduce to the common measure of any metalanguage" (pp. 12–13).

From Graff's evidence and observations, a variety of conclusions may be reached. Graff's own suggestion—that we wage war in front of the children, that the curriculum exploit our incoherence—is an anticlimax: "Do the purposes of liberal education require that the teacher *resolve* [an institutional controversy] before proceeding with his or her task? ... one could bring the controversy itself into the classroom and make it part of one's subject matter" (p. 260). Graff's history has potential healing powers that his suggestions for our behavior lack. Marriage counseling will not unplug our hell machine. Each party to academic literary disputes is in need of deep and individual analysis. *Professing Literature*, a catalogue of patterned eccentricities, has commenced the process. But to progress, we must rightly name and acknowledge the disease.

In our confrontations over method and curriculum, each side is what the other claims to be: Graff documents time and again

The Evasion of Consensus

173

the operation of this mechanism. He shows how Irving Babbitt—traditional humanist, so we thought—was a proponent of the radical view that college literati should teach theory. Graff demonstrates how Helen Vendler—the practitioner of close reading—is a rigorous contextualist. We are each ambivalent in our commitments. We each reject ideas and perspectives that are valid and attractive in order to achieve consistency. We each project perspectives that we cannot bear to lose on individuals who are close (their offices are down the hall) but reliably adversarial. Ambivalence, in other words, is rudimentary consensus; and consensus we will do anything to evade.

A history is required that reaches far behind the nineteenth century and America and the university into a region and a time when, Graff's evidence appears to indicate, an unbearable ambivalence resolved itself in polar conflict. Graff returns in virtually every chapter to examine forms of two old struggles: the battle of ancients and moderns, the opposition of Catholic and Protestant hermeneutics. Graff makes little of the first, less of the second, and nothing of the fact that both struggles date from the period which, since the middle of the nineteenth century, we have called "the Renaissance." The establishment of vernacular, modern literatures as fit subjects for the college curriculum was a more meaningful event than Graff allows, and part of the same antithetic motion that brought Michelet and Burckhardt to reify the Renaissance. What Graff calls "the Humanist Myth"—"the delusion that academic literary studies at some point underwent a falling-away from genuine Arnoldian humanism" (p. 5)—antedates Arnoldian humanism by no less than three hundred years.

Modernity begins, by the humanist accounting, with the rebirth (not mere revival) of antiquity that occurred through the efforts of radical classicists in the fourteenth and fifteenth centuries. At the climax of that achievement, the humanist claim to inaugurate a new age was threatened by reemergence of the Gothic sensibility (the Protestant invaders of 1527 were portrayed as Visigoths by the Roman humanists)—threatened, too, by a new tendency to view the humanist revival not as the characteristic project of modernity but as the work of atavists and pedants. Immediate successors of the humanists accused their opponents of the failure to achieve, or perversion of, or mediocrity in relation to the classical ideal. The antagonism continued, in a variety of forms, down into the period that Graff's study covers. By the mid-nineteenth century the humanist program had come to seem irrelevant to the age it had inaugurated. Modernity was construed more and more as the era of new sciences, new technology, a new economy, and (in the ascendancy of the United States) the era of the New World. The humanists were in retreat until Burckhardt, in his *Civilization of the Renaissance,* altered their battle tactic. By attending to "the Renaissance," instead of to the ancients of whom the Renaissance was the renascence, Burckhardt deprived the opposition of its exlusive claim to being modern and yet arranged to keep what mattered most to humanists: an historical basis on which to invoke standards of classic excellence. On the horizon was a century, so Burckhardt and his colleague Nietzsche thought, that could become a renaissance of the Renaissance, and a rigid axiology would be required to establish and maintain it.

The classic modernists, so-called, each worked to fulfill Burckhardt's hope and Nietzsche's prophecy. In doing so, they rebelled against Matthew Arnold, on the grounds that verisimilitude is the enemy. Joyce and Eliot dismissed Arnold as a philistine *poseur.*[2] His defense of the humanist tradition made him, from the modernist perspective, a classicist in terrycloth: Arnold's project had been to reconstitute so much—no more—of the humanists' dream as was possible within the confines of Victorian democratic culture. The gravest of all fallacies about the relationships among modern literature, modern criticism, and the academy is that professors—Arnoldians, New Critics—were allied with classic modernism. None—not Leavis, not Wimsatt, not Trilling—could commit himself to the ferocious axiology, the antidemocratic values, of a humanist like Yeats or Pound. And Eliot was an Old Critic, a defender of the classical, historical, philological, paleographic, and bibliographical learning (the princely learning instituted by the humanists of the Renaissance) for which Brooks and Warren helped to substitute a pedagogy of the independent text. The New Critics were the bourgeoisie to the Old Critics' aristocracy: a new class that saw its lacks as democratic moral virtues.

The Evasion of Consensus 175

The point: literary studies in the American academy, however multiform, have been profoundly counter-humanist. The Arnoldian (the bourgeois) effort, which neither Nietzsche nor the modernists could stop, was to replicate features of traditional culture inside the progressive culture that destroyed them. Arnoldian culture, its touchstones, their traces in the American curriculum ("Great Books")—a sort of Europeland at Disney World—is what we take to be the classic and conservative milieu within our humanities departments. Graff acknowledges the problem: he notes that it was New Critics, often, who established Great Books courses, such that classic works are taught today without historic context (though in rigid—in totemic?—order of chronology). We defend such teaching, if at all, by reminding that neither the author's intentions nor the beliefs of his coevals can be the final determinant of meaning. In making this argument we are incipient Catholics, in the sense in which Eliot claimed to be wholly so (but was not). A Protestant view holds that the original intention of the Text can and must be contextualized, distilled, and formulated. Graff sees that the polar opposition of these hermeneutics is *specious*: "The pertinent question is not whether we can erase our own feelings," he writes, "but whether we can recognize them as our own, whether we can recognize the modern connotation *as* modern" (p. 203). But he does not observe how the opposition is moreover *obsolete*. There is at work in our bipolar hermeneutics an extinct (so we imagine) theological debate. The fantastic Logology of deconstruction has made increasingly obvious the latent theological content of literary criticism—the fact, put another way, that our poetics descend less from the literary techniques of humanists than from the exegetical doctrines of the churches.

The proliferation of needless enmities, the substitution of *humanist* for terms forbidden, serve to conceal from us that we are bourgeois Christian democrats. Not a fate worse than death, but one which makes too vivid the self-contradiction involved in bourgeois Christian democracy—in democracy, in Christianity, in the middle class. The Christian, the democrat, the bourgeois is a free man or free woman, but to exercise one's freedom against the liberal tenets of Christianity and the middle class and democracy is defined as sin, bohemia, or treason. Graff's account should make us wonder about the function of the university, of academic freedom, in our bourgeois Christian republic. Is it our function as academics to commit high-handed sin, pretend to stand outside the culture, to protect from view the contradictions that are the price of our consensus? It is a measure of the intensity of the experience of reading Graff's new book that so unlovable a question need arise.

Notes

1. Carolyn Heilbrun, "Bringing the Spirit Back to English Studies" (1979) in Elaine Showalter, ed., *The New Feminist Criticism: Essays on Women, Literature, and Theory* (New York: Pantheon, 1985), p. 24.

2. For Joyce on Arnold, see the "Telemachus" and "Circe" episodes of *Ulysses*, in which Arnold appears, respectively, as "a deaf gardener" and as "Philip Drunk." For Eliot on Arnold, see *The Use of Poetry and the Use of Criticism* (London: Faber, 1933), pp. 103–19.

Historical Poe, Theoretical Poe

James M. Hutchisson

Dwight Thomas and David K. Jackson. *The Poe Log: A Documentary Life of Edgar Allan Poe, 1809–1849.* Boston: G. K. Hall, 1987. 919 pp.

I. M. Walker, ed. *Edgar Allan Poe: The Critical Heritage.* London: Routledge & Kegan Paul, 1987. 419 pp.

J. Gerald Kennedy. *Poe, Death, and The Life of Writing.* New Haven: Yale University Press, 1987. 228 pp.

Scholarly interest in Edgar Allan Poe has been consistently high since the Poe Revival of the 1960s. By 1970, the annual number of notes, articles, dissertations, and books on Poe had grown so large that Patrick F. Quinn called for a separate chapter to be devoted to Poe in *American Literary Scholarship.* In 1973, the year that the Poe chapter first appeared in *ALS*, G. R. Thompson reported that more than one hundred articles alone had been published during that year on the author's life and writings. Currently, the number of scholarly publications on Poe hovers around fifty to sixty yearly, and these studies, as Kent P. Ljunquist observed in the most recent volume of *ALS*, have usually fallen into two broad categories: historically oriented scholarship (editions, bibliographies, biographies, and reception studies) and theoretical approaches.[1]

The three books under review here can be placed in one or the other of those categories. Dwight Thomas and David K. Jackson's *The Poe Log* assembles in one volume all the known biographical material about Poe. The authors do more than just make available in one place the facts of Poe's melodramatic life; they clear up many misconceptions about it. In the most recent volume of Routledge and Kegan Paul's *Critical Heritage* series,

I. M. Walker presents much information about Poe's literary career by reprinting part or all of many reviews of Poe's work, limiting his selections to those which appeared between the publication of *Tamerlane and Other Poems* (1827) and the posthumous *Works of the Late Edgar Allan Poe* (1850), edited by Poe's literary executor, Rufus W. Griswold. However, by reprinting only those reviews published during Poe's lifetime and just after his death, Walker's book is not as useful as it might have been: with some minor exceptions, the apparent achievement of *The Poe Log* in gathering all extant contemporary reviews of Poe's work eclipses the value of the *Critical Heritage* volume. Finally, J. Gerald Kennedy's *Poe, Death, and The Life of Writing* constitutes both a theoretical and contextual approach to Poe's art. Kennedy argues that Poe's attraction to death traversed his writing and that Poe's "responsiveness to the problem of death led to self-conscious reflection upon writing and the power of words" in his poetry, fiction, and letters (p. viii). Kennedy ballasts his critical interpretations with a social history of death in the nineteenth century. Some of his readings of Poe's texts—and particularly of his letters—as submerged discourses on the relationship between death and writing appear slightly forced, but the insights into Poe's genius are illuminating, and the arguments are intriguing.

The Poe Log is the first of a projected series of "American Authors Logs" under the general editorship of Joel Myerson. Modeled on Jay Leyda's *The Melville Log*, a ground-breaking research tool which was first published in 1951 and which has proven so useful to scholars that a revised and expanded third edition is now in press, *The Poe Log* contains 919 pages of chronologically arranged entries which weave together all the known documents and events related to Poe. I am certain that it will be an indispensable source for all who do future work on Poe. The book is divided into eleven chapters, each corresponding to a significant period in Poe's life, and each prefaced with a brief summary of the events of those years. Thomas and Jackson have produced a good-looking volume: the pages have ample margins; the typeface is pleasing to the eye; the paper is not wafer-thin; there are seventy illustrations interspersed throughout the

Historical Poe, Theoretical Poe 179

text as well as an eight-page insert of daguerreotypes of Poe; and the volume facsimiles many items that enable the reader to get the flavor of Poe's life: a bill sent to John Allan by Poe's schoolmaster in 1822 (p. 51); an advertisement in the 20 November 1839 *Alexander's Weekly Messenger* for Poe's "The Journal of Julius Rodman" to appear in the next issue of *Burton's Gentleman's Magazine* (p. 277); the first page of the manuscript of "Ulalume" (p. 706). The authors have shown meticulous attention to detail. Each entry contains the date and place of the item and ends with the source for the item. Some ten years in the making, *The Poe Log* represents a large amount of literary detective work, for in tracking down documents relating to Poe, the authors have consulted not just Poe's letters and the letters of people who knew or knew of him, but they have also sifted through newspaper and magazine archives, personal diaries, church registers, legal records, and city directories. These and other sources are listed at the rear of the volume.

The best thing about *The Poe Log* is that, unlike a narrative biography, this documentary life of Poe offers no interpretive commentary about the events that it records. This statement might seem wrong-headed were it not for the many egregious misconceptions about Poe, misconceptions that have existed ever since Griswold slandered Poe after the author's death by rewriting his correspondence in order to malign him. Modern criticism has of course been much more responsible than Griswold was, but many myths about Poe still persist. Scholars have said variously that Poe was a drug addict, that he had a death wish, or, as Thomas and Jackson point out in the introduction, that Poe impregnated someone else's wife (p. ix). In short, because the pathos of Poe's life has generated so much commentary, a book like this, which sets the record straight by scrupulously presenting only the verifiable facts of Poe's life, has been needed for some time. In this same vein, the authors have kept editorial commentary to a minimum. When the authors do interrupt the reader, they do so for good reasons. In their editorial notations, Thomas and Jackson provide concise surveys of scholarship, conveniently pointing the reader to the most significant research that has been done on, for example, the attribution of a text to Poe (as with Benjamin Blake Minor's and Margaret Alterton's erroneous ascription of the tale "Erostratus" to Poe in the July 1836 *Southern Literary Messenger*— William T. Bandy has recently proven that William Duane, Jr., was the author [p. 214]); the textual variants of a piece (as with Burton R. Pollin's work on "The Unparalleled Adventures of One Hans Pfaal" [p. 163]); or the possible source of the name for a Poe character (as with Hervey Allen's discovery that one Thomas Usher and his wife Elizabeth were friends of the Poes [p. 83]).

Sometimes these sources contradict each other, and in one instance, the way the authors handle the conflicting testimony is confusing. Sometime during 1824 or 1825, when Poe was fourteen or fifteen years old, he and a friend, Robert Mayo, swam a distance of six miles in the James River near Richmond, Virginia. The *Log* lists five separate entries for this event. Three of these entries are later references to the event, two by Poe himself on 30 April 1835 and 12 February 1840 and one an allusion to the event by the pseudonymous "Benedict" in the January 1835 *Southern Literary Messenger* in a tale entitled "The Doom" (pp. 149–50; 290; 146). The other two entries are dated "March or Earlier? 1824" and "June? 1824?"—the disputed dates when the event took place. The "March or Earlier?" entry does not tell the reader to look also at "June? 1824?", where the same information is provided, and the same three sources are cited—a *Richmond Evening Journal* article of 1874; a reference to the Baltimore *Sun* of July 1875; and "clippings" in the Valentine Museum in Richmond. With only three months separating the disputed dates, I see no reason to create two entries which contain the same information—i.e., that there are different versions of when Poe accomplished this feat. The *Log* also contains some trivia which I doubt will add to anyone's understanding of Poe. For instance, the authors seem to be keenly interested in how many suits of clothes young Edgar went through. Between 1815 and 1824 the authors list five entries reprinting the boy's tailor bills; the last two record John Allan's receipt of a bill and his ledger notation that he paid the bill. Thomas and Jackson also report how many pairs of shoes Poe wore out (pp. 23, 24, 37, 40,

59, 62, and 63). Some of these entries might have been omitted, but these are picky complaints. More important, the authors' rate of accuracy is nearly one hundred percent. I could detect very few errors. On page 208, under "June 1836," the authors direct the reader to "see July 1836" for more information on *Southern Literary Journal* editor Daniel K. Whitaker's condemnation of the "puffing" of native writers by American magazines, but there is no entry for July 1836. And on page 364, the authors do not designate William A. Jones, a star essayist in the 1830s and 1840s for many leading American periodicals (*The Democratic Review*, *The American Whig Review*, and *The Broadway Journal*, among them), as the author of a piece entitled "Criticism in America," which appeared in the May 1842 issue of *Arcturus*, edited by Cornelius Mathews and Evert A. Duyckinck. Perry Miller identified Jones as the author of this essay as early as 1955 in *The Raven and the Whale*.[2]

But overall there is not much to quarrel with in the *Log*. There is much to praise, notably the information Thomas and Jackson provide about the many literary figures within Poe's orbit. Poe may have been a major protagonist in the often dramatic American literary scene in the 1830s and 1840s, but many minor characters appeared in his story. In 1829, the novelist John Neal, just back from England where he had shamelessly tried to promote himself as the greatest living American writer and overturn the prevailing British condescension toward American literature, expressed guarded optimism in *The Yankee; and Boston Literary Gazette* that Poe might someday "make a beautiful and perhaps a magnificent poem" (p. 98). At the direction of Theodore S. White, Poe wrote the Philadelphia novelist and playwright Robert Montgomery Bird in 1835, asking him to support financially *The Southern Literary Messenger* (p. 175). In 1840, S. Weir Mitchell, then eleven years old, met Poe when the author visited his father, Dr. John Kearsley Mitchell (p. 313). Poe's correspondence with Elizabeth Barrett Browning, to whom he dedicated *The Raven and Other Poems*, is painstakingly documented (pp. 485–89; 525; 531; 591; 620; 627, *passim*). And other literary figures, now virtually forgotten, also play a part in Poe's life. John S. DuSolle, editor of the Philadelphia daily *The Spirit of the Times* (not William T. Porter's New York-based sporting magazine of the same name), unintentionally started a controversy about Poe's integrity by facetiously accusing him of plagiarizing "The Gold-Bug" from a story written by a thirteen year-old girl (pp. 422–26). And Peter S. DuPonceau, a French émigré who became a lawyer in Philadelphia, was contacted by Poe when he was seeking contributors to the *Messenger* in 1836 (p. 212). Two years earlier, DuPonceau had published a fulminatory discourse on the need for a national American literature. These and nearly all of the other figures mentioned in the entries are identified in a thirty-six page section of biographical notes preceding the text. The list is scrupulously accurate and thorough—those persons not listed in the notes are briefly identified in the text of the entry in which they appear. There are only a few figures I would have listed in the notes other than those Thomas and Jackson do list— DuPonceau, for example, or Samuel Kettell, who is designated on page 101 as the author of the three-volume *Specimens of American Poetry* (1829); but we are not told that Kettell, a hack writer, was one of the first and most important of the many ardently nationalistic anthologizers of American literature in the early nineteenth century.

The *Log* makes two other valuable contributions to Poe scholarship. First, it presents a complete bibliography of Poe's writings, a more complete and accurate listing of his literary and journalistic work than that contained in John W. Robertson's *Bibliography of the Writings of Edgar Allan Poe* (1934) and Charles F. Heartman and James R. Canny's *A Bibliography of First Printings of the Writings of Edgar Allan Poe* (1943), both of which were designed for collectors rather than scholars. In citing the periodical or newspaper in which a Poe text first appeared or was reprinted in, the authors also usually list the entire contents of the issue, particularly with *The Southern Literary Messenger* (pp. 151, 172, *passim*). In the entries for the dates Poe's books were published, full bibliographical descriptions are given for the volumes (with the single exception of *Tales of the Grotesque and Arabesque* [1839], p. 278—perhaps no copy is extant). The second contribution the *Log* makes is that it contains the most comprehensive collection of contemporary reviews of Poe's work that has yet appeared. Nearly all of these reviews are reprinted in full; short notices are also listed (and many of them reprinted as well); authorship of the reviews is usually ascribed; and, best of all, private and public commentary on Poe by his friends and enemies is also incorporated, giving a detailed picture of the often internecine war of words that erupted between Poe and the New York literary world from approximately 1835 until Poe's death in 1849. In its usefulness as a collection of nineteenth-century criticism of Poe, then, the *Log* supersedes Eric W. Carlson's *The Recognition of Edgar Allan Poe: Selected Criticism Since 1829* (1966).

The *Log* also supersedes the second book reviewed here, I. M. Walker's *Edgar Allan Poe: The Critical Heritage*. In one sense, it is probably not fair to fault Walker's work by comparing it to the more comprehensive job *The Poe Log* does in its inclusion of so many nineteenth-century reviews of Poe—so many more, as I shall point out, that a scholar studying Poe's contemporary reception would be far better served by using the *Log* than by using *The Critical Heritage*. It was simply unfortunate timing that the two books were published at about the same time. But in another sense, one can legitimately criticize Walker for not expanding his coverage of Poe's literary reputation to include published reviews and general estimates of Poe that appeared after his death, thereby supplementing the *Log*. The book might also have made a more valuable contribution to Poe studies if Walker had included more reviews of Poe's periodical criticism.

But first, a comparison of the reviews contained in *The Critical Heritage* with those in the *Log*. For each book in the Poe canon, the *Log* reprints more reviews than *The Critical Heritage* does; and in nearly all of its entries, the *Log* reprints these reviews in full. Two examples will illustrate the point. For *The Narrative of Arthur Gordon Pym* (1838), the *Log* reprints a total of twenty-nine reviews and notices, eight of them from London quarterlies. Thomas and Jackson have uncovered reviews in such little-known periodicals as the Hartford, Connecticut, *Daily Courant*, the *Ladies' Companion* (a monthly publication which circulated primarily in New York, Boston, and Philadelphia), and the nineteenth-century equivalent of a book club's monthly "preview," *Waldie's*

Select Circulating Library (pp. 249–58). By contrast, *The Critical Heritage* contains only ten reviews and notices, four from British magazines (pp. 91–98). All of the documents in *The Critical Heritage* also appear in the *Log*. For Poe's *Tales of the Grotesque and Arabesque* (1839), the *Log* reprints nineteen reviews or notices (pp. 279–87); *The Critical Heritage* reprints only eight (pp. 109–30). One might argue that *The Critical Heritage* is useful in that it makes it easier for the scholar to locate reviews without having to search through all the other entries contained in the *Log*, but, matters of convenience aside, the *Log* simply outdistances *The Critical Heritage* both in size and substance. In overlooking some of the reviews that the *Log* reprints, Walker has omitted some insightful and exacting criticisms of Poe. The *Log* shows us a more complete picture of the reviewing of periodicals by other periodicals in the nineteenth century. Walker reprints some of the "Supplements" nineteenth-century magazine editors appended to their monthly issues, but the *Log* contains many more. For example, the *Log* reprints nearly the entire "Supplement" for the April 1836 issue of *The Southern Literary Messenger,* a collection of criticisms of previous issues of the *Messenger,* issues which contained some of Poe's most important literary criticism, such as the Drake-Halleck review and his antagonistic remarks about the *New York Mirror*'s puffing of Theodore S. Fay's novel, *Norman Leslie. The Critical Heritage* offers only three selections from this "Supplement"; the *Log* provides eighteen—as wide a sampling as anyone could want. Among them are significant commentaries on Poe's ruthless book reviewing by William Bose in the *Baltimore American* ("the higher the critic places himself, the more fatal will be his blows downwards"—a prophecy which came true) and Nathaniel Beverley Tucker in the *Washington Telegraph* ("there is an occasional severity in some of these strictures which we highly approve") (p. 187).

Finally, Walker's introduction, a well-written account of Poe's literary career, could also have complemented the *Log* by more fully discussing Poe's literary battles. The stories of Poe's book reviewing in the 1830s and 1840s are as dramatic as his fiction. For example, when Poe assumed the "generalship" of *The Southern Literary Messenger* in December 1835 and undertook the responsibility of writing the "Critical Notices" section of the periodical, he started a minor skirmish with the New York literary clique which quickly escalated into a full-scale war.[3] Poe fired the first salvo at Theodore S. Fay, one of the editors (together with Nathaniel P. Willis and George P. Morris) of the *New York Mirror*, a literary weekly. Angered by American publishers and literary periodicals shamelessly puffing the somewhat amateurish literature native writers were producing simply because, as Poe would say four months later in the Drake-Halleck review, it was written by an American, Poe lambasted the *Mirror* for its fulsome praise of Fay's novel *Norman Leslie*. The *Mirror* had printed glowing pre-publication notices of the novel with excerpts from the book on four different occasions between 11 July and 10 October 1835, then evidently enlisted the help of Lewis Gaylord Clark in continuing its campaign to puff the novel. In the November 1835 issue of his *Knickerbocker Magazine,* Clark nearly deified Fay as America's new literary genius. But Walker reprints very few reactions to Poe's attempts to derail this campaign; more disappointing, Walker's discussion of this incident in his introduction is limited to an observation that despite Poe's attacks on the *Mirror* and the *Knickerbocker,* their reviews of *Pym* were "surprisingly mild" (p. 23).

The last section of the introduction, entitled "Changing Fortunes: 1870 Onwards," devotes only three pages to Poe's posthumous reputation and then briefly surveys some of the modern academic work on Poe. But important assessments of Poe such as those by Baudelaire, Rimbaud, Mallarme, Robert Louis Stevenson, Henry James, and Edmund Wilson are missing. In sum, *Edgar Allan Poe: The Critical Heritage* will probably have to stand in the shadow of *The Poe Log* as a source of information about Poe's reception. Had Walker not limited his collection to reviews published only during Poe's lifetime and had he not given short shrift to the reception of Poe's literary criticism, his book would be of greater value to Poe studies.

Finally, in *Poe, Death, and The Life of Writing,* J. Gerald Kennedy investigates Poe's attraction to the problem of death, an idea which Kennedy points out is so "conspicuous" that the lack of critical analyses of the subject is surprising:

Here we find a writer whose entire oeuvre is marked by a compulsive interest in the dimensionality of death: its physical signs, the phenomenology of dying, the deathbed scene, the appearance of the corpse, the effects of decomposition, the details of burial, the danger of premature interment, the reanimation of the dead, the lure of tombs and cemeteries, the nature of mourning and loss, the experience of death, the compulsion to inflict death upon another, and the perverse desire to seek one's own death. [p. 3]

Kennedy maintains that Poe's self-conscious reflections on the problem of death informed his view of the art of writing, and he argues that Poe cast many of his works of fiction, poetry, and prose as allegories about the reciprocal relationship between death and inscription.

Throughout the book, Kennedy adroitly balances critical analysis and historical research. The first chapter investigates the nineteenth century's paradoxical attitude toward death. On the one hand, Victorian America was fascinated by the idea of the Beautiful Death, which sought to make "an edifying aesthetic spectacle out of the banal experience" of dying and thereby to purge from the mind the gruesome reality of dying flesh (p. 10). Social and religious practices conspired to make the fact of dying into a sentimentalized beauty through the proliferation of mourning art, the transformation of funerals into elaborate public spectacles, and the beautification of urban cemeteries. Similarly, American publishers encouraged the publication of literature which sentimentalized mortality by depicting the burial plot as a place for quiet meditation, as in Washington Irving's sketch "Rural Cemeteries," or by offering lugubrious consolation lyrics like those of Lydia Huntley Sigourney. But at the same time, while the nineteenth century evidenced an aversion to the dying flesh and therefore replaced it with a more pleasant aesthetic image, it also displayed a fetishization of the dead body, evidenced by such commemorations of dying as the wearing of memorial jewelry (a ring or necklace that belonged to the deceased), death masks, portraits "in death," locks of hair from the dead body woven into floral designs, and the highly ritualized funeral, in which the corpse was dressed in expensive clothing and placed in a glass-sided coffin so that mourners could look at the body.

Poe was drawn into this cult of death and memory both through its social and religious iconography and its appearance in popular literature. Three of the most popular writers of consolation poetry, in fact, Mrs. Sigourney, Mrs. H. F. Gould, and Mrs. E. F. Ellet, were contributors to *The Southern Literary Messenger*. Further, Kennedy maintains, Poe found in the "conflicted strategy" of the Beautiful Death a metaphor for the relationship between death and writing (p. 11). "MS. Found in a Bottle," for example, manifests two conflicting views of death: "the narrator feels an eagerness for the discovery which means destruction, but he anxiously registers his terror and despair as he tries to describe 'the horror of [his] sensations' as he moves toward extinction" (p. 24). Writing is a means for the narrator to sustain this paradoxical attitude toward death: he "writes to forestall death, yet his every word carries him toward the threshold of silence" (p. 26). Poe's narrator writes on, driven to encounter the repulsive putrefaction of dying, yet he also writes to stave off that event, much as Scheherazade survives by telling one more story in *The Thousand and One Nights*.

Another example of Poe's fascination with death and its analogous relationship to writing can be found in his preoccupation with premature burial, the subject of chapter 2. Again Kennedy ballasts his interpretations of Poe's work with diligent research into such actual phenomena as living entombment. Following the horrors of the yellow fever epidemic that spread through Philadelphia in 1793, a great number of books and pamphlets appeared in the beginning of the nineteenth century that warned of the unsanitary conditions of urban cemeteries and the lack of experience of those who prepared bodies for burial. Such conditions justified the fear of living entombment. Near the end of the 1830s, when Poe had begun to establish himself as a magazinist, periodicals frequently printed comic anecdotes about such dangers in the form of journalistic hoaxes or mock medical "reports." But popular magazines like *Blackwood's* also published stories cast as narratives from beyond (or within) the grave, the silliness of which Poe exploited in "How to Write a Blackwood Article." The idea of premature burial is also commonplace in Poe's more serious fiction; Poe consigned the black cat Apollo and the characters Morella, Fortunato, Ligeia, and Madeline Usher to such a fate. He also had Arthur Gordon Pym and the narrator of "The Pit and the Pendulum" undergo a temporary and symbolic premature burial.

As many critics have noted, Poe was preoccupied with this type of death. But Kennedy is the first to comment on the implications of the premature burial theme for the relationship between death and writing, or, in the case of "Loss of Breath," the relationship between death and the loss of language. The narrator of this tale (published earlier in a different form as "A Decided Loss") is Mr. Lackobreath, who literally loses his breath in a vociferous argument with his wife. For all intents and purposes, the character is dead, or as Poe says, "alive, with the qualification of the dead—dead, with the propensities of the living." But rather than be horrified by his predicament, Mr. Lackobreath is humiliated: Kennedy observes that Lackobreath's misfortunes—the indignities of hanging, mutilation, dissection, and finally premature interment—derive not from his loss of breath but from the loss of words: "he is taken for dead because he cannot speak" (p. 42). This dialectic between speech and death is therefore a variation on the dialectic between writing and death that Poe expressed in "MS. Found in a Bottle." Poe enacted in his scenes of premature burial not just "a culturally shared disquietude" about death, but a lesson in survival: Lackobreath's inscription of the narrative suggests that writing is a means of insulating oneself, at least temporarily, from the threat of death.

Chapter 3, "The Horrors of Translation," situates the theme Poe determined was the "most melancholy of topics most poetical," the death of a beautiful woman, within the conventions of popular literature and the anthropology of death in the nineteenth century. Drawing on examples of works which promoted the idea of the Beautiful Death (the consolation lyrics of Sigourney, Gould, and Felicia Hemans; Irving's lugubrious "biography" of Margaret Miller Davidson; and the Reverend Moses Waddel's *Memoirs of Miss Caroline E. Smelt*), Kennedy demonstrates that Poe "shared the pervasive sentimental view that death intensified female beauty and even brought about a purification of loveliness" in such poems as "Lenore," which idealizes the death of a beautiful woman (p. 67). But Poe also invested his characters with a compulsive need to disconfirm the myth of the Beautiful Death. "The Raven" is a case in point. The narrator pores over "a volume of forgotten lore" in order to find "surcease of sorrow." "Paradoxically," Kennedy says, "he seeks forgetfulness through an act of remembrance" (p. 68). The narrator's response to the raven and the raven's response to the narrator enact a similar ambivalence about death and memory. Although the narrator says that Lenore will remain "nameless *here* forevermore," he perversely whispers her name, the name he is trying to repress. And the raven's response, "Nevermore," suggests both the narrator's desire to forget the departed one—he will nevermore think about her—and his desire to keep some reminder of her death—she is lost forever.

Thus the first three chapters develop a view of the relationship between death and writing largely from a historical perspective; the last three chapters examine the relationship from a more theoretical perspective. Between these sections Kennedy has placed a chapter on Poe's letters, in order "to provide a connection between writing and lived experience" (p. ix).

Kennedy entitles his analysis of Poe's correspondence "The Rhetoric of Dread." He suggests that Poe elaborated fantasies of retribution and triumph in his letters by using language that projected him "as the inevitable victim—of poverty, illness, treachery, or bad luck" and which appealed to its readers to deliver him from his fate (p. 91). Classifying Poe's "urgent messages, letters in which writing functions as a call for help" (p. 91) by three subjects—letters to John Allan, letters to women, and letters to acquaintances in the literary world—Kennedy demonstrates that Poe used a deliberate rhetorical strategy to persuade his correspondent to come to his aid. Poe's letters to other writers were constructed to promote a public image of him as a professional author and, in his letters seeking subscribers for his long-projected but never published magazine, *The Stylus*, to convey the message that his fate depended upon the realization of his great dream. Poe's letters to women constituted a different kind of manipulation; they were marked by a passive melancholy which, Kennedy suggests, was calculated to make his correspondents fear that if they did not return his affection, he would die. The most manipulative of all of Poe's letters, however, seem to be those written to John Allan. Here Poe's appeals for help lay upon his adoptive father the double guilt of being responsible both for his poverty and for his inevitable demise. Unfortunately, throughout this interesting chapter, Kennedy refers to Poe's "epistolary project" and his "immortality project" as if Poe's correspondence constituted some sort of campaign to ease the burden of his "writerly travail" by using the letter specifically as a means of communication, and as if no other avenues of communication were open to Poe (pp. 96, 101, and 89). Such language detracts from Kennedy's analysis of the letters, and its persistent use makes even more jarring this sentence about Poe's letters to Allan, which makes some of Poe's melodramatic prose look like a weak effort: "John Allan's break with Poe became irrevocable on March 27, 1834, when the Richmond merchant passed beyond the reach of earthly correspondence" (p. 96).

Chapters 5 and 6 examine the juxtaposition of writing and death in the context of specific "sets" of texts: those that depict language as verbal revenge and a battle for survival, and those which suggest "the unreadability of death." Kennedy observes that some of Poe's tales like "Mystification" (earlier entitled "Von Jung, the Mystific") and "The Man of the Crowd" anticipate the tales of ratiocination by confounding the reader through misdirection. In "Mystification," for example, the reader, like the narrator in the Dupin stories, is gulled into misreading the evidence. In order to prevent having to respond to a challenge of a duel, Von Jung tells his rival to read a passage in a dueling manual. The passage is in Latin, a language which Von Jung knows his enemy cannot read. Unwilling to admit his deficiency, the enemy is confounded, and Von Jung demonstrates that the pen is mightier than the sword. (The recondite text is actually an account of a duel between two baboons.) Writing, then, is transformed into a weapon with which characters exact revenge, and, Kennedy suggests, with which Poe satisfies his "rage for control" over the reader (p. 118). This view of writing leads Kennedy naturally to a discussion of *Pym*, perhaps Poe's greatest hoax, as revealing the capacity of writing to control its readers. That Poe is alluding slyly to his intentions in *Pym* throughout the novel is by now a commonplace in Poe criticism, due largely to Kennedy's own articles on the wordplay and punning, the digressions, the aesthetic anomalies, and the preface and "postscript" as commentary on the composition of the novel.[4] In this chapter, Kennedy extends that view of *Pym* to suggest that the essential "unreadability" of the novel shows that inscription is a deceptive act, "a plot against the reader" (p. 148). Interestingly, the series of "unreadable" writings are always scenes describing death, leading Kennedy to conclude that in Poe's fictive universe, death can "disrupt or invalidate the act of interpretation" (p. 158).

One comes finally to feel that Kennedy's book is in part an effort to make the reading and interpretation of Poe's writings an acceptable activity for current academics who are interested in post-structuralist criticism—specifically, in deconstruction. Poe critics have always had to fight for their author's place in the canon; Poe has never seemed quite respectable enough, quite difficult enough, for serious attention. "It *is* all right to study Poe," Kennedy seems to be saying. "One *can* find the concerns of post-structuralist critics in his writings. Look here! And here!" Perhaps this is why some of Kennedy's readings seem forced. In discussing one of Poe's many parodies of the premature burial narrative, Kennedy quotes Poe's fictional Mr. Blackwood in "How to Write a Blackwood Article":

There was "*The Dead Alive*," a capital thing!—the record of a gentleman's sensations, when entombed before the breath was out of his body—full of taste, terror, sentiment, metaphysics, and erudition. You would have sworn that the writer had been born and brought up in a coffin.

Kennedy maintains that "to conceive of an author 'born and brought up in a coffin' is to imagine . . . a hermetic inscription delivered, beyond all expectation, from the tomb itself" (p. 33). But this idiom was common to such writing; Poe's character was most likely conforming to such conventions. Similarly, I do not think that when in "The Murders in the Rue Morgue" Dupin confronts the sailor with his knowledge that the murder of Madame and Mademoiselle l'Espanaye was committed by the sailor's orangutan and the sailor stammers, then concedes that Dupin has solved the mystery correctly, and finally drops the cudgel he is carrying, that the sailor is being "literally disarmed by [Dupin's] language," and that it is Dupin's "speech act" that "inflicts a mortification" on the sailor (p. 120). The sailor is mortified because he is surprised (and therefore *speechless,* as Kennedy would have it) that Dupin has solved the mystery. He is not "disarmed" specifically by the words that Dupin utters. In fact, Dupin's interrogation of the sailor is not any more disarming or accusatory than the standard "I-suppose-you're-all-wondering-why-I-asked-you-here" speech performed by the detective-hero in thousands of modern mystery novels: "My reward shall be this," Dupin tells the sailor, who has offered to compensate Dupin for his trouble: "You shall give me all the information in your power about these murders in the Rue Morgue."

With these exceptions, Kennedy's reading of this particular theme in the Poe canon is convincing. However, one wishes that Poe had commented on the reciprocal acts of death and inscription in his essays and criticism. Kennedy admits at the outset of his study that Poe was silent on the subject in his non-fictional writings, but "left traces of such a theory in the writing itself" (p. 18). Kennedy picks up these traces and uses them to advance a sophisticated argument that should stimulate more research into this aspect of Poe's life and writings.

Notes

1. Kent P. Ljunquist, "Poe," *American Literary Scholarship, An Annual: 1985* (Durham: Duke Univ. Press, 1987), p. 43.

2. Perry Miller, *The Raven and the Whale: The War of Words and Wits in the Era of Poe and Melville* (New York: Harcourt, Brace and World, 1955), pp. 198–99.

3. Sidney P. Moss describes this facet of Poe's career in *Poe's Literary Battles* (Durham: Duke Univ. Press, 1963).

4. J. Gerald Kennedy, "'The Infernal Twoness' in *Arthur Gordon Pym*," *Topic,* 30 (Fall 1976), 40–53, and "The Preface as a Key to the Satire in *Pym*," *Studies in the Novel,* 5 (1973), 191–96.

The Lives of Sterne

W. G. Day

Arthur H. Cash. *Laurence Sterne, The Later Years*. London and New York: Methuen and Co., 1986. xx, 390 pp.

Kenneth Monkman. *Sterne's Memoirs, A hitherto unrecorded holograph now brought to light in facsimile*. Coxwold: privately printed for the Laurence Sterne Trust and sold by Heffers, Cambridge, 1985. xxxii, 16 pp.

> This system of Sichelising seems a simple and easy one. Find out the old and original biographies in which the spade work has been done, dates explored and fixed, original letters collected; take the materials and expatiate on them. Take care to approach as from an entirely new point of view, as though you had made discoveries.

This rather tart observation by Percy Fitzgerald, the pioneering nineteenth-century biographer of Sterne, appeared in a review of Walter Sichel's *Sterne, A Study, To Which Is Added the Journal to Eliza*, a volume published in 1910, the year after the first edition of Wilbur Cross's *The Life and Times of Laurence Sterne*.[1] This century has seen a surprising number of *sichelising* lives of Sterne: few other major English writers can have been the subject of thirteen book-length biographies and pseudo-biographies since 1909.[2] There has, of course, been some original work, and this can best be shown by taking the three major offerings in the field and exploring the development of knowledge and methods of presentation. Cross's work was extensively revised; the standard version is the third edition of 1929, of which a reissue appeared in 1967. In 1925 Henri Fluchère announced via the pages of the *Times Literary Supplement* that he was intending to produce a new study of Sterne, and this work appeared thirty-six years later as *Laurence Sterne, de l'homme à l'oeuvre: Biographie critique et essai d'interpretation de* Tristram Shandy.[3] Both these works are now in many ways superseded by Arthur H. Cash's two-volume biography, of which *Laurence Sterne, The Early and Middle Years*, covering the life up to the successful publication of the first two volumes of *Tristram Shandy* in 1760, was published in 1975.[4] *Laurence Sterne, The Later Years* followed in 1986. It is an inevitable result of the late flowering of Sterne's literary output that Cash's second volume, which is concerned with a mere eight years of his subject's life, should be rather longer than the first installment.

Cross's intention, not entirely borne out in his practice, was to employ "the direct method of scrupulous narration" (p. xii). His text is dotted with locutions such as "surely" (p. 18), "likely" (p. 40), "doubtless" (p. 343) and "I fancy" (p. 429); and fancy does indeed appear to take over at points, as when he observes of the arguments in favor of Sterne's education at Heath rather than Hipperholme that it is "a complete and very pretty tale which ought to be true" (p. 20). With slightly more caution Cross noted, "It is a pleasing fancy, if nothing more, that Miss Lumley passed through that traceried door on the morning when she stepped over to the cathedral to become Mrs. Sterne" (p. 43), and, "if the narrative purporting to come from La Fleur cannot be proved authentic, it is at least a very good guess at what really occurred" (p. 394). To the late twentieth-century reader this has more of the air of a fireside chat than of "scrupulous narration," and indeed the whole of Cross's method of tackling the problem of writing the biography of an author reinforces this feeling. Throughout his work he approaches Sterne via the fictions: episodes from *Tristram Shandy* and *A Sentimental Journey* are employed to illustrate moments or putative moments in Sterne's life. The reader is told, for example, that "Uncle Toby's love for the *Iliad*, as well as for chapbooks in which there were soldiers and adventure and much fighting, is undoubtedly only a reminiscence of Sterne's own passion for them" (p. 24).

In terms of reliability Cross's work, in comparison with Fluchère's and Cash's, suffers from one major disadvantage: he could not have before him Lewis P. Curtis's comprehensive and expertly annotated 1935 edition of the *Letters*.[5] The history of the publication of Sterne's letters has been bedeviled by the interference of William Combe, who, shortly after Sterne's death, capitalized on the general interest in the deceased by producing a number of volumes of letters purporting to be original. Combe undoubtedly had access to several genuine letters, and there has been considerable dispute among Sterneans as to the extent to which his productions were forgeries, it being held by many, including Curtis, that some letters though predominantly forgeries contained material which was genuine. Fluchère and Cash followed Curtis's attributions, but it is possible that the whole issue may soon become rather clearer as a result of the discovery of a manuscript notebook of Combe's which contains some of the disputed correspondence.[6] A fair proportion of Cross's argument derives from letters which are no longer accepted as by Sterne, and to this extent the reader has to approach with caution. To counterbalance this, Cross provides in extensive appendixes a full transcript of Sterne's letterbook in the Pierpoint Morgan Library and a detailed bibliography. This bibliography is gradually being superseded by those being prepared by Kenneth Monkman for the Florida edition of the *Works* of Sterne, of which *Tristram Shandy* has appeared, with the *Sermons* volume nearing completion. Until all of Monkman's researches are published Sterne scholars will continue to need to have Cross available.

Where Cross was seduced by the seeming reality of Sterne's fictions into the *si non e vero, e ben trovato* school of biography, a school which still flourishes, as witness the section on Pope's childhood in Maynard Mack's recent book,[7] Henri Fluchère attempted to separate *l'homme* from *l'oeuvre*, though as his title indicated he set out to use the former to illlustrate the latter, thus reversing Cross's method. Readers who use Barbara Bray's translation and abridgment, *Laurence Sterne: From Tristram to Yorick*,[8] may be misled as to the nature of Fluchère's work as the abridgment involves the almost total excision of the biographical essay which fills over 200 pages of the French edition. And where

Cross provided an appendix dealing with the bibliography of Sterne's publications, Fluchère gave his readers an extensive, if idiosyncratically organized, bibliography of useful secondary material. This too disappeared in the abridgment.

Fluchère's opening sentences made clear that his work was not to be an example of surreptitious *sichelising*:

> Excellente à tous égards, la biographie monumentale du Professeur Wilbur C. Cross sera, pour l'étude de la vie de Sterne, notre guide et notre soutien. Nous avons, en toute occasion possible, confronté sa documentation avec les textes originaux, et nous l'avons toujours trouvée minutieusement informée.... Ajoutons à ce livre de base le receuil le plus récent des *Lettres* de Laurence Sterne, publié par M. Lewis Perry Curtis en 1935, qui contient une foule de renseignements très utiles sur bien des points de détail. [pp. 15–16]

His extended essay provides a useful touchstone with which to test the achievements of both Cross and Cash. He employed the new evidence provided by Curtis to correct minor details in Cross—thus the name of the doctor in whose house Mrs. Sterne expired was noted as Linières rather than Lionières (p. 202)—but where Curtis's endeavours did not enable positive decisions to be made about disputed elements of Sterne's life, a somewhat cavalier approach was adopted. And the cavalier nature of some expressions is made all the more surprising in view of one's expectations of the comprehensiveness of French doctorats d'état. Cross had devoted a good deal of space to the conflicting claims of Heath and Hipperholme to be Sterne's school. Fluchère simply wrote, 'Hipperholme, près de Halifax, ou Heath, proche de Woodhouse—qu'importe!' (p. 22). Cash subsequently came down firmly on the side of Hipperholme and provided extensive documentation. Fluchère's piece is a biographical essay functioning as a preliminary to his interpretation of *Tristram Shandy*. He expected his readers to have access to both Cross and Curtis and did not duplicate their references. The reader wishing to go further into detail needs all three books in front of him. Nevertheless, for the general reader Fluchère's essay remains the best introduction to the subject.

Arthur H. Cash's two volumes are essential reading for anyone who wishes to write about Sterne. The documentation is punctilious, and the statement of intent, which comes rather late on in the first volume ("The purpose of this biography is to throw light upon Sterne's work by the study of his life, not the other way around" [p. 197]) is adhered to with a considerable degree of success. It is inevitable that a scholar so steeped in the details of Sterne's life and works should be ever conscious of the epigraph to the first volume of *Tristram Shandy*: "Men are tormented with the Opinions they have of Things, and not by the Things themselves,"[9] and Professor Cash is to my mind at times unduly on the defensive when he offers his opinions on readings of Sterne's fictions. Discussing Volume VII and the possible interpretations of Tristram's character, for example, Cash develops the notion that "the lesson he teaches is how to get through an ironic world cheerfully" (p. 199) and provides a footnote which both acknowledges his indebtedness to Melvyn New's *Laurence Sterne as Satirist*[10] and indicates a wariness as to whether New would agree with the argument at this point. Now while it is admirable in a footnote relating to fact to indicate the reliability of the detail, the circumvallation at this point seems unnecessary. Cash's view of the character of Tristram is consistent with the account he gives of Sterne the man at this point of his biography. The footnote only serves to undercut.

Only rarely in either volume does Arthur Cash hypothesize about Sterne's activities at those periods of his life where we have minimal documentation: sentences such as "If there was a music society at Jesus, Sterne would have been a member" are few and are mainly confined, as is this example, to the first volume (p. 55). Errors of fact and misleading constructions are even thinner on the ground; indeed they are so few that at the risk of appearing carping I think they should be recorded here.

We are told that "ten page numbers representing the missing Chapter 24 of Volume IV are omitted in all good editions of the novel" (p. 86). It is true that every modern edition of *Tristram Shandy* with aspirations to scholarly status omits ten pages at this point, and to this extent the statement about "all good editions" is valid. It is worth noting though that no modern edition accurately represents Sterne's bibliographical jest at this point. Editors have always followed Sterne's words:

> —No doubt, Sir—there is a whole chapter wanting here—and a chasm of ten pages made in the book by it—but the book-binder is neither a fool, or a knave, or a puppy—nor is the book a jot more imperfect, (at least upon that score).... [11]

In the first edition this statement occurs at the top of a recto page. The immediately preceding verso is numbered, quite properly, 146; the recto is numbered '156'. The actual gap is nine, not ten, pages. This may seem trivial, but there is a knock-on effect; for the whole of the rest of Volume IV through five signatures, all recto pages are even-numbered. This is, so far as I am aware, the only occasion in the history of English printing when this happens. It may be a matter of opinion as to whether page numbers are parts of a text: but it is indisputable that such consistent disregard for a long-standing convention can hardly be accidental. The page numbers in Volume IV may not be essential to our understanding of *Tristram Shandy*, but they do add to the air of dislocation which Sterne so effectively fosters in his use of bibliographical bizarreries, and it seems rather surprising that "all good editions" take such care to duplicate the black page, marbled page, lines of plot, and the flourish of Trim's stick, and that all fail to reproduce this one device. A little later Cash says of *The Life, Travels, and Adventures of Christopher Wagstaff, Gentleman, Grandfather to Tristram Shandy*, one of the large number of parasitic works attempting to capitalize upon the success of the early volumes of *Tristram Shandy*, "This thin volume opens with a preface that attempts to demonstrate that Sterne had copied John Dunton's *Voyage Round the World* (1691), but the narrative which follows is a new fiction that had nothing to do with Dunton" (p. 114). The *Wagstaff* volume does prefix an explanatory essay which claims to show that Sterne used it as a source for *Tristram Shandy*, but the rest of the book is essentially Dunton's text with minor alterations to accord with the *Wagstaff* hack's effort to make the book closer to Sterne's and thus a more likely source.

One additional zero in a footnote on page 111 should have bibliomanes waving the volume at their antiquarian bookdealers as evidence that, the standard work on Sterne citing a print run for Volumes V and VI of 40000 rather than the more conventional 4000, prices for these two volumes should drop radically.

These examples are minor.[12]

That on the evidence available to Cash in the writing of these two volumes this should constitute the list of errors noticed argues a good deal for the attention to detail one finds throughout. Cross's ideal of "scrupulous narration" appears to have been attained. Moreover, in the tradition of Cross and Fluchère, each volume concludes with informative appendixes: in *Laurence Sterne, The Early and Middle Years* there is a checklist of portraits of Sterne, describing, locating, and assessing the authenticity of twenty-one portraits and an even larger number of copies and states of engravings; *Laurence Sterne, The Later Years* publishes seven unedited Sterne letters and discusses at some length the John Hamilton Mortimer caricature group of 1767 which, among its eighteen figures, depicts Sterne displaying the locket of Eliza on his bared chest. It is typical of the care taken in the presentation of this book that the caricature group which adorns the wrapper, and thus will probably be thrown away by most libraries, is reproduced within the text together with an numbered overlay which greatly helps the reader in the following of the argument relating to identification of the various figures. It is unfortunate that Cash merely provides details of the locations of the five various articles which were published between 1951 and 1968 detailing eleven letters not known to Curtis rather than printing the texts of these letters together with the seven he has located since. This would have provided his readers with a very handy single supplement to Curtis.

Those who have worked on Sterne cannot fail to be impressed by the immense labor which these two volumes represent. Any effort to add to the pile of Sterne biographies in the immediate future will inevitably be a case of *sichelisation*. There are two areas, though, where scholars in the next century may be in a position to revise and expand. In his preface to *Laurence Sterne, The Early and Middle Years* Arthur Cash acknowledges indebtedness to former biographers and indicates where he has had the advantage of access to particularly the works of L. P. Curtis. Two sentences refer to his debt to Kenneth Monkman, the Hon. Curator of Shandy Hall, who "has kindly shared with me a number of documents he has found. Others will be brought to light with the publication of Monkman's own book on Sterne's early writing career" (p. xiii). Some indication of the impact of Monkman's researches can be deduced from the publication, just before Cash's second volume, of *Sterne's Memoirs, A hitherto unrecorded holograph now brought to light in facsimile*. Sterne's *Memoirs* had first been published by his daughter Lydia in her edition of his letters in 1775. Curtis demonstrated the unreliability of Lydia Sterne as an editor: she excised passages unfavorable to her mother, changed names within letters, and falsified recipients' names. And a letter of Hannah More to her sister in 1776, reprinted in her *Memoirs* in 1834, records the even more disturbing detail that, having heard from Wilkes that he had either burned or lost all the communications he had had from Sterne, "the faithful editor of her father's works sent back to say, that if Mr. Wilkes would be so good as to write a few letters in imitation of her father's style, it would do just as well, and she would insert them."[13] In view of this the letters have always been approached with some caution, a caution made keener by the knowledge of the possible intrusion of Combe's underhand activities. The *Memoirs* on the other hand has generally been accepted as reliable: Cross and Fluchère were openly dependent on it for much of their discussion of Sterne's early days, and when writing his first volume Arthur Cash did not know of the existence of the holograph. The publication, with introduction and commentary by Monkman, of the recently discovered manuscript of rather more than two-thirds of the *Memoirs* provides further detailed evidence of Lydia Sterne's manipulation of the material. Possibly the most important of her excisions was of the date occurring toward the end of the section reproduced here. It has always been assumed that this brief but lively autobiographical sketch was written by Sterne, the famous author, at a time when he realized that his daughter might wish to know of his history. The date in the manuscript, which his daughter chose to remove, shows that in fact the first two-thirds at least had been written before *Tristram Shandy* had been started. This excision was deliberate: at another point Lydia appears to have been merely careless and miscopied one letter of her father's quite legible spelling of the name of his mother's first husband. Arthur Cash is entitled to feel quite irritated at having expended so much energy pursuing what now turns out to have been a blind alley because of a single erroneous letter.

The volume of *Memoirs* has been beautifully produced, providing the reader with a facsimile of the holograph, a reduced facsimile on a fold-out sheet of the text as issued in Lydia Sterne's edition to allow for easy comparison, and an introduction and comprehensive annotation. It is difficult to think what more could be said on this matter, and as the book is privately printed for the Laurence Sterne Trust in a numbered limited edition of 500 copies, all profits from which go to the upkeep of Shandy Hall, the reader who has not bought one is recommended to rectify the position.[14]

It is, though, Monkman's work on Sterne's early career which ultimately will have the greatest effect on Cash's biography. As the editor of Sterne's minor writings for the Florida edition I have been shown some of the material involved, and the sheer volume and the time span involved will lead to major revisions of commonly held notions about the development of Sterne's style. This will only affect the first of Cash's two volumes: *Laurence Sterne, The Later Years* is the definitive account of Sterne's most productive years.

Notes

1. New York: Macmillan, 1909; new ed., New Haven: Yale Univ. Press, 1925; third ed., New Haven: Yale Univ. Press, 1929; reissue, New York: Russell and Russell, 1967. The Fitzgerald comment is quoted in the preface to the third edition (p. x).

2. In chronological order, and omitting those discussed here at length: Walter Sichel, *Sterne, A Study, To Which Is Added the Journal to Eliza* (London: Williams and Norgate, 1910, unaccountably reprinted New York: Haskell House, 1971); Lewis Melville [pseud. i.e., Lewis Saul Benjamin], *The Life and*

Letters of Laurence Sterne (London: Stanley Paul and Co., [1911]); Arie de Froe, *Laurence Sterne and His Novels Studied in the Light of Modern Psychology* (Groningen: P. Noordhoff, 1925); Alfred Hoyt Bill, *Alas, Poor Yorick* (Boston: Little, Brown and Company, 1927); Rudolph Maack, *Laurence Sterne im Lichte seine Zeit* (Hamburg: Friederischen, de Gruyter, 1926); Lodwick Hartley, *This is Lorence: A Narrative of the Reverend Laurence Sterne* (Chapel Hill: Univ. of North Carolina Press, 1943); Thomas Yoseloff, *A Fellow of Infinite Jest* (New York: Prentice-Hall, 1945); Willard Connely, *Laurence Sterne as Yorick* (London: Bodley Head, 1958); Overton Philip James, *The Relation of Tristram Shandy to the Life of Sterne* (The Hague: Mouton and Co., 1966); David Thomson, *Wild Excursions: The Life and Fiction of Laurence Sterne* (London: Weidenfeld and Nicholson, 1972).

3. Paris: Librairie Gallimard, 1961.

4. London: Methuen and Co., 1975.

5. Oxford: Clarendon Press, 1935.

6. I hope to publish a detailed account of this notebook in *The Transactions of the Cambridge Bibliographical Society*.

7. *Alexander Pope, A Life* (New Haven: Yale Univ. Press, 1985).

8. Oxford: Oxford Univ. Press, 1965.

9. Sterne's title page printed the Greek of Epictetus, from chapter 5 of the *Enchiridion*. The English version here is that provided by Charles Cotton to his translation of Montaigne's *Essais*, London, 5th edition, 1738, I, 285.

10. Gainesville: Univ. of Florida Press, 1969.

11. *The Life and Opinions of Tristram Shandy, Gentleman*, ed. Melvyn and Joan New (Gainesville: Univ. Presses of Florida, 1978), p. 372. In a textual note (p. 855) the editors do draw attention to the disparity between Sterne's claim and the actual gap, but justify their decision to follow the former on the grounds that it avoided an "awkward situation" which would have continued for the rest of the work. I think this could be read as an implied criticism of the shortcomings of modern printing technology.

12. In a review of Cash's volume, Pat Rogers provides a small number of further examples. "Oddity's Rainbow," *London Review of Books*, 8 January 1987.

13. Quoted by Cash, p. 352.

14. As a member of the Council of the Laurence Sterne Trust, I should declare an interest at this point.

Thomas Wolfe and His Biographers

Richard S. Kennedy

David Herbert Donald. *Look Homeward, A Life of Thomas Wolfe*. Boston: Little Brown and Company, 1987. xix, 579 pp., with 32 pages of photographs.

Athough fifty years have passed since the death of Thomas Wolfe, David Donald's *Look Homeward* is the first really adequate biography of Wolfe that has emerged. The reasons for this long dearth are worth setting down for the annals of scholarship.

In the early 1940s, Maxwell Perkins, as Wolfe's literary executor, appointed an official biographer, John Terry, an assistant professor at New York University who claimed long-standing friendship with Wolfe, going back to his college days at Chapel Hill. (He had been named at the insistence of Wolfe's mother, Julia E. Wolfe.) Although Terry had an M.A. degree from Columbia, he was inadequately trained as a scholar and was a very lazy man. He first produced an edition, *Thomas Wolfe's Letters to His Mother* (1943), which was so chronologically jumbled and so ill-transcribed that it had to be re-edited, a task carried out very ably by C. Hugh Holman and Sue Fields Ross in 1964. Even though Terry had exclusive access to Wolfe's papers before they were sold to the Harvard Library in 1946, he did not produce a line of the biography during the fifteen years he held the position of official biographer. All he did was accumulate random notes and sequester a large number of Wolfe manuscripts in his apartment and refuse to give them up to the Harvard Library. cruelly satirical portrait of him as the grossly fat sentimentalist, Jerry Alsop, in *The Web and the Rock*, for he was able to prevent any competent aspirant from producing a worthwhile biographical study of Wolfe for a decade and a half.

Meanwhile Maxwell Perkins had died, Edward Aswell was

named administrator of the Estate of Thomas Wolfe, and the Wolfe papers at Harvard became available for research. In 1949 Edward Aswell allowed me access to the Wolfe papers in order to write a Ph.D. dissertation, "A Critical Biography of Thomas Wolfe to 1935." He saw no interference with Terry's exclusive right: he considered me just a "Ph.D. chaser." But when I finished the dissertation, I requested permission to publish and to proceed to Volume II of the work I was writing. I told him that the Oxford University Press had expressed an interest in my book.

Just at this juncture John Terry died, and Aswell appointed Elizabeth Nowell as official biographer. He refused my request to publish and denied me further access to the Wolfe papers at Harvard, regarding me now as a disruptive intruder into his new plans for an official biography. However, Elizabeth Nowell, who was a friend of mine, interceded for me with Aswell, who relented to the extent that he allowed me to use the Wolfe papers if I would alter the emphasis of my work to make it a critical study of Wolfe. He further stipulated that I could not consider publication until Nowell's biography appeared.

Elizabeth Nowell, who had been Wolfe's literary agent, was the second official biographer who had no scholarly training, but unlike Terry she was a person of good sense and a tireless worker. Her book, *Thomas Wolfe, A Biography*, published by Doubleday in 1960, told the story of Wolfe's life in a lively style, but it was badly weakened by the fact that one-fifth of the text was made up of passages from Wolfe's fiction, quoted as if they were fact.

Shortly afterward Edward Aswell died, and my own book, now a single volume, was finished. When I traveled to New York to see Pincus Berner, the new Administrator of the Wolfe Estate, I discovered that Aswell had signed a contract with Doubleday agreeing that no competing publication drawing upon the Wolfe papers would be permitted until five years after the appearance of the Nowell biography. Berner himself had been too busy to see me and had asked me to talk with a new young man in his law office, Paul Gitlin. When Gitlin saw my down-heartedness and heard the story about the long delay in getting my work to publication, he told me to go ahead and put my manuscript in shape with as little biographical detail as seemed reasonable in a book about Wolfe's literary career and to send it to the Estate for approval when I found a publisher.

The University of North Carolina Press accepted my book under these conditions but, in order to conform with Gitlin's guidelines, made me remove an account of Wolfe's relations with Aline Bernstein, a complete chapter about Wolfe's teaching of composition and literature at New York University, and a good many other passages. Meanwhile, Pincus Berner had died suddenly and Paul Gitlin was appointed as Administrator of the Wolfe Estate. He approved my manuscript, and this "non-biographical" book, *The Window of Memory: The Literary Career of Thomas Wolfe*, was issued in 1962. I honestly think that if Edward Aswell had continued to live, my book would never have seen print.

Andrew Turnbull, the author of a successful life of F. Scott Fitzgerald published by Scribner's, was the next to try a biography of Thomas Wolfe. Turnbull, a historian teaching at Massachusetts Institute of Technology, had wanted to do a biography of Maxwell Perkins but Scribner's had decided that the subject would not have enough commercial appeal and had deflected him into developing a book on Wolfe instead. His *Thomas Wolfe* (1967) was a more satisfactory handling than the Nowell book had been and was especially successful in its extended portraits of Maxwell Perkins and Aline Bernstein. But it seemed to reflect little awareness of Wolfe as a literary artist. In Turnbull's presentation, Wolfe might as easily have been a baseball player or an opera singer.

As the years passed, editors and scholars had published a great many works that accumulated information about Wolfe's life. *The Letters of Thomas Wolfe*, edited by Elizabeth Nowell, had been issued as early as 1956. Two volumes of *The Notebooks of Thomas Wolfe*, edited by me and Pascal Reeves, came out in 1970. *My Other Loneliness: Letters of Thomas Wolfe and Aline Bernstein*, edited by Suzanne Stutman, and *Beyond Love and Loyalty: The Letters of Thomas Wolfe and Elizabeth Nowell*, edited by me, were published in 1983. *Thomas Wolfe Interviewed*, edited by Aldo Magi and

Richard Walser, appeared in 1985. Over the years, Walser had published a book and two monographs about Wolfe's ancestors, his parents, and his college days at Chapel Hill. Also dozens of short memoirs of Wolfe had been published in *The Thomas Wolfe Review* and elsewhere, especially because interest in Wolfe had been stimulated by the Wolfe Fests held annually at St. Mary's College in Raleigh, 1975–81, and by the annual meetings of the Thomas Wolfe Society since 1979. A wealth of new material was now available to a new Wolfe biographer.

David Donald—an American historian, a Pulitzer prize winner, and a southerner—seemed the ideal person to pick up the challenge, and now that *Look Homeward* has come before us, all expectations have been fulfilled. Beyond exploring the riches of recently published source material, Donald went on to wade through the daunting quagmire of the Wolfe papers at Harvard, the extensive Wolfe collection at the University of North Carolina, the Scribner archive at Princeton, the family papers in the Braden-Hackett Collection in Memphis, and to pursue scattered items in libraries all over the country. Moreover, he had sought out for interview every living person who knew Wolfe, a good many of them obscure figures, difficult to find.

The result is a well-written, carefully organized narrative of Wolfe's life that brims over with facts and testimony. It presents Wolfe as a tortured genius, an egoistic personality who burned up his energies expressing his responses to life in fiction but who was unable to function without the guidance of editors and mentors. An unsavory picture of Wolfe's personal life predominates: he is seen as a man full of racial and ethnic prejudices, crude and selfish indulgences of appetite, and rages against imagined enemies. Donald seems to take special relish in details of Wolfe's sex life or his bodily functions. As a consequence, the unpleasant side of Wolfe gets so much space that the reader is somewhat distracted from seeing Wolfe as a writer.

I do not wish to leave the impression that Donald neglects Wolfe's literary career. Indeed, he discusses carefully most of the work that Wolfe published before his death and, in so doing, handles it more sensibly than many literary commentators have done. But Donald is an historian, and his inclination is to gather evidence, to select and record it, and to organize his narrative and sprinkle it liberally with anecdotes. What troubles me is his seeming reluctance to interpret Wolfe in order to provide understanding of his unusual personality and relate it to his literary achievement or his literary shortcomings. If one's subject is a writer, the countless details of his life are less important than a consideration of why he wrote the kinds of books that he did and how they came to be.

A case in point will illustrate what I mean. Donald was given access to a document written by Edward Aswell that had long remained in the files of the Estate of Thomas Wolfe and that no other biographer had ever seen, "Love as Art and Vice Versa: An Erotic Experience as Told to Me by Thomas Wolfe," which not only records Wolfe's views on sex but reveals his observations on a connection between sexual stimulation, even autoerotic manipulation, and literary creativity. Donald does not do much with these observations: he uses them for narrative anecdote and neglects the opportunity to relate them to Wolfe's literary endeavors.

What is new in Donald's biography? There is a great deal about Wolfe's love affairs, especially about Clair Zyve, a young schoolteacher who helped him get over the break with Aline Bernstein, and about Belinda Jelliffe, the vivacious, beautiful wife of the psychiatrist, Dr. Smith Ely Jelliffe. There is a much fuller picture of the Wolfe family life than found anywhere, even in Walser's monographs. There is more about his relations with colleagues and students at New York University, more about his associations with Robert Penn Warren and the Vanderbilt group, more about his appearance at the Writers Conference in Boulder, Colorado, in 1935, more about the secretaries who did his typewriting.

As a biographical narrative this a work of high quality, yet I must call attention to two weaknesses. Like other Wolfe biographers (Walser is the shining exception), Donald occasionally falls before the temptation to use quotations from fiction as if they presented fact. This offense is most troublesome when he quotes dialogue from characters in a Wolfe or Bernstein novel as if it were spoken by Wolfe or Bernstein. I read this manuscript before publication and indicated to the author all of these misuses of quotation. He corrected some but not all of these lapses.

The second weakness is rather a matter of emphasis. Donald is much too hard on Edward Aswell as an editor of Wolfe's final manuscript than he should be. No one excuses Aswell's keeping silent about his editorial presence until 1941 when he published "A Note on Thomas Wolfe," explaining, with some obfuscation, his role as an editor. But Donald's final judgment of Aswell's cutting and editing is unduly harsh. This seems especially so because in his close examination of the situation Donald appears uncertain about his opinion of Aswell's procedure. He points out the editorial alternatives that Aswell might have followed and then rejects them all. Further he concedes that Aswell tried to fulfill Wolfe's purposes as best he could understand them and states, "It is certain that another editor, with a different temperament and with a different literary sensibility, would have made different decisions. Yet it is not clear that another editor could have made better, or even considerably different, novels out of Wolfe's manuscripts" (pp. 483–84). Even so, his pronouncement on the matter is uncompromising: "Far from deserving commendation, Aswell's editorial interference was, both from the standpoint of literature and of ethics, unacceptable" (p. 482).

When I read through the Donald manuscript before publication, I pointed out to him a mistaken conception he had of the material that Aswell had on hand to carry out his editorial task: Donald had thought Aswell drew upon the entire treasury of Wolfe's manuscripts in order to bring Wolfe's novels into print. But this was not the case. Aswell was only able to use the manuscript materials that Wolfe gave him; the crate containing the rest of Wolfe's manuscripts was sealed after Wolfe's death and shipped to Perkins, the literary executor. What this means is that Aswell had in hand a body of material that Wolfe had assembled and that Wolfe knew needed to be made congruent with the advice of his editor. Aswell did not range freely among Wolfe's total manuscript accumulation in bringing the last novels into their publishable form. Nor did he have any help or aid to understanding from that crate of other Wolfe manuscripts; he had to work with what Wolfe had given him. It was an extraordinarily difficult editorial task, and despite Aswell's early silence about his editorial cutting, changing, and rearranging, it was a commendable achievement to bring before the reading public forty percent of Thomas Wolfe's lifetime work in coherent form.

For the final version of his biography, Donald corrected all the statements that were based on his misapprehension about how much material Aswell had to work with, but he did not make any change in the stern judgment that I have quoted above. I think it should have been modified. Scholars will continue to differ in their opinions on this matter. They will have further evidence to consider when Leslie Field's *Thomas Wolfe and His Editors* is published later this year.

These strictures on Donald's book do not alter my overall view of it. Donald has produced, through his research and his mastery of an overabundance of documents and testimony, a first-class biographical work. It will endure as a standard biographical reference along with the editions of Wolfe's letters and his notebooks. In time, someone with critical perceptiveness will be able to use this great accumulation of scholarly research to offer a more sensitive interpretation of Wolfe's unique literary personality. The opportunity awaits.

Glimpses of the Henry James Who Earned His Living

Hershel Parker

Michael Anesko, *"Friction with the Market": Henry James and the Profession of Authorship.* New York: Oxford University Press, 1986. xiii, 258 pp.

A tried-and-true way for a reviewer to annoy readers and to outrage an author is to suggest that the book under review did not fulfill its platonic ideal—that it struggled, and failed, to become another and of course better book. Folks, try to forgive me for saying that parts of Michael Anesko's *"Friction with the Market": Henry James and the Profession of Authorship* belong to the marvelous book he should have written (and did partly write), while parts (if they had to be written) should have been published as a forgettable critical essay. The wholly admirable portion of the book as published consists of the scattered but substantial and original contributions to the history of James as a professional author. If a dabbler in James's publishing history like me responds to Anesko's information with almost pathetic gratitude, how must long-starved Jameseans respond to a mass of new facts (often mustered with charm and cogency) about James's relationships with his publishers? The ho-hum part of the book consists of "readings" of James novels as bearing on his relationship with his publishers and audiences. Lord knows what happened. Maybe the dissertation director or the committee decided that a history of James as a professional writer was altogether too unimaginative for the graduate program in the History of American Civilization at Harvard in the Decade of Theory and that the author, at the least, should dress up his deplorably un-chic story of contracts and sales figures. More likely (to judge by some comments I quote below) Anesko himself was torn between the desire to tell a new story based on his researches and the desire to prove himself capable of interpretation. (Never underestimate the power of critics and theorists to make a scholar feel inferior.) Whatever happened, the book as published embodies (literally embodies, in the self-trashing which occurs in several chapters) the devaluation of scholarship which has prevailed in American universities since the 1950s. If Anesko had written a book really about (not just subtitled) *Henry James and the Profession of Authorship,* a chronological account of James's relationships with his American and English publishers and his responses to conditions in the literary marketplace, he would have won the lavish and enduring gratitude of students of Henry James and of nineteenth-century publishing. As it is, he has won much gratitude mixed with considerable exasperation.

Anesko in his preface reveals an admirably self-conscious and detached sense of just where he came into the continuum of work on James. "Ever since the New Criticism began to explore the 'poetics' of fiction, we have been in danger of ignoring the fact that novelists write to be purchased and read." Critics have usually ignored the abundant evidence that James's works "were shaped not merely by the imagination alone, but by a constant and lively 'friction with the market.'" Breaking with tradition, Anesko has worked through "sources that have previously gone unexamined—publishers' records, correspondence between James and his editors, and documents pertaining to the novelist's literary income" (p. vii). (Anesko himself ignores the relatively little part of this work that other scholars such as Sister Stephanie Vincec and S. P. Rosenbaum have already done.) He describes his book as "an essay in the sociology of literature, an attempt to reconstruct the social and economic contexts of the production of fiction, and to bring that reconstruction to bear upon the interpretation" of James's work (pp. vii–viii). He continues with what is apparently an elliptical reference to his own friction with his readers at Harvard or at Oxford University Press: "As such, this book cannot easily be classified either as literary criticism or literary history, and I have deliberately resisted the advice of some readers to make it look more like one or the other" (p. viii).

The Henry James Who Earned His Living

Anesko's introduction (which counts as the unnumbered Chapter I) continues his helpful overview and places his study securely in the history of work on James in particular and twentieth-century criticism in general. Of two early Jameseans who set the terms of criticism, Anesko says that Percy Lubbock was not interested "in exploring the work-a-day realities of Henry James's career," while Theodora Bosanquet portrayed James "as a 'writer who had fasted for forty years in the wilderness of British and American misconceptions without yielding a scrap of intellectual integrity to editorial or publishing tempers'" (p. 5). Jameseans of "the great revival years of the 1930s and 1940s," such as R. P. Blackmur, F. O. Matthiessen, and Lionel Trilling, were not interested in the James who wrote in order to earn a living:

> In the drive to legitimate their preference for detailed scrutiny of texts, the high priests of modernism were quick to impress James into their ranks, claiming his critical premises as their own and deriving their conviction from the magnificently isolated heroism of his example. While some of these commentators recognized the danger of excessively abstracting James from his immediate historical context, the remarkable zeal that they brought to the study of James's work was not matched by a complementary interest in the relevant circumstances of his career. [p. 6]

The "modernist critics," in short, "exaggerated the distinctiveness of James at the same time that they evaded some of the key questions his example ought finally to have raised" (p. 6)—questions about James as earner of his own living. Anesko gives due credit to Leon Edel's intermittent attention to James's "descent into the market-place," but fairly concludes that Edel's preoccupation is with James's psychology rather than with his professionalism (p. 7). Rightly observing that the "gap here in critical understanding is not peculiar to James scholarship" (p. 7), Anesko points out that William Charvat's pioneering study of the profession of authorship in the United States has rarely been followed up by later students, whether of James or of other writers. The tribute to Charvat which concludes the introduction is altogether apt, for Anesko at his best belongs in the great Charvat tradition.

The portion of this book which is about James and the profession of authorship is unfashionably based on real work. Nowadays professors in American English departments are perfecting the technique of writing literary history (not just criticism and theory) without the inconvenience and mess of research. Parker exaggerates, you say? Look, oh skeptic, at *American Romanticism and the Marketplace,* which Michael T. Gilmore wrote without consulting a single publisher's or author's archive (and which Sacvan Bercovitch hailed in the *Times Literary Supplement* [January 9, 1987] as "a model of literary-historical revisionism"). Anesko went to the Henry James papers at Harvard, at Duke, at the Library of Congress, at the New York Public Library, at Virginia, at Yale. He went to publishers' archives at Harvard, at Columbia, at Princeton, at the New York Public Library, at the British Library, at the University of Reading, at the National Library of Scotland, and elsewhere. Whenever he is working from the documents he is wonderful, whether he is correcting impressionistic comments from the experts or (more often) telling stories the experts never knew because they never slogged through the archives. Unlike most of the experts, Anesko knows what he is talking about—knows more about James's career as a publishing writer than anyone has ever known. As you might expect of any young scholar zeroing in on his first big research project, Anesko becomes fuzzy-sighted when he glances away from what he knows better than anyone else. His generalizations about nineteenth-century publishing conditions are sometimes dubious: does he know how thoroughly the Harpers advertised at midcentury? (see p. 53); does he know beyond any doubt that Hawthorne's relationship with Ticknor was typical of the time? (see p. 87). Furthermore, his information derived from older scholars (even his hero and mine, William Charvat) is sometimes wrong: was *Pierre* published "on the half-profits system"? (see p. 215, n. 87). This sort of vagueness or imprecision is easy to forgive, since it is rarely presented in a dogmatic way, but it makes the reader wary, particularly when some valuable recent scholarship is not cited.

But Anesko is not content to work in the Charvat tradition. The imp of the perverse hops in, unwilling to let well (or wonderful) enough alone. The symptom emerges in the deplorable title, *"Friction with the Market": Henry James and the Profession of Authorship*—deplorable if only because quotation marks within a title cause problems every time the book is cited. Furthermore, some perfectly competent people will read the first word as "Fiction," do a doubletake, then remain uncertain as to what the correct word is. I'll bet you the amount James earned from *Confidence* that the title will soon appear in bibliographical citations with "Fiction" instead of "Friction." You learn the source for the quotation and adjust to it, sort of (though you never adjust to the misapplication of such a quotation as "publishing scoundrel" [p. 64]). The descriptive subtitle ought to have been the title and the impulse to be cute should have been resisted, or yielded to only in the subtitle.

The conflict between an overpowering urge to be "literary" and a happy determination to shape the documents from the archives into a coherent story runs through the book (and displays itself openly in those chapters where the artsy part goes as main title and the substance is relegated to the subtitle). Chapter II, "Stuff as Dreams Are Made On: Henry James and His Audience," contains an account of James's writing for the theatre which corrects Leon Edel's treatment of that work "as an anomalous interlude" in James's professional career (p. 19), but it is mainly devoted to a perhaps plausible but overly elaborated reading of the architectural plan of the house in Albany at the start of *Portrait* as a model of James's "own professional situation" (p. 13). Chapter III, straightforwardly entitled "Henry James and the Profession of Authorship" briefly continues the comparison between Isabel Archer and James—a comparison that may have some validity but is not very useful, and takes up the space which ought to have been filled even fuller with the enthralling account of the economic footing on which James's built his career, particularly the arrangements for the publication of *A Passionate Pilgrim* and *Transatlantic Sketches* and James's "siege of London" (p. 37), his siege of Macmillan in particular. In the largely irrelevant Chapter IV, "James's Hawthorne: The Last Primitive Man of Letters," an account of how James came to write and publish his *Hawthorne* is distractingly overshadowed by a self-indulgent digression on *The House of the Seven Gables* as "patterned loosely" on Hawthorne's "family history" (p. 67). Chapter V, "Melodrama in the Marketplace: The Making of *The Bostonians*," starts with a fascinating account of the way arrangements for publication affected the growth of the manuscript, but the chapter veers off the track as Anesko pushes a reading of *The Bostonians* as an allegory of James's search for a share of the literary market. And I am baffled that Anesko does not cite Sister Stephanie Vincec's classic study, "'Poor Flopping *Wings*': The Making of Henry James's *The Wings of the Dove*" (*Harvard Library Bulletin*, 24 [January, 1976]), as corroboration for his conclusion that other critics "have sometimes apologized for James's digressive treatment of his subjects, but few have offered convincing explanations for them" (p. 85). Chapter VI, "Between the Worlds of Beauty and Necessity: Hyacinth Robinson's Problem of Vocation" (after lingering over *The Bostonians* for several pages) gets on track with a discussion of the impact that the fortunes of the publisher Osgood had on *The Princess Casamassima* but veers off again, leaving us stalled between Information and Fancy. Chapter VII, "Accommodating Art and the World: The Primary Motive of *The Tragic Muse*," after an enlightening account of James's diminishing income in the late 1880s goes off the track in treating the problem of success in *The Tragic Muse* as a parallel to James's problems. In the last chapter, "The Eclectic Architecture of Henry James's New York Edition," Anesko tells a story that had always been badly told until 1983, when he published a version of this chapter in the *New England Quarterly*. Final evidence of the divided nature of the book comes when essential material is relegated to appendices. Appendix A, "Henry James and the Movement for International Copyright," should have been told in the appropriate places in the (platonic) narrative. Appendix B, "Henry James's Literary Income," should have been elaborated as the stuff of many undreamlike pages throughout that narrative. As it is, most of Appendix B consists of tables which are unusable unless you go to the third edition of *A Bibliography of Henry James* and find the titles of the pieces of fiction which Anesko identifies only by the numbers assigned to them there.

There are distractions, such as the gauche references to "famous" letters or anecdotes—see pp. 26, 50, 73, 87, 120, and 127 (twice). One typographical error should cause deep blushes at Oxford University Press: Michael Sadlier (p. 36). I see other mundane typos on pp. 42, 80, 111, 115, 124, 146, and 226, along with a mystical reference to "the king of intelligent criticism" (p. 4). Such gaffes are trivial. What counts is that Anesko did research of high significance then seized some of his opportunities to present the results of that research to the world while intermittently throwing away other chances to tell us what he alone knows. At his scholarly best Anesko is infinitely better than any of those flashy critics he seems to want to emulate.

G. Bernard Shaw: Losing or Saving Him

A. E. Wallace Maurer

Dan H. Laurence. *Bernard Shaw: A Bibliography.* The Soho Bibliographies XXII. Oxford and New York: Clarendon Press, 1983. 2 vols. xxiv, 516 pp.; vi, 542 pp.

Stanley Weintraub, ed. *Bernard Shaw: The Diaries, 1885–1897.* University Park and London: The Pennsylvania State University Press, 1986. 2 vols. vi, 682 pp.; vi, 560 pp.

In 1956 Professor Archibald Henderson declared that on 24 February 1903 his mode of life had changed without warning. Led on that far-off day against his will to see a play (*You Never Can Tell*) by Bernard Shaw, a playwright of whom he had never heard, he now, half a century later, apocalyptically marked the day's event as the beginning of his inextinguishable interest in Shaw: "With the close of this day I was, all unconsciously, taking the first step toward becoming, in the near future, the biographer of a new immortal."[1] This past year, 1987, Professor Harold Bloom used rough-and-ready revisionist language in "the hope of arriving at a freshly balanced estimate" of Shaw. Indeed, in a short headnote to a collection of fourteen essays on Shaw, twelve, including his own introduction, published within the last twenty years, he quite unapocalyptically aimed at a balanced estimate that is not even of the whole Shaw, but of something less, namely of his "limitations" and "his varied achievements as a comic melodramatist." In his own re-examination, Bloom severely collapsed the immortal into an embarrassingly recognizable and unexceptional mortal who rode atop "copious intellectual debts," displayed "dialectic cunning" and "crafty" irony, harbored a "passion for himself" that was "nobly unbounded," and had "no style to speak of."[2]

At the risk of banality, I juxtapose a shift in my own intellectual behavior regarding Shaw which overlaps the time span separating the opposed attitudes of Henderson and Bloom. As a freshman in the late 1930s at a university which plunged us directly into "literature" rather than "composition," demanding mastery of the latter by creative panic if such mastery were not possessed on arrival, I read with unanticipated delight Shaw's *Caesar and Cleopatra*. (I also had not heard of Shaw before.) The following summer I read his works and his pronouncements non-stop, happily astonished at *his* mastery of composition, and insatiably curious about its nature and cause. Assured by friends that I would "specialize" in Shaw, I said no, despite my delight in his work, and have held firmly to that decision. But now I find myself impelled to write on Bernard Shaw, just once.

The completion of a 180-degree turn in attitude towards Shaw from positive to negative over thirty years (signalled in the antithetical observations of Henderson and Bloom), my compulsion to write on Shaw, and the appearance of Professor Dan Laurence's *Bernard Shaw: A Bibliography* and Professor Stanley Weintraub's *Bernard Shaw: The Diaries, 1885–1897*—all around the same moment—are not coincidental happenings. The bibliography and the diaries come with uncanny timeliness to empower the crucial sector of a bifurcation in Shaw studies since 1950. My compulsion to write is prompted by Bloom and Henderson. I wish to interpret the historical implications of the bibliography and the diaries. Can they help us approach, if not fully establish, fair and full truth about Bernard Shaw to the extent that our epistemological self-awareness and our concomitant conception of the meaning of things over time allow?

There is a datable starting point for the shift in critical response to Shaw, not just the particular one evident in Henderson and Bloom, but also the general shift from a vantage point within passionate personal involvement to one of inquiry *de novo*. In the history of Shaw scholarship, specifically of theories of his durability and utility, the year 1950 (the year of his death) is a watershed. Before 1950, writers on Shaw had always to face the real possibility that their work could—as indeed at his choice it did—fall under the scrutiny of his forward-darting and preternaturally alert intelligence. There was also his legal keenness and economic power, which he exercised to the moral hilt. After 1950, writers on Shaw no longer had to be aware of the presence of Shaw as a self-contained intellectual judicial system. Now they felt free to inquire in all areas and by all the usual critical modes. Not that pre-1950 writers ever persuasively complained that Shaw kept them from saying what they saw, for they found new light and dimension in his reproofs and corrections; nor that post-1950 writers breathed a sigh of relief at the prospect of divulging what he seemed to have wished suppressed. But the man presiding over the works, the man prompting instant planetary wire-release, was gone.

Whether he will die out in the sense that, say, Chaucer, Shakespeare, Milton, Anna van Schurman, Dryden, and all other literary practitioners have done, to be revived and painstakingly reconstructed only, after all is said, approximately, or whether he unfurled the potentiality of human endowment and carried the reactivating capacity of language beyond what any of the writers of the past have done—this constitutes my preoccupation with Shaw. It also constitutes my argument for the supreme essentiality at this moment of the works of Laurence and Weintraub here under review.

These two works come at the end (but are not the end) of a scholarly movement into Shaw's works and milieu that began on both sides of the Atlantic after 1950, but had indestructible roots and recollective inspiration in the pre-1950 era of the tireless G.B.S. In those days his every pyrotechnically prescient word, from the beginning of his prime in the 1880s, but especially in the twentieth century, until the day of his death, circumnavigated the planet more swiftly, quotably, and penetratingly than had any writer's before him. Within post-1950 Shaw scholarship lies a micro-history which reflects the course of interests in Shaw up to now—a critical moment—and which hints, inconclusively as yet, at the destiny of Shaw's place in the world. This microhistory, transpiring most noticeably within the Shaw journals, which reflect prevailing interests in Shaw, is the succession of changes in the mastheads. These changes come with no formal announcements and can indeed pass by the reader unnoticed. But they reflect shifts in the judgment of Shaw and in the conceptual direction of Shaw studies. Unheralded and fragmentary, these changes are either on a road to unrecognized extinction, or they have assisted in the perpetuation of the magnitude and quality of Bernard Shaw. One must trace this easily overlooked phenomenon in order to interpret the Henderson-to-Bloom graph, my own shift in perceptions and intent, and the significance (high and mighty) of the works of Laurence and Weintraub.

Scholarship exists to search out the truth about the nature and destiny of the race. It is a drive towards omniscience as our epistemology gives us to see it. It is impossible now to keep track of it all in one human memory, in anyone's, and even within a sector of it like Shaw studies it is hard to be sure of incentives, tensions, or probable ends. In retrospect it does appear as if the initiative of scholarly action on Shaw since 1950 took head in the channels cut by societies established to do something *with* or *for* Shaw. What was done manifested itself in their journals, of which three have persisted, one of them with tremendous vigor because associated with the scholarly energy of the American universities.

Vast although this scholarship is becoming, one can detect in it a dialectic. The Shaw journals are powered by a tension between two elemental intellectual motivations: passionate espousal and unaligned curiosity and inquiry. Both have in common wholly alert and undivided attention to Shaw. Whether the one or the other, or both together, will clarify the question of Shaw's merit is central to the argument of this review. A portion of the mastheads of the journals, while seemingly infinitesimal, is barometric in a charting of the dialectic in Shaw studies. In the two smaller but infectiously informative and by no means ineffectual journals, the elements of the dialectic are evident. In the presently largest one, the two tendencies in the dialectic (the tendency towards the research of espousal and the tendency towards research *de novo*) emerge to cut directions in Shaw studies in ways that radically, though ultimately not solely, determine the losing or the saving of the whole phenomenon known as G. Bernard Shaw.

The scholarly cadres founding themselves after 1950 did not post on the mastheads or title pages of their journals proclamations of freedom from any prepossessions. Instead they hoisted watchwords out of Bernard Shaw himself. In December 1953, the first number of *The Shavian,* of the Shaw Society of London, upon absorbing Number 51 of the precedent *Shaw Society Bulletin,* put gleaming on its first banner page Shaw's unrelenting challenge to the human being: "'This is the true joy of life, the being used for a purpose recognised by yourself as a mighty one; the being thoroughly worn out before you are thrown on the scrap heap; the being a force of Nature instead of a selfish little clod of ailments and grievances complaining that the world will not devote itself to making you happy.'"[3] So potent was this injunction on page one that on page two the enterprise was thrown into an apparent inferiority complex. In its "Prefatory" salutation there it found itself sheepishly letting Shaw take over the first sentence again with his own corrective warning: "'I am not a Shavian,' once said Bernard Shaw."[4] In its statement on "Objects and Membership Terms," *The Shavian* enjoined members to apply their minds freely and vigilantly, to leave nothing unexamined, but its editors found in Shaw the best statement of that injunction and presented it in italics: *"You must always let yourself think about everything. And you must think about everything as it is, not as it is talked about. . . . We should never accept anything reverently until we have asked it a great many very searching questions."* After demanding relentless inquiry via Shaw's definition, the editors fostered the marriage between scholarship, which is to "promote a wider and clearer understanding of Bernard Shaw's life and work," and underlying partisan affection for Shaw, which will provide "a rallying point for the co-operation and education of kindred spirits and a forum for their irreconcilable controversies."[5] The quotation disappeared from the first page after the third number, but it joined the other quotation on the policy statement page beginning with the fourth number in May 1955. That page appeared off and on until May 1957, when it appeared for the last time, in the new larger format, with the simultaneous inauguration of a new tradition, signalled by a quotation from Shaw on the "Contents" page. This quotation lasted through summer 1973.[6] Between 1953 and 1973, then, the affectionate and philosophic centrality of Shaw in *The Shavian* underwent some subtle de-emphasis through diffusion.

On this side of the Atlantic, in one of the early scholarly ventures devoted to Shaw, there occurred a similar and somewhat more decisive contraction of guidelines directly out of Shaw. No sooner did *The Independent Shavian*, organ of the New York branch of the Shaw Society of London, in October 1962 eschew hero-worship and proclaim its contributors' desire to extract and test the universal elements in Shaw, than it helplessly drew its finest watchword and touchstone for procedure from Shaw himself, who asserted that the great artist "'is not a lump of genius to be gaped at, but a combination to be analyzed.'" It posted his caution "'never accept anything reverently, without asking it a great many very searching questions.'" And it seized upon his rule of inquiry and judgment: "'The way to get at the merits of a case is not to listen to the fool who imagines himself impartial, but to get it argued with reckless bias for and against.'"[7] In short, this commendable American enterprise, in the very exercise of banishing idolatry, climaxed each of its three major paragraphs of apologia with incandescent statements out of Shaw, statements that displaced from memory the honest plans of the journal's directors. *The Independent Shavian* steered readers' minds into full radical cerebral activity in behalf of Bernard Shaw, according to the injunctions for self-correction educed by Shaw himself—unparaphrased, unmatched, and unimproved. After the proclamation in its opening issue, however, *The Independent Shavian* subsequently bore no guiding quotation from Shaw and defined no scholarly intent on its masthead. While on the cover it engraved the signature "G. Bernard Shaw" in gilt, it non-committally described membership and publication in facts and figures. In the second number the then president accepted as a matter of course the inseparability of the logic of "scholarship," viz., independence going where it must concerning its subject, and the logic of "fellowship," viz., a fundamentally affectionate espousal of its subject.[8] In 1979, when the

New York Shavians became "The Bernard Shaw Society," they retained the marriage of scholarly inquiry and scholarly espousal when they declared their purpose to be the "furthering [of] appreciation of Bernard Shaw and his work."[9] In 1980 that statement vanished. First-hand memory of the visual reality of Shaw was decreasing; on the title page from then on until the latest issue (1986) a series of characteristic portraits of Shaw—sketch, cartoon, photograph—kept alive the affectionate realm of the dialectic.

Both those post-1950 journals exhibit the inception of the ongoing dialectical condition of which I have already spoken. But the incitements in the dialectic—sympathetic bias for Shaw and unattached inquiry into an item called Shaw—and the particularities and intensity of study of Shaw are most discernible in the third journal preoccupied with Shaw since his death. This journal, by and large, tends to take position and become one major side of the bifurcation in Shaw studies. The bifurcations are not adversarial, or fatuously hostile, or mutually exclusive. Only a conceptual and perhaps temperamental line divides them. The history of the masthead, again, is instructive. On Shaw's ninety-fourth and last birthday, 26 July 1950, The Shaw Society of America, Inc., founded *The Shaw Bulletin* under the sponsorship of some fifty figures, from Archibald Henderson to Gene Tunney to Albert Einstein. In the first number, the Society committed *The Shaw Bulletin,* as late as its seventh page, to furthering the understanding and appreciation of Shaw's life and work. But it had happily launched itself on page one with a corrective response of the Shaw of ninety-four. With sage exhaustion he averred, "I am so old that to me the Bernard Shaw of fifty years ago is as dead as the infant of 90 years ago." And he beat Professor Bloom to the punch as well: "The utmost I can claim . . . in my best days," he wrote, "is that I was one of the hundred best playwrights in the world, hardly a supreme distinction." There followed two additional claims, large political, geopolitical, and meta-political ones, made by "the ancient dodderer I am now." "I was one of the inventors of Fabian Socialism," wrote Shaw, and "I helped to set the religion of Creative Evolution with its feet on the ground because I saw that no established religion in the world is wholly credible, and that without religion men are political timeservers and cowards."[10] In January 1959 *The Shaw Bulletin* turned into *The Shaw Review*, which in 1981 in its turn became *SHAW: The Annual of Bernard Shaw Studies*, which it has so far remained.

Like the other post-1950 journals, this one has displayed a shift in the tone and perspective of discourse on Shaw that has transpired during the years since 1950 through the morning of 30 December 1987, when I most recently consulted its latest number. Until now, this shift has been from helpless idolatry at worst and celebration of genius at best to the cumulative play of analytic inquiry. The shift in this journal, as in the other two, is gradual, like the change in angle of the sun over the seasons. Nonetheless it is datable, like an equinox. When the last *Shaw Review* in 1980 became the first *SHAW: The Annual of Shaw Studies*, an omission silently occurred. Early on, *The Shaw Bulletin* (I, no. 5, May 1954) had begun the practice of placing a Shaw quotation on the title/contents page, a practice which took on the happy familiarity of a convention. Occasionally a citation from someone else, drawn by gravity to Shaw, had appeared.[11] Though outnumbered by about five to one, these substitutions prefigured the shift signaled by the new format of 1980–81, when the quotations disappeared altogether.

Shaw the performer, immanent in his works, alive before the reader and spectator, tended to give way to Shaw the discrete item for inquiry. Shaw died—almost. The transition between the presence and the item was made in a *Shaw Review* issue of 1960 and was carried across into the first *SHAW*, of 1981, and retained, except in *SHAW 2* and *SHAW 3*, thus far into *SHAW 7* (1987). G. Bernard Shaw has become material for the energy and ardor of contemporary scholarship. Yet the moving shade of Shaw bobs about in the interstices of the typography. What figure in and out of the canon, even "Will Shakespeare," is called by his contemporary trademark, "G.B.S."? And for which writer's uncommon all-out exercise of make-up, his tireless reach for comprehensiveness, remains the lingering admiration that resides in the phrase "his assumed province"?[12]

These bits of admiration for the mighty pre-1950 G.B.S. are

signs, very broadly, of a path never quite abandoned. The essential character and achievement of Shaw could perish in random welter of inquiry into Shaw, sympathetic and unsympathetic, indifferent and insatiable, discrete and synthetic, obscurantist and prophetic. The research in the *SHAW*s is not by any stretch of the term partisan; it is wide-open, prepared for fundamental alteration, should evidence be persuasive. But it proceeds with the intent of elucidation for increased appreciation of an uncommon figure. That is, at the moment, the major drive of Shaw scholarship represented by *SHAW*. It is impelled by the principle that retention of the whole phenomenon of Shaw rests on reconstruction of micro-points of memory even as they dim or have not yet been recovered.

Thus, the robust scholarship of the first seven *SHAW*s responds to the brute facts of life span. Thirty-six years after Shaw's death, fewer readers of his works remember him alive than encounter him as a figure of preceding times. Hence the thrust of *SHAW* is in reconstruction of milieu. Driven by the desire to overlook nothing and focused on certain imperatives, *SHAW* finds that it must "deal with Shavian nuances which escape the printed page or were enhanced by performance."[13] Contributors must write on plays heretofore untouched in order to enrich "our collective sense of the range and depth of the Shavian canon."[14] They must follow abroad with his wife the Shaw who had meticulously researched foreign settings for his plays before he had visited the countries themselves.[15] They must perceive the moral and intellectual fertility of Shaw's religion.[16] Alternating with the issue-centered volumes have been three concerned with a range of topics, from Shaw's vegetarianism to his qualifications as a systematic psychologist to an uncanny aerial view of Pointe Bernard Shaw, Iles Radisson, Ungava Bay, Quebec, Canada, to a corrective revaluation of Shaw's concept of science. In these diverse inquiries, the happy assent to Bernard Shaw biases the tone, as in Bradbury's "Shaw the God"; Brunger's alertness to Shaw's "left eye, his nose and hirsute mouth and chin"; and the tender vignette of Einstein moved by the spectacle of Shaw's fragile hip broken by his fall in his garden in his ninety-fifth year.[17]

Broadly speaking, *SHAW* tends to draw scholars who respond perforce with respect, if not universally with admiration, to the discoverable and recoverable magnitude of achievement in Shaw's works. Again broadly speaking, scholarship outside of *SHAW* tends to carry no brief for Shaw, to approach him with noncommittal openness or with skepticism, or with groundbreaking iconoclasm. When I later discuss the reductive element in Shaw scholarship, I shall describe the second major area of scholarship on Shaw. Practitioners in this area, if their intuitions and findings prove right, may reduce Shaw to size in time. If they are wrong, they will only reaffirm Shaw's strength.

As the foregoing minuscule history of the mastheads suggests, the post-1950 journals on Shaw reflect a movement from ardent sympathy for him towards dissociation from him. That small history is the skimmed top of vigorously growing commentary on Shaw, generally taking the broad form, during our decades, of a dialectic with the outcome as yet indeterminate. But that dialectic is fraught with possibilities for the future of Shaw; it is both the drama of and the dynamic incentive behind scholarship on Shaw. How it will go depends in part on who and what affect it. At this time, out of the flow of commentary on Shaw, come two works of colossal industry. Both are unabashedly inspired by the magnitude of Shaw's importance. That the scholars who produced them—Professors Dan Laurence and Stanley Weintraub—should be so inclined is not surprising. Both are reasonably young patriarchs who early took a lead in Shaw studies, the former having assumed the editorship of the *Shaw Bulletin* in May 1954 and the latter, in November 1956, retaining that position through the transition to *SHAW* and on to the present.

Convinced of the genius of Shaw, Laurence has devoted more than thirty years to producing a bibliography of colossal proportions.[18] It treats Shaw's publications in more than twenty-four countries and fourteen languages; it is indebted to some three hundred collectors, bibliographers, librarians, and scholars, and to approximately one hundred libraries and institutions, to say nothing of hosts, hostesses, and compositors (II, 937–46). There are eleven sections of listings, some fifty blank pages for "Ad-

Losing or Saving Shaw   229

denda," and an index of over one hundred pages. The bibliographical record of Shaw occupies two volumes, totaling 1,058 pages, and sells for $169.00, a pittance when measured in hours of labor.

A few vignettes suggest the reconstructive ardor with which Laurence worked. On 23 November 1952, at the first and only meeting of the Shaw Society, finding that Dr. Fritz Erwin Loewenstein had abandoned his bibliographical mission, new member Dan Laurence, then a graduate assistant, began this project with an "angry determination" sustained for more than thirty years (I, ix–xiii). He strove for a comprehensive bibliography which would treat not only the texts but also the fly-sheets and dust-wrappers, items all and equally touched by Shaw's mind. Each entry for a first edition or a subsequent printing (with Shaw inveterately revising towards the best of cascading alternatives) became a monument to dauntingly meticulous collation. Information from countless sources was collected on publication, genesis, process, and history. To establish so fugitive an item as Shaw's drafting of a pamphlet for James Timewell, a master tailor and Honorary Secretary of the Police and Public Vigilance Society, Laurence pieced together records on contributions to the Society funds, a January 1898 note by Shaw on his current projects, and a letter to Ellen Terry (I, 32–33). Laurence's sorting out of proofs and rehearsal texts is excruciatingly painstaking, involving encounters with Shaw's mischievous veiling of authorial identity. In the first Rehearsal Copy of *Pygmalion,* for example, Shaw referred to the author as "a Fellow of the Royal Society of Literature" (I, 375–78). Laurence's sources constitute the passing scene of two half-centuries of persons and events struck by Shaw's intelligence. Works noted range from three stanzas of a poem recovered in a surviving page of a lost book to a lecture syllabus drafted by him for the Fabian Society in 1923 (I, 421, 437). Even jacket blurbs give us a glimpse of Shaw making a note on the length of time it took him to read a work or writing a terse evaluation of the account of the Scott expedition to the South Pole by its sole survivor.[19]

To test comprehensively the accuracy and reliability of Laurence's bibliography is beyond me at this point. Swift thought that to review a writer's work should take "more Pains and Skill, ... Wit, Learning, and Judgment" than it took the author to produce it.[20] I do not have thirty years to produce this particular review. Some tiny flaws there are—Stanley Weintraub in his review has already noted two limitations in foreign translations and correspondence.[21] My own checking argues for painstaking care. Out of some seventy Shaw items in the Rare Books Room of my university library, I checked the collations of nineteen against Laurence's. Seventeen revealed flawless description. Two are discrepant, perhaps involving typographical or transcription error, or perhaps revealing variant states to be recorded on the blank pages in the rear.

Laurence's *Bernard Shaw: A Bibliography* is electric with fascinatingly direct flashes of Shaw in word or act. It is also packed with the history, economics, and sociology of the age. For instance, in statistics on printings, what elsewhere would be dry-asdust here becomes endlessly intriguing demography of intellect. Laurence's *Bibliography* also makes possible the reading and re-reading of Shaw. It is the biggest push of the intellect, next to Shaw's own, inspired by the desire to preserve him whole. And the labor has been performed by a scholar impinged upon by the author, for Laurence is old and young enough to have observed G. Bernard Shaw whole. That, as we shall see, is important.

The second work under review here is Stanley Weintraub's edition of Shaw's diaries. The diaries of 1885–1897 are the centerpiece of this enterprise, but the extension of the title—*With early autobiographical notebooks and diaries, and an abortive 1917 diary*—and the introductory essay add information on Shaw's earlier attempts at diarymaking in the 1870s and early 1880s. Also included are the small pocket engagement books that Shaw began carrying at least as early as 1904 and continued to carry until 1950. Weintraub's work gives a conspectus of all autobiographical material not intended by Shaw for publication. Shaw relied on it for his own short-range practical use and drew on it, for a larger purpose, as a record of what he did with his time and money.

Weintraub aims at a faithful reproduction of the diaries, which record activities in shorthand and expenditures in longhand,

and at explanatory reconstruction of persons, events, and circumstances. Weintraub traces the spectacular physical history of the diaries: in 1892, for instance, some of them were rescued from "debris" picked up by a bookseller called by Shaw's mother, and diaries of other years were discovered in a warehouse to which they had been transferred when a World War II bomb hit Shaw's aunt's house where they had lain (I, 2). Throughout the entire work Weintraub engages in the much larger rescue of the exact contents of the diaries from two previously attempted transliterations. One was by Blanche Patch, Shaw's secretary from 1920 until his death. She made her transliterations furtively, apparently afraid that Shaw would destroy them. The other attempt was by the late Professor Stanley Rypins of CCNY, who worked on the diaries from 1950 until his death in 1971. Neither transliteration was complete or accurate. Using the Rypins as starting-point, and following Shaw's microscopic Pitman shorthand, Weintraub aims at faithful completeness, drawing annotations from his own research of more than two decades on Shaw. Among Weintraub's finest provisions for thorough presentation of the materials (beyond his cross-checking of Patch, Rypins, and subsequent transliterations) is a microfiche reproduction of the original documents, made to go with his edition.

Weintraub's edition follows his past scholarly pattern of preserving Shaw both via himself and through reconstruction of the fading milieu. "New" in themselves, the diaries detail twelve years in Shaw's life. We glimpse Shaw's attendance at debating societies to develop speaking skills, his associations with radical political and intellectual groups, the life at his mother's place, his hand-to-mouth economy, his relations with women, his writing of articles (sometimes under street light) on art, music, and theater, his inability to spell "macaroni," his voracious reading in the British Museum. Reconstructing the London milieu of a century ago, Weintraub follows trails until they end in thin air. For instance, annotating Shaw's entry for 14 February 1885—"Went to Barton's in the evening. Burkinyoung, Graham, French and another"—Weintraub loses the clueless "another," but locates a probable candidate for Graham, and finds the other two (I, 61). Weintraub fills in the pictures that Shaw could recall for himself by a single word. He points, for instance, to Shaw's use of the German word *Trennung,* acute and total for him, signifying the end of his closeness to Florence Farr (I, 5). Statistics tell the story of Weintraub's detective work: annotations make up a fifth of the 1,150 pages; a sixty-page index presents seventy names per page, principally of persons, but also of organizations, places, and works.[22]

Weintraub's awareness of the significance of the twelve years of Shaw's life covered by the diaries at once impelled and justified his industry. Unavailable to Shaw when he wrote his prefaces and essays, they provide a contemporary record with which his allusions to his past can be compared (I, 3). Further, while the diaries record events ledger-like, with none of the intellectual drive that marked Shaw's published works, they reveal, as Weintraub underscores, Shaw following the interests which were eventually to dominate him. When they did, the diaries dried up.[23] As Michael Holroyd has noticed, they disclose "the long and arduous labour pains of bringing GBS to birth, . . . the man behind the superman."[24]

Will Henderson prove right about Shaw's merit and durability or will Bloom? A good deal—though not all, as I shall indicate—will hinge on the outcome of the dialectic between the scholarship of espousal and the scholarship *de novo,* the latter sometimes shading into revisionist skepticism and iconoclasm.

Scholarship *de novo* is the rule of survival: it guards against illusion and delusion, exposes error, discovers, expands the base of thought, helps locate our destiny. But scholarship *de novo* on Shaw, especially that which is iconoclastic in cast, is *now*—whatever it might become—reductive. It is reductive not correctively, but substantively. I have singled out Bloom as a representative careful skeptic. His skepticism appears to be founded on his own shrewd observation in *The Anxiety of Influence* about the making of great poets. While Shaw was not part of Bloom's illustrative matter, he can certainly seem to exemplify the hypothesis incidentally and directly. First, the gradual disappearance of Shaw from the masthead and title page of the journals looks a lot like the growing decision of strong intelligences to snap the leading strings of Shaw, that is, to get out from under Bloom's six-way delineated "agony of influence."[25] To maintain their independence, scholars of Shaw must cast off his influence and see him afresh.

More directly, Shaw himself might seem a perfect case study for Bloom's hypothesis that great poets are those who have freed themselves of the influences of their most admired and towering precursors. In his recurring self-directed debate over whether he was better than Shakespeare, Shaw can look like Bloom's poet in the toils of anxiety over Shakespeare's haunting stature in world drama. But the stakes for which Shaw was playing were higher. Bloom distinguished the triumph over the precursor of the "aboriginal poetic self," of "*the poet in a poet*," thus: "Weaker talents idealize; figures of capable imagination appropriate for themselves."[26] Not only did Shaw fit Bloom's *second* clause exponentially, like Shakespeare, in that he "appropriated" all predecessors whom he scrutinized, from Sophocles through Shakespeare, Bunyan, Ibsen, Henry George, and on and on, but he also rendered Bloom's dual categorization of human capability limited and misleading. For what Shaw discovered in his predecessors was the universal normality of genius. To Shaw there were no "weaker talents," only undiscovered talents, undiscovered by their possessors. Once Shaw saw his, he turned them loose without a backward look on precursors except to be sure that he had missed nothing useful. His predecessors were not influential precursors to be wrestled out of priority in his system, but kindred spirits venturing and probing on our epistemological edge of certainty and obscurity. "Whether it be that I was born mad or a little too sane," he remarked, "my kingdom was not of this world: I was at home only in the realm of my imagination, and at my ease only with the mighty dead."[27]

To apply to Shaw the term "influence," even when done by a scholar of espousal like Professor Frederick McDowell, is reductive, but also staggering. In 1975 he enjoined scholars of Shaw to spend the rest of the century in "the detailed study of Shaw's relationship to those who were formative upon him, so that a more precise impression can emerge as to the exact contours and configurations of his mind."[28] I would be the last to disagree. I cannot help but see, however, that a Shavian response to the realities of that assignment would simultaneously collapse and multiply it infinitely, proposing that every person in his life, from the coast guards who were in stitches over his learning to ride a bicycle, to Charlotte Payne-Townshend, to the borough council, to the heckler who at an open-air socialist speech asked him what exactly he would do with £100, to every author he read in the British Museum were continuously and immeasurably influential. Laurence has found that at "the British Museum Shaw applied for more than three hundred books a year, each year that he was a frequenter of the Reading Room.... In December 1948, when he was in his ninety-third year, we find him asking the librarian: 'Is there a book in the library on the Elephantine papyri?'"[29] How does one trace the influences on a mind going for all there is? One tries, but must sense the scale of the intelligence being gauged.

Shaw never stood still intellectually long enough for a thought system to describe him. Dame Sybil Thorndike recalled Shaw's readiness to talk ardently with anyone as soon as he discovered the cutting edge of their informed curiosity. He fell, for instance, into professional exchange with her chauffeur on the insides of cars.[30] That impulse to press on the edges of perception has so far generally rendered "critical approaches" inconsequential, though their most painstaking practitioners have now and again enriched what is known. Thus, of the psychoanalytic criticism done in the late 1970s and early 1980s, the potentially most penetrating treatment (based on Shaw's own observation that "if a man is a deep writer, all his works are confessions") acknowledged, while trying to locate the limits of Shaw's self-consciousness, that the best critics "crawl far behind his darting intelligence."[31] Similarly, a scholar who initially delighted in Shaw as a champion of women, but who came to distrust him and his works, remarked two years after the study appeared, "It may ... be proved that, after all, he was his own best interpreter."[32]

Such glimpses by scholarship *de novo* of the range and clarity of Shaw's vision are, however, not the rule. More often than not, serious commentary becomes reductive as memory or knowledge of Shaw fades. Two randomly picked instances suffice. With faintly amused condescension, a recent work considers Shaw "a man of boundless ambition [whose] longing for power had been cruelly thwarted . . . , [who] aspired to be a world leader," but had to settle for the obscure post of "Vestryman of St. Pancras at the age of forty-one and nothing more."[33] I do not presume to construct Shaw's response. But its ingredients are everywhere in his work and in the vanishing past. As vestryman Shaw demonstrated exemplary studiousness, lucidity, economy of action, practicality, but not a trace of condescension or frustration over applying his mighty intelligence to a pin-point on the geopolitical complex. He would have been tickled to learn that a fantasy "of governing a nation"[34] had gnawed at the GBS who had teased or jolted the world at will through wireless, newspapers, stage, movies, and early television. He had the whole world conceptually and theatrically—the ultimate power if that is what one wants—in hand.[35] In *St. Joan* he had delineated the intellectual crux of the western world: Protestantism, or freedom of the individual, versus Roman Catholicism, or institutional preservation of the individual from chaos. So fully had he portrayed Roman Catholic logic that he was asked whether he planned conversion. He paused only to boom, "There is not room enough in Rome for two Popes."[36] His political stakes were higher than the prime-ministership (which, if assumed, would have glowed as a rare historical moment, whether one of fifty years or five minutes in duration). Lecturing a captive audience of all the world's politicians and their constituencies, while in the pay of none, was supreme political power.

Elsewhere, to judge Shaw's preface to a play as failed explication of that play is to miss Shaw's discrimination between his spectators for a play and his subsequent readers of a preface to that play. Between both audiences, an interval of ferment had produced the need to show the full scope of thought empowering the play. The prefaces were not for dramaturgic explication, which was the play's own business. Rather, a preface engaged in no less than sufficient "saturat[ion] with letters" and proper "credit[ing of] English literature" to demonstrate that the source of thought for the play (*Major Barbara,* in this case,) was not in major European heresiarchs, as the critics of that time confidently but incorrectly claimed, but in the vision of "a revolutionary writer" in a world of maddening ironies ("our laws make law impossible; our liberties destroy all freedom").[37]

Scholarship *de novo,* were it now to gain ascendancy, unlimited by the other bifurcation in Shaw studies, would lose Shaw, because it has not witnessed, or has forgotten, qualitative elements of the whole Shaw. Often it "cannot *hear* Shaw's voice."[38] Where scholarship *de novo* will lead or what purposes it will serve are unpredictable. In any event, while its practitioners are deeply absorbed, none as yet has felt compelled to spend thirty years in discrediting or pulverizing Shaw.

For retention or recovery of the whole Shaw *now,* reconstruction of detail and perspective, *quantum sufficit,* is essential. Shaw's writing was a performance for a live, monitored audience in time. He, they, and the resultant work impinged on one another and constituted the substance and art of the work. In the vanguard of the scholarship of espousal, Laurence and Weintraub have provided massive, timely means to preserve Shaw. Laurence has saved the Shavian corpus. Weintraub has opened a chamber of Shaw's brain. Both have restored segments of the disappearing past necessary to save G. Bernard Shaw whole.

But having done this, perhaps in the nick of time (*Pro captu lectoris habent sua fata libelli*),[39] they have really helped make possible only what, after all is said, Shaw alone, through his written words, can achieve. He knew that. To each reader of the sturdily bound volume of his collected plays, he wrote,

When you once get accustomed to my habit of mind, which I was born with and cannot help, you will not find me such bad company. But please do not think you can take in the work of my long lifetime at one reading. You must make it your practice to read all my works at least twice over every year for ten years or so. That is why this edition is so substantially bound for you.[40]

There is fired into Shaw's style (I use the word in its radical sense of an instrument for cutting a mark) something which cuts deep and unforgettably. Cosmic alertness, clear conceptualization, tireless purpose, dialectical cross-examination, arch rapport—all lodge with nascent energy in every word. Shaw's words were "straight as a ray of light," once wrote H. M. Tomlinson, "such as we get once or twice in a few centuries, as the result of passionate morality that happens to be gifted with the complete control of full expression."[41] Through his style, Shaw can rise phoenix-like off the page. Laurence has saved the pages. Laurence and Weintraub point the way to supplant fading memory or to inform the curious and the forgetful.

Except for a compulsive act now and then by spirits kindred to his, the rest is up to Shaw.

Notes

1. Archibald Henderson, *George Bernard Shaw: Man of the Century* (New York: Appleton-Century-Crofts, 1956), p. xiii.
2. Harold Bloom, ed., *Modern Critical Views: George Bernard Shaw* (New York: Chelsea House, 1987), pp. vii, 2, 8, 19, 20.
3. *The Shavian*, 1.1 (1953), 1.
4. *The Shavian*, 1.1 (1953), 2.
5. *The Shavian*, 1.1 (1953), 24.
6. *The Shavian*, 4.7–8 (1973).
7. *The Independent Shavian*, 1.1 (1962), 1.
8. *The Independent Shavian*, 1.2 (1962), 1.
9. *The Independent Shavian*, 17.3 (1979), 1.
10. *The Shaw Bulletin*, 1.1 (1951), 1.
11. Bunyan cited at Shaw's funeral in 1.10 (1956); Mencken's admiration in 2.1 (1957); Henri Bergson's depiction of Shaw's dramatic intelligence in 4.3 (1961); H. G. Wells' iconoclastic persiflage in 6.1 (1963); Frank Swinnerton's witty praise in 7.2 (1964); Yeats' acknowledgment of Shaw's dialectical intensity in 12.2 (1969); Jorge Luis Borges on the power of Shaw's plots in 16.1 (1973); Chesterton on Shaw's encyclopedic intelligence aimed at human improvement in 17.2 (1974); Martin Quinn on the Dickens element in 20.3 (1977); Timothy G. Vesonder on mythical aspects of Shaw's work in 21.2 (1978).
12. See *The Shaw Review*, 3.2 (1960), inside front cover; and *SHAW* 1 (1981), verso of the title page.
13. Daniel Leary, "From Page to Stage to Audience in Shaw," *SHAW*, 3 (1983), 1.

14. Alfred Turco, Jr., "Introduction," *SHAW*, 7 (1987), 3.
15. Rodelle Weintraub, "Introduction," *SHAW*, 5 (1985), 1–4.
16. Charles A. Berst, "In the Beginning: the Poetic Genesis of Shaw's God," *SHAW*, 1 (1981), 6.
17. Ray Bradbury, "GBS and the Loin of Pork," *SHAW*, 2 (1982), 1; Richard F. Dietrich, "Shavian Psychology," *SHAW*, 4 (1984), 149–71; Alan G. Brunger, "Pointe Bernard Shaw—Identification and Naming," *SHAW*, 6 (1986), 1–3; Desmond J. McRory, "Shaw, Einstein and Physics," *SHAW*, 6 (1986), 35, 63–64.
18. Timothy Kidd, "Taking Shaw to the Limit," rev., *Times Higher Education Supplement*, 4 May 1984, p. 26, typifies stunned acclaim: the "scale" is "staggering."
19. II, 854 (E 6); 854 (E 8).
20. Jonathan Swift, *A Tale of a Tub*, eds. A. C. Guthkelch and D. Nichol Smith (Oxford: Clarendon, 1958), p. 10.
21. Weintraub, *Times Literary Supplement*, 18 May 1984, p. 563. David Leary, rev., *The Independent Shavian*, 23.1 (1985), 14, found one omission in 1,058 pages.
22. Slips occur: the "Rubinstein" in the index should not be "Arthur," but "Anton" of the text (I, 558); "Philipp Spitta" does not appear on I, 32. See also Julia Biggs, rev., *Times Higher Education Supplement*, 7 November 1987, p. 15.
23. Shaw bequeathed the diaries to the London School of Economics (I, 1).
24. Michael Holroyd, rev., *The Sunday Times*, 5 October 1986, p. 55.
25. Harold Bloom, *The Anxiety of Influence* (New York: Oxford Univ. Press, 1973), pp. 5–16.
26. Bloom, *Agony*, pp. 11, 5.
27. Hesketh Pearson, *G. B. S. A Full Length Portrait* (1942; Garden City: Garden City Publishing Co., 1946), title page.
28. Daniel Leary, "The State and Future of Shaw Research: The MLA Conference Transcript," *SHAW*, 2 (1982), 187.
29. Dan H. Laurence, *Shaw, Books, and Libraries* (Austin: Humanities Research Center, 1976), p. 13.
30. Allan Chappelow, *Shaw the Villager and Human Being* (London: Charles Skilton Ltd., 1961), p. vii.
31. Arnold Silver, *Bernard Shaw: The Darker Side* (Stanford: Stanford Univ. Press, 1982), pp. 2, 21:
32. Margot Peters, *Bernard Shaw and the Actresses* (Garden City: Doubleday, 1980), pp. xiii–xiv; Peters, "The State and Future of Shaw Research: The MLA Conference Transcript," *SHAW*, 2 (1982), 177–84.
33. Maurice Valency, *The Cart and the Trumpet: The Plays of George Bernard Shaw* (New York: Oxford Univ. Press, 1973), p. 351.
34. Valency, *The Cart and the Trumpet*, p. 351.
35. "Where there is no vision, the people perish." Proverbs 29:18.
36. The comment is imperfectly recalled in Pearson, p. 342.

37. J. L. Wisenthal, *The Marriage of Contraries: Bernard Shaw's Middle Plays* (Cambridge: Harvard Univ. Press, 1974), pp. 57–86; Bernard Shaw, *Prefaces by Bernard Shaw* (London: Constable, 1934), pp. 115, 135, 137.

38. A fierce charge against Arnold Silver, *Bernard Shaw: The Darker Side*, by Alfred Turco, Jr., "Attila, Adolf, and George," rev. in *SHAW*, 4 (1984), 192.

39. Terentianus Maurus, *De Litteris De Syllabis De Metris*, 1. 1286, in Heinrich Keil, ed. *Grammatici Latini* (Hildesheim: Georg Olms, 1961), VI, 363. (According to the whim of the reader, books have their fates.) Professor Charles B. Wheeler once drew my attention to the line; Professor Clarence A. Forbes found its source.

40. Bernard Shaw, *The Complete Plays of Bernard Shaw* (London: Odhams Press Limited, 1937), p. vi.

41. Cited by Michael Holroyd. See, above, note 24.

Studying the Studiers: A History of the History of American Literature

James J. Martine

> Kermit Vanderbilt. *American Literature and the Academy: The Roots, Growth, and Maturity of a Profession*. Philadelphia: University of Pennsylvania Press, 1986. xxii, 609 pp.

The most recent *bon* story making the rounds of academic conferences from Kalamazoo to Santa Cruz and back to Boston asks, "What do you get if you cross a deconstructionist with a *mafioso don*?" The requisite response is, "Someone who makes you an offer you can't understand." Kermit Vanderbilt's book, intelligent, informed, and, best of all, readable, is the perfect antidote to the deconstructionists, reconstructionists, circumcisionists, and other modern attempts to re-revise American literary study. Maybe John Barth was only half right in 1967—we do not have a literature of exhaustion, but we may by now have arrived at a literary study and criticism of exhaustion. Perhaps the remedy is to send contemporary students and readers back to names they do not know but should: names like Samuel Knapp, the Duyckinck brothers, and Van Wyck Brooks. Professor Vanderbilt will serve as a knowledgeable guide.

It is, apparently, time for studies to study themselves. Witness just a few random samples: Robert V. Bruce, *The Launching of Modern American Science, 1846–1876* (New York: Knopf, 1987), an institutional, and not so institutional, history of the American scientific community; Gerald Graff, *Professing Literature: An Institutional History* (Chicago: University of Chicago Press, 1987), a history of academic literary studies in the United States, roughly from the Yale Report of 1828. *Professing Literature* is not as careful or as fully developed as Vanderbilt's volume and not merely because it is 315 pages to Vanderbilt's 609. Graff's book is more pedagogical, philosophical, and polemical than historical. Graff is interested in literary theory rather than history, more interested in the theoretical than the biographical. Graff is disposed to give greater credit to works such as Yvor Winters, *Maule's Curse* (1938) and Leo Marx, *The Machine in the Garden* (1965) than Vanderbilt does. Vanderbilt's book is more historical and biographical. Both books are enjoyable. Graff's is the after-dinner cigar; Vanderbilt's is the meat and potatoes.

All this interest, differences aside, in the record of the *study* of things is suggestive. Perhaps it is time to know once again who Moses Coit Tyler, C. F. Richardson, and Fred Lewis Pattee were and what they contributed. Perhaps it is time to re-evaluate some thematically structured courses in the American college classroom and rediscover the merit of an historical approach. Isn't it important that students know that Emerson and Hemingway were not contemporaries? Isn't it moderately absurd that students of American literature do not know it is significant that Whitman wrote before Allen Ginsberg? Thus, a book like Vanderbilt's is not just interesting and intelligent, it is important.

Vanderbilt is candid about the genesis of this volume. Inspired by the unrest, in reaction to the Vietnam crisis, at the 1968 Modern Language Association convention in New York City, and by the 1969 Denver MLA disturbances, Vanderbilt began the reflections that would eventually lead him to his attempt at an historical perspective on where we are in teaching and scholarship in American literature and how we got there. It is, and Vanderbilt knows it, requisite to remember that the pioneering professors of American literature had every bit as much trouble as, if not more than, present day colleagues would concede, or know about. Tracing the background, birth, and growth of this profession is a fantastic journey, one that has fascinated more than a few of us—and for a long time.

The structure Vanderbilt provides for his history delivers what his subtitle promises. The volume is divided into three "Books." The first, appropriately called "Roots" (pp. 1–240), covers the profession of the study of American literature from its beginnings up to 1921. Book Two (pp. 243–410) is called "Growth" and covers the years *l'entre deux guerres*, 1921–1939. The final major section, Book Three (pp. 413–534), bears the title "Maturity" and covers 1939–1948. There is a brief epilogue (pp. 535–43) pointing to "New Directions." As well, there are three gatherings of photographs of representative American literature scholars, one group of photographs at the conclusion of each "book." It will seem to even the most discriminating eye that the balance of the volume is right—that is, the weight of pages devoted to each section, and chapters within sections, is appropriate.

Moreover, Vanderbilt as an historian of the profession provides a more subtle, unannounced structure. He sees the publication of the *Cambridge History of American Literature* (1917–1921), *The Reinterpretation of American Literature* (1928), and *Literary History of the United States* (1948) as *the* watersheds—indeed they may conveniently be seen so—and he uses these works as principal organizational devices for his material, although he does not neglect major scholarly works by individual authors such as Vernon Parrington, to whom he devotes an entire chapter.

The book is not without apparent flaws. Some questions might be raised about elements of its organization. After Chapter 2: "Organizing the *CHAL* Team," on the "birth" of an academic profession, Vanderbilt returns to earlier scholars and scholarship—the gestation period of a previous century. Chronology, however, is not the only way by which books can be arranged, and the teller must be allowed his tale. Moreover, the chapter clearly demonstrates that Vanderbilt has waded through a mass of correspondence and through Carl Van Doren's journal entries to reconstruct the fabliau of editing the *CHAL*. Vanderbilt's choosing of the publication of *CHAL* from 1917–1921 as *the* occasion needed to bring scholars together to "create the esprit required to create a profession" (p. 3), while convenient and defensible, may give some present-day scholars a moment's pause. No one would deny the significance of the *CHAL* in its time, but to claim that this volume and its compilation "ushered in the distinctive profession of American literature scholarship" (p. 3) seems historically late. It is, however, Vanderbilt's declared intention to write a "biography of an academic profession" (p. xx); once he gets to the biographies and works of individual scholars like William Peterfield Trent, the "story" begins to take shape, and it is an exciting one. All the individual biographies and relationships that go into the larger "biography" of the Academy and American literature are interesting and well written, and the tale as presented by Vanderbilt reads like a great adventure story—which, in a sense, it is. Vanderbilt's section (pp. 471–74) on F. O. Matthiessen as a *teacher* in the classroom is among the most beautiful sections in the book; his brief treatment of Matthiessen's tragic personal life among the most sensitive.

Vanderbilt does have some mildly annoying stylistic quirks. Sometimes he informs his reader of something, then lets it drop. For example, of Trent he writes, "He also possessed a volatile temper" (p. 7), but he never lets the reader see that volatile temper or explains why it was important enough to mention in the first place. Thus what might have been an important detail becomes a gratuitous irrelevance. Likewise, Vanderbilt writes, "The University of Washington welcomed Parrington after he was fired from Oklahoma" (p. 189) without saying here *why* Vernon Parrington was fired. Vanderbilt might have known that when he raises his reader's interest he must be prepared to satisfy it, even if all that is required is adding a phrase or clause such as "of which, more later." For Vanderbilt finally does describe why Parrington was fired by the University of Oklahoma—on page 303, some 114 pages later. If you're going to tell it at all, and if you have judged that your audience does not know the tale, then tell it when first you mention it or beg your reader's patience with some little rhetorical sign. One final example will illustrate: the author whets the reader's interest with "Van Wyck Brooks . . . returned from a personal crisis" (p. 365); then it is not until eight pages later that he writes vaguely of Brooks's emerging from "a four-year breakdown" (p. 373). Vanderbilt might have been better advised to deal with Brooks's "season in hell" at first mention.

In a book this outstanding generally, the smallest stylistic flaws seem, perversely, most annoying. Vanderbilt has another odd habit of repeating things that give his reader a sense of *déjà vu*. Compare the following two passages on Moses Coit Tyler: "Distracting, too, were incidents of faculty unrest at Cornell, compounded by Tyler's intermittently poor health" (p. 93), and "After returning to Cornell, Tyler suffered the disruption of faculty unrest, soon compounded by periods of poor health" (p. 135). What is distracting is that the author mentions it twice and doesn't specify what caused the "incidents of faculty unrest." An academic audience will certainly want to know. Another slight yet distracting redundancy involves Pattee's *A History of American Literature* (1896); Pattee's book, we are told, "finally sold some quarter of a million copies" (p. 133) and "Pattee reported an eventual market of one-quarter million" (p. 175). The footnotes to each cite an identical (and familiar) source. Again, we have H. L. Mencken on Stuart Sherman's quaint "maxim that Puritanism is the official philosophy of America, and that all who dispute it are enemy aliens and should be deported" (p. 212) followed by "Sherman, who had given the younger generation strict warning 'that Puritanism is the lawful philosophy of the country, and that any dissent from it is treason'" (p. 218). Yet again, the prose reproduces itself, this time on a topic dear to the peripatetic professoriate, the annual bacchanalian rite known as the Modern Language Association conference: "The New York meeting in 1942 and the 1943 convention were canceled due to transportation difficulties attending World War II" (p. 425), and "The MLA did not hold an annual meeting during the war years of 1942 and 1943" (p. 490). By the time the reader gets to each of the second passages, he feels like Fonzie on the popular old television sitcom *Happy Days* saying, "I knew that." These *déjà vu* episodes, however, are small matter.

Something else again can be the *handling* of quoted material. Vanderbilt opens Chapter 13 on "A New Era" by quoting Pattee's *Century Readings for a Course in American Literature* (1919). Vanderbilt's quote reads, "The recent manifestation of American patriotism, the new description of Europe of the soul of America, the new insistence upon the teaching" (p. 243) while

Pattee's "Introductory Note" actually reads "The recent manifestation of American patriotism, the new *discovery by* Europe of the soul of America, *and* the new insistence upon the teaching" (italics mine). This kind of irregularity in the handling of quoted material will not seem a serious flaw to a popular audience, and perhaps it is not, but it makes scholars uneasy. A random check of a dozen or so other citations, however, shows the quoted material is *verbatim et literatim*, so the flawed passage may be an editorial aberration.

All in all, these are small concerns in a book this substantial. There are lists and catalogues that include titles of the earliest textbooks and describe the first university and college course offerings in American literature (pp. 32–34); a compendium of the first colleges and professors to offer courses in American literature (pp. 110–11); a listing of the first doctoral dissertations in American literature (p. 128). As the study of American literature grows, Vanderbilt provides statistics, data, percentages which reflect that growth (p. 495), but he is aware of quality as well as quantity. He carefully traces the campaign for the development of a national literature year by year from the earliest decades of the nineteenth century. These sections include observations on the contributions of William Cullen Bryant, Washington Irving, and James Kirke Paulding. The author identifies noteworthy contributions to the early polemics over literary nationalism by Noah Webster, John Greenleaf Whittier, and William Ellery Channing leading up to the culmination of Emerson's much-celebrated oration on 31 August 1837 at Harvard. These may have little to do with "the Academy" of the book's title, but readers, even those familiar with this part of the story of the development of American literature, will remain interested. Vanderbilt's prose style is hardly riveting, but he has done a great deal of work in his research and done it well, and the story itself is compelling. This is a story worth telling. It is a story worth knowing. Vanderbilt has gathered a great part of it into a single volume, a volume worth owning.

After several crowded chapters devoted to Rufus Griswold, the Duyckincks, and American literary controversies, Vanderbilt returns in Chapter 6 to the academy and the pioneering efforts of Moses Coit Tyler, a scholar he calls the "founding father of our scholarly profession" (p. 81) and "the Homer of our literary history" (p. 93). There are, as well, interesting chapters on C. F. Richardson and Barrett Wendell, although later it will occur to some readers that Vanderbilt relies too heavily on the *CHAL* for the shape of the first part of his book. For a volume presented as a "biography of our profession," much of the weight is devoted to the history of published histories of American literature, and Vanderbilt makes the publication of Volume One of the *CHAL* a publishing event somewhere in importance between the signing of the Magna Carta and Moses' descent from Mount Sinai with the stone tablets, although, in truth, one must allow that Vanderbilt is fully cognizant of, and treats fairly, the problems with that volume, especially those created by the presence of multiple authors who were not always in concert (the schizophrenic effect, for example, of Paul Elmer More's chapter on Emerson following the chapter on "Transcendentalism" by Harold C. Goddard, who was far more enthusiastic about Emersonian "liberation" than More).

If Vanderbilt devotes perhaps too much space to the *CHAL*, he gives six chapters, nearly 100 pages (or almost twenty percent of his text), over to the *LHUS*, yet some of the material is wonderful. Chapter 22, for instance, is a thickly gossipy chapter about the problems and politics that preceded and went into the creation of the *LHUS*, as much fun to read as a novel of international espionage. Vanderbilt, an impeccable historian, does not take sides in the disputatious, internecine, and *in camera* wrangling among the members of the scholarly brotherhood (then almost exclusively male). There are no bad guys and good guys here. They are all good guys—although some are clearly gooder than others. Throughout the volume, one of the most respected Americanists, Robert E. Spiller, who, along with Louis Budd and Warner Berthoff, read Vanderbilt's entire manuscript and made suggestions and corrections (an advantage for any scholar), is in all the battles clearly the legitimate heir to the throne as boss American literary historian. No one today would disagree. Chapter 21 contains meaty descriptions of the battles (political) between the MLA and the then American Literature Group (ALG).

A present-day American literature scholar will find prescient a 1930s Jay B. Hubbell letter to Spiller insisting that ALG should be a separate organization. Some Americanists still feel that perhaps now is the time to pull away from the bloated MLA which each year looks more and more like a huge gas-filled bladder floating in the Macy's Thanksgiving parade.

The book can as well be suggestive: Vanderbilt raises interesting questions about graduate study requirements for the Ph.D. in American literature—in the light of recommendations of a blue-ribbon panel of "name" scholars as early as 1926, although he acknowledges that "intramural political realities had to be faced" (p. 264). Moreover, he examines the logic of the separate American literature department, a recommendation first made more than fifty years ago.

It is clear throughout that Vanderbilt has made heavy and good use of the Hubbell Center at Duke University and of scholarly collections elsewhere. There are forty pages of notes and a usable index. In his text, all the advocates get their turn in turn. He treats fairly four leftist histories written during the Depression. Russell Blankenship, V. F. Calverton, Granville Hicks, and Bernard Smith all are established at various degrees portside on the political compass. Hicks is particularly remembered here because he lost jobs at both Smith and Rensselaer because of his economic and social beliefs.

As well, other advocates of various stripe are treated objectively and intelligently: Humanists, Agrarians, Freudians, and Nationalists. Vanderbilt demonstrates an impressive breadth of reading and an historian's ability to synthesize apparently disparate elements, movements, and schools of thought. Inevitably his scholarly method is to follow his own *précis* and evaluation of major works with a representative selection of contemporary critical reactions to them—that is, after having his say about the genesis of a book and its content, he always includes a sampling of reviews and the reactions of others on the occasion of publication; Vanderbilt does, moreover, provide his reader with the long view as well. For example, after listing the praise by Spiller, Howard Mumford Jones, Matthiessen, and others for Alfred Kazin's *On Native Grounds* in 1942, Vanderbilt identifies the book's more obvious deficiencies apparent to an audience of the 1980s.

Vanderbilt has, in addition, collected not-so-well-remembered episodes; he has a nice historical eye for the ironic and demonstrates it several times. For example, he recounts how it was that John Macy, socialist and anti-academic critic, should die in the midst of a series of lectures on the rebellious nature of American literature—delivered not on a college campus but to trade-union workers at Unity House, Stroudsburg, Pennsylvania. Furthermore, he concludes the long story of the making and reception of the *CHAL* with a retelling of an interesting if little-recalled episode involving the censorship of an American scholar; the episode became the center of a controversy that eventually made the front page of the *New York Times*. It concerned Woodridge Riley's original essay for the *CHAL* on Mrs. Eddy, Christian Scientists, and the Mormons. It is a pithy tale.

Chapter 11 is clearly one of the liveliest chapters in the book and this is so, in part, because the subject matter is lively. It is also true that when one quotes enough H. L. Mencken, the prose pace accelerates and the narrative inevitably becomes more readable. This chapter explores "the larger cultural debate of the second decade of this century" (p. 183), the insurgent critics versus "the professors."

Perhaps this book should be required reading for all young Ph.D.s about to enter the "profession" of teaching, and doing research in, American literature. That way, they would know (at least) who were the great players, the Babe Ruths, Mel Otts, and Cy Youngs in their chosen field and who were the Bob Ueckers and Buddy Biancalanas. It is wonderful to have retold the celebrated events of the past—the war between the academics and the critics who did not have a university affiliation. The American literature scholars were barely comfortable in their battle against academic colleagues antagonistic to American literature when a new front of hostility opened, with large shells lobbed in by Van Wyck Brooks, John Macy, Randolph Bourne, Waldo Frank, and the ol' disturber of the peace himself, H. L. Mencken. It is a story one generation of Americanists should tell to the next around a campfire. Since we cannot, it is handy that Kermit

Vanderbilt tells it and tells it well. The old soldiers will enjoy his tale every bit as much as will the new recruits.

Chapter 16 describes the inevitable and necessary establishment of an official journal, *American Literature*, yet the chapter also illustrates how the old-boy network came into being and how it operated; the chapter provides a keen view of the privileges secured by rank and seniority, by friendly reviewers, and by strategic maneuvering and infighting on the professional scene from the 1920s on. What makes it all so much fun to read is that the names of the players shimmer and gleam. These are the stars in the American Literary Scholarship Hall of Fame. It turns out that Richard Ohmann and Louis Kampf did not invent politics. It is just that the early generations played a different sort and were very good at it.

On a higher plane and a more serious level, Vanderbilt's book portrays the intellectual curiosity, profound insight, remarkable judgment, and just plain hard work of generations of critics and scholars. Further, it makes clear that the call for an aesthetic approach, the "careful and intelligent reading of the literature itself" (p. 282), must precede the techniques and principles of *explication de texte*. There is a true development in the study of American literature. This book stands as a tribute to the scholars who have gone before us. As in building a house, the foundations must be laid by the masons before the craftsmen can place the cornices.

It is a commonplace, but a justifiable one, to conclude comments on a book of this caliber by saying that it is a must for all libraries, all Americanists, and anyone interested in American literature. The book is significant enough and well enough produced to serve scholarly investigators and researchers for years. It will best serve those who read it, for pleasure, straight through, especially if the reader professes to the professoriate of that literature.

Crisis and Conversion in Jewish-American Literature

Andrew Gordon

Mark Shechner. *After the Revolution: Studies in the Contemporary Jewish-American Imagination*. Bloomington: Indiana University Press, 1987. ix, 261 pp.

The paradox of contemporary Jewish-American literature is that the Jews made it in American life and culture even as their Jewishness seemed to be disappearing. Many critics have commented on this paradox, although Leslie Fiedler was one of the first to point it out, in his 1964 essay, "Zion as Main Street": "The very notion of a Jewish-American literature represents a dream of assimilation, and the process it envisages is bound to move toward a triumph (in terms of personal success) which is also a defeat (in terms of meaningful Jewish survival)."[1] The title of a 1971 book by Allen Guttmann tells the story: *The Jewish Writer in America: Assimilation and the Crisis of Identity*. According to Guttmann, Jews had assimilated into American society so well that they were in danger of vanishing. The writers were chroniclers of that successful process of Americanization and secularization.

Today, it is taken for granted that the assimilation of the Jews into America is over and that the "crisis" of Jewish-American identity has ended. The Jews have not vanished. Most American Jews feel comfortable with their hyphenated identity, and some are even rediscovering their Jewish heritage. But that also means that the historical moment of the ascendancy of the Jews in American culture has passed. While authors such as Saul Bellow or Philip Roth are still undeniably *major* figures, they no longer seem quite so *central*; other minorities, such as black women, are now having their moment in the literary limelight. Therefore, criticism of Jewish-American literature or culture no longer has the same immediacy or urgency that it did in the 1950s and 60s, and tends to take on a historical cast. The remarkable success story of the Jews in America is celebrated in nostalgic histories like Irving Howe's *World of Our Fathers* and sociological studies like Charles E. Silberman's *A Certain People*.

Now that an era is past or passing, it is certainly the time for retrospective studies of the great achievements of twentieth-century Jewish-American writers. The focus of some recent books is not only on how Jewish writers became Americanized but on how they affected American literature and American identity in the process, and on what was left on the end that could still be called "Jewish." One difficulty that all of these books face is that there is still no general agreement on whether "Jewish" refers to a religion, a people, a culture, a way of life, or some combination of these elements. Murray Baumgarten's comparative study, *City Scriptures: Modern Jewish Writing*, argues that modern Jewish writing—not just Jewish-American literature—centers on one informing myth of the Jew moving from the tribal realm of the *shtetl* (village) into the freedom and complexity of the city. Baumgarten classifies the fictional protagonists as either freethinkers, who validate the new at the expense of the old, or critical thinkers, who invent ways of bringing traditional values into the modern world. Sam Girgus's *The New Covenant: Jewish Writers and the American Idea* discusses how Jewish history was transformed by the idea of America as a counter to the various forms of oppression of Europe. Jewish-American writers often led the effort to make the idea of America relevant to an urban, industrial age, and contemporary Jewish intellectuals have taken upon themselves the task of explaining America to herself. Even as they reinvented Jewish identity in America, Jewish-American writers helped to reinvent American identity.

The debate still continues about Jewish-American literary responses to the holocaust. Dorothy Seidman Bilik argues in *Immigrant-Survivors* that the Holocaust has inspired renewed interest in the Jewish past, as evidenced by the appearance of immigrant characters in Jewish-American fiction since 1957. And R. Barbara Gitenstein in *Apocalyptic Messianism* claims that the mystical works of the *kabbalah* have influenced the response of contemporary Jewish-American poets to the Holocaust. However, Alan C. Berger in *Crisis and Covenant* finds most contemporary Jewish-American fiction writers theologically ignorant or indifferent to covenant Judaism; therefore, most of their Holocaust fiction is "a spurious literary response to the *Shoah*."[2]

But the most original of the recent studies of Jewish-American literature is the book on which I will focus, Mark Shechner's *After the Revolution: Studies in the Contemporary Jewish-American Imagination*. Shechner's book is a lively, witty, learned work of intellectual history about the "crisis and conversion" of Jewish-American writers who abandoned Marxism and in the post-WWII era found a radical substitute for it in psychoanalysis (p. 4). Shechner focuses on the "non-Jewish Jew," the restless thinker "who is the inventor of the Jewish imagination in our time" (pp. 12,13). In particular, he deals with writers born between 1915 and 1926, offering chapters on Saul Bellow (b. 1915), Isaac Rosenfeld (b. 1918), Norman Mailer (b. 1923), and Allen Ginsberg (b. 1926), and glances at others of the same generation of New York Jewish intellectuals, including Delmore Schwartz, Arthur Miller, Paul Goodman, Alfred Kazin, Irving Howe, and Leslie Fiedler. The exceptions are his chapters on Lionel Trilling (b. 1905) and Philip Roth (b. 1933), whom he takes as, respectively, *paterfamilias* and prodigal son to this generation of writers.

What this generation had in common was a shattering experience of conversion: disillusioned with Marxism, which had been their "substitute Judaism" (p. 8), they were forced not only to change their politics and their culture but also to remake themselves. In the 1940s, Jewish writers began to have a major impact on American letters by focussing on certain obsessive and interrelated themes: "*alienation, anticommunism, modernism,* and *therapy*" (p. 10). Therapy provided a remedy for alienation at the same time that it validated alienation as the normal human condition in what was perceived as the sick and disorienting postwar era. Psychoanalysis also gave these writers a radically skeptical, flexible point of view which never rigidified into an ideology like Marxism.

Shechner's book is both engaging intellectual history and

sharp literary criticism. He places this generation of Jewish-American writers in the context of the intellectual politics of their time ("It is sometimes hard to tell the Jewish literary scene from gang warfare" [p. 3]) and he assesses their careers. As the subtitle *Studies in the Contemporary Jewish-American Imagination* suggests, he shows the creative uses to which the writers put the materials at their disposal, how they responded imaginatively to the personal, political, and intellectual crises of their era. He focuses in particular on the politics, sexual politics (Freudian or Reichian), relation to psychoanalysis, and relation to Judaism of each writer.

Although Shechner admirably documents the "crisis and conversion" of a group of Jewish-American writers, I had some reservations about his larger conclusions. First, his selection of writers is narrow, primarily *Partisan Review* alumni, and includes no women. Some major New York writers, such as Malamud and Heller, are omitted. Second, he needs to test his thesis against these Jewish writers' WASP contemporaries: is this process of conversion from Marxism to psychoanalysis a peculiarly or exclusively Jewish phenomenon? Or is it a more widespread process which took on a "Jewish" coloring among these groups of writers? For example, the careers of non-Jewish writers of the same generation, such as Ralph Ellison and Robert Lowell, suggest a similar trajectory away from Marxism and towards psychoanalysis. *Invisible Man* is also about "alienation, anticommunism, modernism, and therapy." In other words, although he makes some frequently brilliant observations, Shechner may not have fully accounted for the phenomenal rise of Jewish-American writers to a central role in American culture in the post-WWII period.

His title, *After the Revolution*, echoes Robert Alter's *After the Tradition: Essays on Modern Jewish Writing*, and Shechner seems to have learned from Alter. As Alter writes, "One cannot . . . discount the possibility that some essentially Jewish qualities may adhere to the writing of the most thoroughly acculturated Jews . . . certain modes of imagination or general orientations toward art and experience that seem characteristically Jewish, even where the writer scrupulously avoids all references to his ethnic origins."[3]

Unlike Alter's, however, Shechner's critical approach is strongly (although not exclusively) grounded in psychoanalysis, so that he is not only interested in the Jewishness but also alert to the characteristic moods and defenses of each writer. Shechner is a supple psychoanalytic critic, like Isaac Rosenfeld, who "never fully subordinated his exquisite discriminations to Reich's clumsy diagnostic machinery" (p. 110). Nevertheless, I eventually grew tired of the repetition of such terms as "therapeutic," "symptomatic," and "diagnostic," because they tended to turn these very different writers into the same *kind* of writer: a clinician of his own emotions, writing semi-autobiography as self-therapy. That may indeed be a part of what they (or any group of contemporary writers) are doing, but it is not necessarily the best or the only part.

Shechner considers the Jew in Isaac Rosenfeld's familiar term: "the specialist in alienation" (p. 14). As has often been pointed out, Jewish-American intellectuals suffered a double alienation, "first *as* Jews, second *from* Jews" (p. 16). Because young Jewish intellectuals felt so rootless, they found a shared identity in the experiences of their generation: Marxism in the 1930s and alienation in the 1940s. Today, however, Jewish writers are no longer disaffected, and alienation now "strikes us as anachronism, a relic of a more sentimental age" (p. 22). This progress has meant an imaginative loss.

When the Jewish writer first took center stage in American literature, he did so by divorcing himself from the Jewish middle class, emphasizing not continuity but discontinuity, loss of traditional culture and beliefs, and alienation. This is a point that Alter emphasizes: how is the Jewish writer to create a tradition "when most of the grounds for continuity have been cut away"?[4] Shechner's answer is that in the 1940s, Jewish-American intellectuals made the concept of alienation central to their own and to American thought, importing ideas from European existentialism. The new hero of the late 40s was not a traditional American optimist but an alienated loser like Arthur Miller's Willy Loman.

All of the major Jewish-American writers of the late 40s and 50s "strike the familiar note of isolation and drift" and sing "the Jewish blues" (p. 29). But their lament over the Holocaust and over their own alienation from America was also a celebration. Paradoxically, the crisis had released their creative energies.

Although the Jewish intellectuals broke with their middle-class origins, it was never a total break: even as they turned inward to become alienated modernists, they still paid attention to the social world. They could never entirely forget the lessons of the ghetto, the Depression, and Marxism. The novel, not poetry, attracted them because its "drama of class conflict" reflected their experience as Jewish-Americans (p. 48). Thus, even as they embraced modernism, they still loved nineteenth-century realism. Shechner makes a useful distinction: Jewish-American intellectuals are an intelligentsia, not an avant garde, and they remain devoted to questions of reason and social justice that strike most of the avant garde as irrelevant or hopelessly bourgeois.

Among the Jewish writers of the 1940s, only Delmore Schwartz was a pure modernist, uninterested in politics. Shechner sees Schwartz as a writer of grandiose ambitions and minor achievements, a tragic warning figure. He argues that Schwartz's work failed because Schwartz was not Jewish enough: "Lacking the leaded keel of a traditional culture, he adopted poetry as a surrogate culture" (p. 51). His argument resembles Irving Howe's claim that Philip Roth's fiction is unsatisfactory because it comes out of a "thin personal culture."[5] But there is some evidence to counter such a claim about Schwartz, who once said that being the child of Jewish immigrants was for him "a matter of naive and innocent pride" and that "the fact of Jewishness has been nothing but an ever-growing good to me, a fruitful and inexhaustible inheritance."[6]

Shechner goes on to argue more persuasively that disillusioned ex-Marxists flocked to psychoanalysis in droves in the postwar era, in search of a replacement grand theory. Psychoanalysis made the ambivalent neurotic into a modern hero and put writers in touch with all the neurotic protagonists of modernist literature. Freudianism could be put to many different political uses because there were two different Freuds: sometimes "affirmative and liberal," other times "disconsolate and conservative" (p. 63).

One use to which psychoanalytic liberalism could be put is illustrated in Shechner's chapter on "The Case of Lionel Trilling." Trilling's cure for the "disease" of modern life and culture was psychoanalysis and the novel. But his own novel is too removed from social reality and therefore smells of "the seminar room" (p. 81). Although Shechner admires some aspects of Trilling's criticism, he finds him politically wrongheaded; whereas Delmore Schwartz damaged only himself by divorcing himself from social reality, Trilling damaged the liberal tradition in the 1950s. Trilling wanted an art and a politics of dignified sensibility and balance, but only helped make liberalism politically irrelevant, "without a program of reform" (p. 90).

In contrast to Freudian liberalism is the psychoanalytic radicalism of the writers who followed Wilhelm Reich. Leslie Fiedler in *Waiting for the End* pointed out the appeal to many Jewish writers in the 1950s of Reich, "one-time brilliant exponent of Freudian insights, and later independent *magus* and healer, who taught that through full genitality man could conquer the ills of the flesh and the corruptions of society."[7] Critics have since detailed the influence of Reich on certain novelists, but Shechner's treatment is the most comprehensive so far, until someone devotes an entire book to Reich's impact on Jewish-American and Beat writers.[8] As Shechner explains, Reich seemed to promise disillusioned intellectuals in the 1940s and 50s that you could abandon the tedium of conventional politics; all you had to do was get laid, which became a socially and politically significant act. Reichianism was a very American sort of therapy: it was pragmatic, offered self-help, and could be done at home. Reichianism was particularly appealing to writers because it promised to free the imagination. Some 50s writers, attracted by "a certain romance of violence," tried to liberate themselves by turning against the superego as they had formerly railed against the bourgeoisie (p. 100). Among those Jewish-American writers influenced by Reich were Goodman, Ginsberg, Mailer, Bellow, and Rosenfeld.

Isaac Rosenfeld was perhaps the most zealous convert to Reichianism; Reich became his substitute for Marx. He wanted a "literature grounded in conflict, alienation, and neurosis," true to his own inner torments (p. 107). As a critic he championed Reichian standards—the release of feelings—but, ironically, his own fiction is mannered. When Jewish intellectuals joined the Establishment in the 1950s, Rosenfeld remained alienated. He was an unstable personality, a manic-depressive, attracted in his manic phases to Reichianism and later to Hasidism. He began as a hedonist and ended as a monk. Shechner claims, "Rosenfeld fashioned himself into the last ghetto Jew" (p. 120). But this claim seems unconvincing, since it is unclear whether Rosenfeld's problem was in his identity as a Jewish-American or in his personal neurosis. It is difficult to prove that in his self-denial Rosenfeld was simply imitating a "ghetto Jew."

Shechner's chapters on Bellow and Roth are the longest and best in the book; unquestionably these are the writers to whom he responds most strongly. He is put off by Trilling's "squeamishness" and "fussiness" (p. 89) and appalled by Rosenfeld's self-destructive survivor guilt; he dislikes Schwartz and Mailer for apparently cutting themselves off from their Jewish roots; he is disappointed by Ginsberg's authoritarianism. However, he is deeply attracted by the personalities and the range and style of both Bellow and Roth: Bellow's "variousness and possibility" (p. 158) and Roth's "volatility" and "continuing invention" (p. 238).

Bellow he categorizes as a writer of "fiction of character," like Dickens, interested in mental causes but more intrigued by social behavior (p. 121). From Reich, Bellow got a psychology similar to Ben Jonson's psychology of humors, a way of classifying personality types by physical appearance. Shechner calls a Bellow "a diagnostic novelist specializing in the diseases of civilization and the distortions of the emotional life that underlie them" (p. 123). Although Goodman, Mailer, Ginsberg, and Kerouac also followed Reich in the 50s, Bellow did not share their revolutionary social program; he was more interested in reforming the individual. Bellow uses Reich in an ironic, comic way in his fiction in the 1950s, but his heroes' quests for personal liberation are deadly serious. The Bellow hero wants desperately to live but doesn't know how; Bellow's "great theme has been the pain of achieving emotional clarity" (p. 124). Because his works depend on a therapeutic morality, at their worst they can be tedious and smug. His heroes "are typically most endearing when they are sunk in troubles and least believable when they appear to be working things out" (p. 124). Shechner's major insight is to notice the manic-depressive cycles in Bellow's novels: typically, after a manic novel such as *Augie March* (1953) comes a depressive one like *Seize the Day* (1956). He sees in Bellow's style "a classic depressive's aesthetic" (p. 126).

He also traces the influence of Reich in *Seize the Day* (1956), which ends in a therapeutic moment for the hero, as he breaks down weeping, and in *Henderson the Rain King* (1959), a "comic farewell to Reich" (p. 134). Shechner astutely observes that there is something in Reichian therapy alien to the "spirit" of novels, which are more concerned with social relationships and character than with releasing repressed psychosexual energy (p. 138). Shechner ranks *Herzog* (1964) as Bellow's best work, a fable of psychoanalytic regeneration which succeeds both as psychological novel and novel of manners. But he deplores *Mr. Sammler's Planet* (1970) and *The Dean's December* (1981) as mere polemics, and believes that the "main line of Bellow's vitalism" is in the comedy of novels like *Humboldt's Gift* (p. 149). As the manic-depressive cycles of his fiction continue, Bellow remains an elusive, changeable writer who tries to give his changing moods "image, form, and stories to tell" (p. 158). He continues to be capable of surprising us with new work because he remains perpetually skeptical about all solutions, including his own.

Shechner's treatment of Bellow is admirable, but perhaps a bit too schematic in its dichotomies: he sees manic novels alternating with depressive ones, and comic novels with polemical ones. Bellow himself thinks *Seize the Day* is a comedy; he was disappointed that the film version of the novel was not very funny. And Shechner dismisses *Sammler* and *Dean's December* as "potboilers" (p. 154), anomalies in Bellow's career. Perhaps they might instead be considered as part of the main line of Bellow's development, for the manic always fights with the depressive within his fiction, and the comedy is often polemical. Bellow's most memorable comic creations are eccentric and preachy cranks like Tamkin, Dahfu, and Humboldt, but that may be because Bellow himself is also something of a crank. Thus the same impulse that leads him to create these comic figures can also lead him into tedious diatribes.

Shechner next analyzes how Norman Mailer turned the therapeutic to revolutionary ends in *Advertisements for Myself* (1959). With this book, Mailer transformed himself from a Marxist novelist into a sexologue calling for a sexual revolution inspired in part by Wilhelm Reich. According to Shechner, Mailer's "White Negro" was an "enabling myth" which liberated Mailer and his writing and also prefigured the explosions of the 1960s (p. 178).

Many critics, myself included, have referred to the "White Negro" as a mythical figure or traced the influence of Reich on Mailer.[9] Schechner's achievement is to shift the focus onto Mailer's personal sexual politics and to argue the driven, desperate character of *Advertisements*. The "White Negro," as he correctly points out, was not simply a myth but also the beginning of the automythology by which Mailer has ruled his career ever since. After feeling impotent and irrelevant on the literary scene throughout the 1950s, Mailer faced a choice of either collapsing or reinventing himself. However, I wish that Shechner had treated Mailer in greater depth; whereas he discusses the entire careers of the other writers, he limits himself to Mailer in the 1950s, admittedly an important transitional phase in Mailer's career, but one which has already been exhaustively covered by both critics and biographers.[10]

After Mailer, Shechner considers another psychoanalytic revolutionary, Allen Ginsberg; like Mailer, Ginsberg remade himself and created and lived his own myth. For me, this is his least successful chapter. Shechner is concerned primarily not with Ginsberg the poet but Ginsberg the public figure, the culture hero who had great moral authority in the 1960s peace movement and promoted a politics of imagination and play. Shechner follows with disillusionment Ginsberg's evolution from Marxism to Reichianism to a sort of "Buddhist fascism." Shechner too easily dismisses Ginsberg's poetry by saying that Ginsberg is no

Whitman. Although it is true that Ginsberg has done nothing comparable in scope and power to *Leaves of Grass* and that Ginsberg's influence has waned, nonetheless he was a major poet and a major influence not simply on countercultural politics but also on American poetry in the 1950s and 60s. *Howl, Kaddish*, and a handful of his shorter poems were breakthroughs for the form, style, and subject matter of American verse in his time. Moreover, for Shechner to record his political disillusionment with Ginsberg is not to say anything particularly new, since the episode on which he focuses—Ginsberg's subordination in the 1970s to the autocratic Buddhist guru Trungpa—has been widely written about. As Shechner admits, Ginsberg's life has been as meticulously documented as the life of a saint, so that those who care to know are well aware by now of his lapses from grace. Although Shechner is good at analyzing Ginsberg as a "hero for the therapeutic age" (p. 187), his disillusionment with the poet shows that he may once have too readily accepted Ginsberg's myth of himself. Shechner's disappointing conclusion is that the hero and saint is just a fallible human being after all.

Shechner sees Philip Roth as another writer who, like Mailer and Ginsberg, has created his own myth, one with two phases: "The myth of the man in the trap and that of the man who got away" (p. 197). He interprets Roth as a "clinician of his own experience" who has adopted Freudian myths to his own purposes (p. 197). Roth is in truth a "son of the New York intellectuals themselves"; he came up through the same journals they wrote for and was influenced by Isaac Rosenfeld and the *Partisan Review* checklist of modernist writers. But the late 60s "culture of desublimation" finally gave Roth license to rebel against his literary fathers (p. 206). Roth has always seen himself as a Jewish son plagued by a weak father. In his fiction, most relationships are pitched battles; the child wars against the parents but can never grow up to become a parent himself. Shechner compares Roth to Hawthorne for sustained self-analysis, except that Roth has the advantage of knowing Kafka and Freud! This is high praise indeed, and may help to counter some of the critics who put down Roth for his supposedly narcissistic self-absorption.

Roth's early novels are about repressed heroes whose only release is the temper tantrum. *Portnoy's Complaint*, in 1969, is his "emotional breakthrough," but the novels after it testify to "the return of the repressed" (p. 209). *Portnoy* is "the most spectacular instance of Freudian fiction in postwar American literature" (p. 210). *My Life as a Man* (1974), although not as spontaneous as *Portnoy*, is more profound. Roth now begins to contradict *Portnoy*: the mother is not to blame for all the son's problems. This novel questions all explanations, including those of psychoanalysis. *The Professor of Desire* (1977) is a "convalescence novel" about the regenerative power of love, but sweetness is not Roth's strong suit. He is at his best as a novelist of "incipient panic" (p. 225).

Roth's novels are not exactly autobiography but "fables of identity" (p. 225) about the forms of martyrdom, the traps one can fall into. The critical attacks on Roth, such as Irving Howe's, play into his "sense of martyrdom" (p. 226). Sometimes Roth fights back against his critics, but other times he placates them with a restrained, civilized novel like *The Ghost Writer* (1979). However, that means putting "his gift for mad improvisation into escrow" (p. 227). Although Roth tries to create the public persona of a sane, civilized writer, the real power of his fiction comes from exposing "the hidden, the recessive, the shameful" (p. 236). He is an unsettled artist whose volatility gives "promise of his continuing invention" (p. 238). The recent publication of Roth's novel *The Counterlife* would seem to bear out Shechner's prediction.

Shechner's chapter on Roth is a valuable reassessment of the career of a major writer who has often been unfairly attacked, denigrated, or underestimated. Although I agree in general with what Shechner says about Roth, I cannot entirely agree with all of his judgments on particular works. For example, if Roth's "gift for mad improvisation" is one of his greatest talents, then what went haywire with such mad improvisations as *The Breast, Our Gang*, and the *Great American Novel*? I would also rank *The Ghost Writer* much higher in the list of Roth's achievements. Roth isn't placating the critics here; on the contrary, the young narrator Nathan Zuckerman is incensed by the philistine Judge Wapter, who attacks his fiction. Moreover, the contrast between the two writers, the repressed Lonoff and the turbulent Zuckerman, successfully embodies the struggle between Roth's opposing tendencies as novelist (the "paleface" versus the "redskin"). And Roth certainly exercises his gift for mad improvisation in Zuckerman's elaborate fantasy about Anne Frank.

In his conclusion, Shechner writes that the decline of American Marxism paradoxically "released geysers of creative and intellectual power" in disillusioned Jewish-American writers (p. 239). These "non-Jewish Jews" wrote dynamically because of their "divided allegiance" (p. 241). What distinguished their generation was their conversion from Jews to Americans and from Marxist radicals to convalescents. For a time, Wilhelm Reich provided the radical therapy many of them needed to change their lives and their writing. But in middle age, this group of "ambivalent converts" returned to Judaism in odd ways: Trilling as a Victorian rabbi, Ginsberg as "a Buddhist rebbe" (p. 241), Roth as "the spiritual stepchild of Franz Kafka" (p. 242), and so on. Despite their many conversions, they remain "unmistakably Jewish" (p. 242). This conclusion is reminiscent of Robert Alter's assertion that even in thoroughly acculturated Jews, there remain "certain modes of imagination . . . that seem characteristically Jewish." Such a proposition may sound vague or debatable to many, but perhaps it is the best we can do with a term so elusive and multifarious as "Jewish."

Few recent critical works are such a pleasure to read as *After the Revolution*: the prose is lucid, witty, and at times positively elegant. Mark Shechner has a talent for coining memorable, epigrammatic phrases. My only quibble is that he can sometimes be compulsively or distractingly witty—a lit-crit version of S. J. Perelman. What I want most to emphasize is that *After the Revolution* is an extremely valuable contribution to the study of Jewish-American literature and postwar intellectual history. Although, as I mentioned, I am not entirely persuaded that this process of painful "conversion" is exclusively the province of Jewish-American writers, nevertheless Shechner links a generation of writers in new and interesting ways. His treatments of the less critically discussed writers Lionel Trilling and Isaac Rosenfeld are knowledgeable and judicious. The chapters on Saul Bellow and Philip Roth are brilliant and incisive, indispensable for any critic of these two major writers.

Shechner calls Bellow's *Henderson the Rain King* an affectionate farewell to Reich, both an homage and a spoof. *After the Revolution* too is a witty and tender homage to the writers on whom Shechner comments, for he writes out of a personal engagement with his subject matter. Shechner sees these writers as ambivalent Jewish sons in exile, trying to make a home for themselves in American life and culture. But they are also his literary fathers, and in criticizing them he is implicitly re-evaluating himself and his own experience of "crisis and conversion," his skeptical involvement with Judaism, leftist politics, and psychoanalysis. He is trying, as we all do, to locate or to create the father he needs. Judging from the qualities he admires or rejects in the various authors he discusses, the composite father figure who emerges from his book would be a writer somewhat similar to Shechner himself: humane, warm, wry, skeptical, and a *mensch*. No wonder, then, that he is so attracted to Bellow and Roth: these are not bad models for a Jewish son to follow.

Notes

1. Leslie Fiedler, *Waiting for the End* (New York: Dell, 1965), p. 70.
2. Bilik, *Immigrant-Survivors* (Middletown: Wesleyan Univ. Press, 1981); Gitenstein, *Apocalyptic Messianism and Contemporary Jewish-American Poetry* (Albany: State Univ. of New York Press, 1986); Alan L. Berger, *Crisis and Covenant: The Holocaust in American Jewish Fiction* (Albany: State Univ. of New York Press, 1985), p. 13.
3. Robert Alter, *After the Tradition: Essays on Modern Jewish Writing* (New York: Dutton, 1969), p. 18.
4. Ibid., pp. 10–11.
5. Irving Howe, "Philip Roth Reconsidered," reprinted in *Critical Essays on Philip Roth*, ed. Sanford Pinsker (Boston: G. K. Hall, 1982), p. 236.
6. Quoted in James Atlas, *Delmore Schwartz: The Life of an American Poet* (New York: Avon, 1977), p. 20.
7. Fiedler, p. 93.
8. See, for example, Eusebio Rodrigues, *Quest for the Human: An Exploration of Saul Bellow's Fiction* (Lewisburg: Bucknell Univ. Press, 1981), and Andrew

Gordon, *An American Dreamer: A Psychoanalytic Study of the Fiction of Norman Mailer* (Cranbury, N.J.: Fairleigh Dickinson Univ. Press/Associated Univ. Presses, 1980).

9. On Mailer's "White Negro" as myth, see, for example, Robert Solotaroff, *Down Mailer's Way* (Urbana: Univ. of Illinois, 1974), p. 92; Laura Adams, *Existential Battles: The Growth of Norman Mailer* (Athens, Ohio: Ohio Univ. Press, 1976), p. 59; Jean Radford, *Norman Mailer: A Critical Study* (New York: Harper, 1975), p. 92, and my *An American Dreamer*, p. 42.

10. For a discussion of Mailer's career in the 1950s, see the abovementioned books by Solotaroff, Adams, Radford, and myself, among others, and two recent biographies: Hilary Mills, *Mailer: A Biography* (New York: Empire, 1982), and Peter Manso, *Mailer: His Life and Times* (New York: Simon and Schuster, 1985).

Jacobitism and Alexander Pope

Vincent Carretta

Douglas Brooks-Davies. *Pope's* Dunciad *and the Queen of Night: A Study in Emotional Jacobitism*. Manchester: Manchester University Press, 1985. x, 190 pp.

Was Pope a Jacobite? That is, did he believe that James II (*Jacobus* in New Latin) and his descendants were the de jure monarchs of England and later Great Britain (after the Union of 1707) because their claim to the throne was based on divine right and therefore indefeasible? Did he believe that William III and his eventual Hanoverian successors were illegitimate, merely de facto, rulers? Brooks-Davies's valuable study to a large extent begs these questions, as if the answers are no longer in doubt. On a personal level, as Maynard Mack points out in *Alexander Pope: a Life* (1986), Pope's Jacobitism will probably never be known, but his public actions and statements make him an unlikely candidate for the label.

During the last decade some scholars, most notably John Aden in *Pope's Once and Future Kings* (1978) and Howard Erskine-Hill in several essays, have returned to one of the earliest critical approaches to Pope's works—reading them in light of his alleged Jacobitism. What had been the basis for accusation in John Dennis's *Reflections Critical and Satirical, Upon a Late Rhapsody, Call'd*, An Essay Upon Criticism (1711) has become the grounds for accolades among those who at times appear to be seeking a Jacobite poet laureate to legitimate a lost cause. Someone no doubt will soon renew the nineteenth-century inclination to see Pope's unfinished "One Thousand Seven Hundred and Forty. A Poem" as a veiled call for a Jacobite restoration. Or perhaps the time is right for a full-scale elaboration of contemporary charges that Swift, too, was a Jacobite.

Since I have reviewed Aden's book elsewhere, I shall consider here some of Erskine-Hill's findings, which Brooks-Davies cites as support for his own study.[1] The place to begin is his "Literature and the Jacobite Cause," which convincingly demonstrates that Jacobite writers, like non-Jacobite opponents of the government, in an age of press censorship frequently had to rely on innuendo and indirection to express their views.[2] But when Erskine-Hill turns to the concrete example of Pope, assertion tends to replace argument. For instance, in his "Under Which Caesar? Pope in the Journal of Mrs. Charles Caesar, 1724–1741," *RES* (1982), he shows that Pope had been asked to write a Jacobite poem, but is this evidence of Pope's Jacobitism when Pope apparently refused to comply?

The problem of establishing Pope's Jacobitism is part of the larger historical argument about the role of Jacobitism in eighteenth-century British politics. The recent bibliography on this question is the subject of Frank McLynn's review essay, "Jacobites and the Jacobite Risings" in *History Today* (1983). McLynn's most recent book-length contribution to the argument, *The Jacobites*, is disappointingly superficial and reassigns Pope's most direct renunciation of the Jacobite premises—"May you, may Cam and Isis preach it long! / The RIGHT DIVINE of Kings to govern wrong"—from Dulness in *Dunciad* 4: 188–189 to an unidentified voice in *An Essay on Criticism*. He also accepts Samuel Johnson as "the quintessence of the Jacobite type."[3]

Since her contribution to Romney Sedgwick's *History of Parliament: the Commons, 1715–1754* (1970), Eveline Cruickshanks has established herself as the leading spokesperson for the position that until its death after the failure of the rising of 1745 the Tory party was essentially a Jacobite party. Others deny the real threat of Jacobitism after the defeats of 1715–16: in "Popular Politics in the Age of Walpole," in *Britain in the Age of Walpole*, H. T. Dickinson perceives "Jacobite symbolism" as "little more than a gesture of popular defiance to the ruling oligarchy"; in "A Client Society: Scotland Between the '15 and the '45," in the same collection, Bruce Lenman dismisses Walpole's fear of a Jacobite rebellion as "carefully cultivated paranoia."[4] Paranoia or not, however, the fear had undeniable domestic and foreign consequences, as Paul Fritz in *The English Ministers and Jacobitism between the Rebellions of 1715 and 1745* (1975) and Jeremy Black in *British Foreign Policy in the Age of Walpole* (1985) and *Natural and Necessary Enemies: Anglo-French Relations in the Eighteenth Century* (1986) remind us. The most extended rebuttal of Cruickshanks's identification of Tory and Jacobite is Linda Colley's *In Defiance of Oligarchy: the Tory Party, 1727–1760* (1981). By perhaps relying not skeptically enough on the surely self-serving Stuart papers, Cruickshanks accepts almost any reference to Jacobite correspondence as evidence of sympathy with the cause. Similarly, in his *Pope and Bolingbroke* (1984), Brean Hammond attributes to Pope a kind of guilt by association because of his friendship with Tories and former Jacobites like Cornbury and Bolingbroke. The presumption of Pope's Jacobitism, although never quite directly addressed, pervades Hammond's *Pope* (1986). But, as Lenman (whom McLynn calls the "curmudgeon" of Jacobite studies) points out in *The Jacobite Risings, 1689–1746* (1980), correspondence was a form of political fire insurance rather than a certain sign of collaboration. If the latter, Marlborough was a Jacobite. And why must Pope remain a Jacobite when Bolingbroke is widely accepted as having left the fold? Presumably because Pope was a Roman Catholic. Lenman's *The Jacobite Cause* (1986) is now the most even-handed and informed book on the subject.

In effect, Brooks-Davies assumes that the Erskine-Hill / Cruickshanks position is a given and reads the *Dunciad* as a Jacobite poem needing decoding. The result is often more assertion than argument, marked by frequent leaps from "it may be" to "at the back of Pope's mind lies." Such associative leaps enable us to overcome the restraints of chronology: "It is thus not performing too much of an historical anachronism to use the 1738 part of [William Warburton's] *The Divine Legation* in order to help elucidate the political implications of the three-book [1728] *Dunciad*" (p. 125). Although Brooks-Davies acknowledges that Pope mocks the divine right thesis in the *Dunciad* and admits that Pope was not enthusiastic about the person of James Francis Edward Stuart, the Old Pretender, he does not mention Pope's implicit denial of indefeasibility in *An Essay on Man*: "For Forms of Government let fools contest; / Whate'er is best administer'd is best" (3: 302–3). Nor does he quote Pope's remark to Joseph Spence that the reign of James I "was absolutely the worst reign we ever had, except perhaps that of James the Second." Curious statements for a Jacobite.

Pope in fact has very little good to say of any of the Stuarts, with the oft-noted exception of Anne in *Windsor-Forest*. But she was the de facto ruler and as such received similar praise from many, like Sir Richard Blackmore, whom no one would call a Jacobite. To a strict Jacobite, moreover, she was not the direct heir to the throne. In his later satires against Walpole and his Hanoverian master, what are we to make of Pope's praise of John Campbell, second Duke of Argyll, defender of the Hanoverian succession in the Privy Council and on the battlefield in 1714 and 1715, and thereafter leader of the anti-Jacobites in Scotland? Must praise for a reigning Stuart or discontent with a ministry identify one as a Jacobite? Are all of Pope's political comments, particularly in his correspondence, to be ignored as so much cant or subterfuge? Did his political position remain unchanged over the period between the 1728 and the 1744 *Dunciads*?

The "emotional Jacobitism" of Brooks-Davies's subtitle refers to a tentative and almost completely undeveloped suggestion that typifies his method of presentation:

Then again, did Pope's commitment to the ideal represented by Queen Anne have something to do with his relationship with his mother, with whom he lived for most of his life and whom he anxiously tended throughout her eighties and early nineties until her death, only eleven years before his own, in 1733? If it did, his dedication to the maternal model might suggest that his Jacobitism was not so much practical as emotional: that it was, in essence, regressive, a statement of Pope's reluctance to move from home in the senses of the comforting female. . . . [p. vii]

Of course, Brook-Davies's question is unanswerable, but I suspect that the poet's mother might have declined the honor of being supplanted by "the maternal model" of Dulness, especially five years before her death. Is this a case of proleptic displacement, another anachronism made possible by the author's thesis? In his definitive biography, Mack is far more cautious in dealing with Pope's possible emotional ties to Jacobitism, concluding that he "was in essentials simply a Roman Catholic nonjuror . . . capable of deep sympathy with friends more Jacobite than he" (p. 265).

My reservations about his Jacobite thesis notwithstanding, Brooks-Davies has much to offer to students of Pope, many of whom may agree with Paul Korshin's judgment that this book "is an extraordinarily interesting study . . . , a much better book than its two predecessors by Aubrey Williams (1955) and John Sitter (1971)," an opinion Thomas Faulkner shares.[5] Brooks-Davies confesses to a "congenital zeal for the obscure" (p. viii), and therein lies his work's principal appeal. His leaps of association are often dazzling, if not to me always convincing. As other reviewers of his book have noted, he has gathered a great deal of out-of-the-way information. Brooks-Davies presents persuasive arguments for the influence of Virgil's *Georgics* and *Aeneid*, John Gay's *Trivia*, Milton's *Paradise Lost*, as well as poems by Cowley, Boileau, and Garth, on Pope's *Dunciad*. And he offers fascinating information on possible effects on that poem from processions, the Eleusinian mysteries, Egyptian and Hebraic sources, among many other things. *Pope's* Dunciad *and the Queen of Night* is worth having, despite its primary thesis.

Notes

1. *JEGP*, 79 (1980), 129–31.
2. See Howard Erskine-Hill, "Literature and the Jacobite Cause: Was There a Rhetoric of Jacobitism?" in Eveline Cruickshanks, ed., *Ideology and Conspiracy: Aspects of Jacobitism, 1689–1759* (Edinburgh: John Donald Publishers, 1982).
3. Frank McLynn, *The Jacobites* (London: Routledge and Kegan Paul, 1985), pp. 78, 151.
4. Jeremy Black, ed., *Britain in the Age of Walpole* (London: Macmillan, 1984), pp. 61, 69.
5. See Paul Korshin, "Recent Studies in the Restoration and Eighteenth Century," *SEL*, 26 (1986), 572, and Thomas Faulkner, *Scriblerian*, 19 (1986), 55.

Through the Looking-Glass, Shrewdly: C. L. Dodgson and the Marketing of Lewis Carroll

Barry Menikoff

Morton N. Cohen and Anita Gandolfo, eds. *Lewis Carroll and the House of Macmillan.* Cambridge: Cambridge University Press, 1987. x, 384 pp.

Publishing history has never been at the forefront of literary criticism. It would be fair to say that until the last ten or fifteen years publishing history has usually been an acquired taste, the kind of scholarship reserved for people attracted to books as physical objects. (I am setting aside here the separate and considerable genre of publishing house histories.) With a few exceptions, notably William Charvat, whose *The Profession of Authorship in America* continues to be cited, the scholars who traditionally have worked in this field have been bibliographers and librarians.[1] Their major concerns have never been the developing movements in criticism and theory. For these scholars publishing history largely has meant the history of the printed book, and the periodicals in which they have published—*Studies in Bibliography* and *PBSA,* for example—have focused almost exclusively on matters pertaining to the physical text.

But the past decade and a half has witnessed a profound change in the entire field. For one thing, the movement in textual studies from medieval and Renaissance works to those in the nineteenth and twentieth centuries opened up a whole new area for publishing history. No longer were editors restricted to the problems presented by older texts, which put constraints on what they could investigate simply because of the scarcity of primary materials. Instead they could utilize the massive modern sources available to them: publishers' records, authors' correspondence, newspaper files, and trade journals. For the first time it was possible to explore in detail the history of a text *prior* to its publication. The undertaking in the 1960s by the Center for Editions of American Authors to produce authoritative texts of major American writers spurred this process. Every text was of course described in terms of its conventional printing and bibliographical history. But each was also examined in terms of its larger history: How did the book come to exist in the first place? What determined the relations between author and publisher? What were the terms of their contracts? What factors determined the success or failure of the book?

Publishing history suddenly had a wider potential audience. Rather than the exclusive province of the bibliophile it became the domain of the social and cultural historian. For the issues of how books got published, and by whom, and how and where they were sold, and how received, were recognized as nothing less than indices of a culture's attitudes and practices. Therefore, instead of isolating the book as an artifact, scholars began to study it within a larger context, as the material consequence of a complex series of interactions between a large number of people with varying viewpoints and interests—author, editor, agent, publisher, printer, art designer, bookseller. Where the traditional bibliographers and librarians focused on the history of the *book,* the newer historians transferred their interest to the history of its *production.* By doing so they opened the door to a wider discourse on "publishing history."

The movement toward critical theory in literary studies also had the effect of developing and broadening the interest in publishing history. This may seem paradoxical, for the scholar devoted to the properties of the book would appear to have nothing in common with the critic determined to find its meaning. But if publishing history is seen as a cultural and social investigation, then the two inquiries share a common purpose. They are both concerned with theories of the text, or at least with questions about the genesis of texts, and in practice they both diminish the importance of the author. If deconstruction demonstrated the illusion of an author's power, of his inability to incorporate his "intentions" in his own text, then the impulse behind that method had its parallel expression in publishing history. For the two are fundamentally concerned with process, with the cultural/social/political/sexual factors that determine the structure of texts, and that contribute to their success or failure. To the deconstructionist, authors are merely agents in that process, some admittedly more powerful than others, some more astute, but all caught in the process and powerless to determine its outcome. For the publishing historian, the author, although reduced in size, nonetheless replaced the book as the focus of interest. And the author's relations with his publisher were viewed as the crucial first step in studying the origins of the text. Insofar as those relations are determined within the intricately reticulated "world" of publishing, then those relations constitute publishing history.

The establishment at Oxford University of *Publishing History* in 1977 is a signal mark of the advance which this line of inquiry has made. And the publication in a recent *TLS* (15–21 January 1988) of an essay entitled "R. L. Stevenson and the Authors-Publishers Debate" suggests the general interest the subject holds for readers. Because book publication, or the history of the book, has been re-viewed as a cultural rather than a bibliographical enterprise, publishing history has entered the mainstream of critical discourse. It has done that directly in studies that draw on publishers' archives, providing specific information on the details of the publishing process and the writer's role in that process, and indirectly in studies that draw on theoretical sources and are often quasi-Marxist in their approach.[2] These latter studies emphasize the production and reception of texts. Issues of the "marketplace" and the writer's relation to a bookbuying audience are the major concern of these critics, and publishing history is treated primarily as a political or economic issue, as in Michael T. Gilmore's *American Romanticism and the Marketplace*, or a sexual one, as in Jane P. Tompkins' *Sensational Designs*.

Lewis Carroll and the House of Macmillan is the second volume in the Cambridge University Press series "Studies in Publishing and Printing History." It was, on the face of it, an excellent choice. In the figure of Lewis Carroll (or Charles Dodgson) the editors of the series had an author universally known, possibly even loved, under his pen name; in Morton Cohen they had the advantage of a senior editor familiar with Lewis Carroll's letters from the publication of a two-volume edition of that correspondence by Oxford University Press;[3] and in the correspondence between Charles Lutwidge Dodgson and the house of Macmillan they possessed a collection both voluminous and virtually complete in its coverage. Dodgson met Alexander Macmillan in 1863. His first letter to him was wrtten in November 1864. *Alice's Adventures in Wonderland* was published in 1865. Dodgson's last letter is dated 15 December 1897, just one month before his death at the age of sixty-five. The correspondence in this volume contains 351 letters spanning those years, and this is only a selection from the 479 originals that Morton Cohen and Anita Gandolpho have identified.

Dodgson was a prodigious letter-writer even by Victorian standards. Cohen estimates that he wrote more than 100,000 letters during the last thirty-seven years of his life. He kept a letter-register, in which he recorded a précis of each letter sent and received. As he wrote once to Macmillan in 1895, trying to unravel some old dispute, "*I* only record a précis of each: but *I* could easily give, for any year since about 1865, the *substance* of our correspondence for the year" (p. 313). Since he as a private individual could manage that, he expressed mild shock that Macmillan, as a major business firm, was unable to recover more exact information.

But before we begin with these "numbers," or get caught up in the numbers, we might remind ourselves just who Charles Dodgson/Lewis Carroll was. That he was the author of two of the most successful books in children's literature goes without saying. Every schoolchild has read *Alice's Adventures in Wonderland* and its more interesting sequel, *Through the Looking-Glass*. And everyone knows that Charles Dodgson was an Oxford don who taught mathematics. He was also an ordained clergyman, although he never held a pulpit. According to the editors, "Dodgson was deeply and genuinely religious," and charitable as well (p. 9). He came from a very large family and helped them with gifts and money whenever he could. He never married, lived most of his life in his rooms at Oxford and spent time occasionally at the family home at Guildford. He travelled little, although he made one extended trip to Russia in 1867. These are well-

The Marketing of Lewis Carroll

known facts about the man who told a story to please three small girls—the Liddell sisters—who were the children of the Oxford Dean of Christ Church. They clearly inspired *Alice* one bright afternoon on a summer outing—a trip which was to give the world one of its favorite treasures.

But this does not begin to suggest the nature of the man, nor of his accomplishments. Dodgson was extraordinarily talented—Cohen says "gifted" but many would use the term *genius* to describe him—and he possessed technical as well as imaginative skills. He was a great entertainer and from childhood put on puppet shows and small theatricals to entertain his own family. He loved the theater and retained a lifelong devotion to the stage, although it was one area of his life that seemed to run counter to his religion. He was inventive, frequently designing ingenious devices that he was intent upon producing and selling. His rooms at Oxford were full of these devices. One of his biographers, Derek Hudson, suggests that "by instinct he was . . . a graphic and visual artist."[4] For example, he illustrated the original version of *Alice* himself. His mechanical skill, allied with his visual instinct, led him to take up photography in its very early days, and there is common agreement that Dodgson was one of Victorian England's great portrait photographers. As almost everyone now knows, he specialized in photographing young girls, and he is notable if not notorious for his nude photographs, a very few of which were reproduced for the first time in 1978. Of his photography it has been said that had he not written the *Alice* books he would be known for his contribution to child and portrait photography, even to the field we now call "art" photography. Because of his complete disregard for the Victorian conventions of background and furnishings, there is a consensus among art historians that his work was far in advance of its time.

Then there is Dodgson's work in his chosen field—although it is sometimes difficult to say exactly what his chosen field is—of mathematics. He wrote books on geometry, including *Euclid and His Modern Rivals,* demonstrating that modern efforts to improve Euclid for the purposes of teaching were misguided and ineffective. He wrote on logic, where he still maintains a relatively high position, and has influenced philosophers of language. It is in his work on logic that his fables (*Looking-Glass*) and his mathematics come together in a discourse on language and meaning that makes him a figure of such interest for academic theorists of language. He had a modest influence on Wittgenstein, and he has been cited by jurists for questioning the meaning of justice in *Looking-Glass*. Add to this the inventiveness of his nonsense verse—*The Hunting of the Snark* and "Jabberwocky"—and the questions they raise about the meaning of words, indeed the very existence of words, and we have a man who had so many talents that it is hard to know where or how to place him.

It should be said at the outset that these letters are not for casual reading. However much Lewis Carroll is noted for humor and gentle satire and nonsense, Dodgson's letters to his publisher are strictly formal and exclusively concerned with business. Perhaps those warmer qualities were reserved for his family and close friends, particularly his "child-friends"—a term we can use only because it was Dodgson's. One wonders how someone could maintain a relationship for more than thirty years with his publisher and never resort to any mode of discourse other than the formal. The editors explain this as a Victorian convention, and as Dodgson's particular kind of conventionalism, perhaps even stodginess, although that is not a term they would use. Dodgson was not stodgy, and certainly not conventional in any usual way; but the terms of the correspondence do demand an explanation. From the point of view of Cohen and Gandolpho, these letters are the necessary communication between an author and his publisher, involving all aspects of the publishing of books under Lewis Carroll's name, or, in the case of mathematics texts, under the name of C. L. Dodgson.

But is that really the case? At the time of Dodgson's meeting with Alexander Macmillan the latter had recently moved to London and, along with his brother, had established the firm which was to become one of the largest and most influential in British publishing history. Dodgson cast his lot with them, and the relationship proved mutually advantageous. The *Alice* books were enormously successful. In fact, they were a steady resource, always being reprinted, and unfailingly reliable for Christmas sales and special editions. But the *Alice* books were only the staples of Dodgson's publications with Macmillan. Poetry, mathematics texts, puzzles for people who (like Dodgson) had insomnia and needed to keep their minds occupied while they were awake late at night, logic texts, and the final "children's" books that had such a disappointing reception, *Sylvie and Bruno* and *Sylvie and Bruno Concluded*. In short, Dodgson's relationship with Macmillan covered the publication of everything that he wrote. Nor did the relationship stop there. Dodgson drew on the house of Macmillan for a variety of non-publishing services. He was constantly requesting them to get him theater tickets for his regular visits to London. The publisher was always obliging. Dodgson regularly requested them to consider for publication manuscripts of friends. Macmillan almost always agreed to look at the manuscripts, or at least suggest other possible publishers. Throughout this correspondence Dodgson treats Macmillan as a resource capable of providing information and even performing services of use to an Oxford academic who is removed from the dynamic world of London.

This aspect of the publisher-author relationship parallels the experience of Robert Louis Stevenson with Scribners. Stevenson was forever making demands on his American publisher for books that he wanted to purchase, in effect using Scribners as a personal bookseller. But Stevenson *was* in Samoa, which is not exactly the same as being in Oxford. There is little doubt that Dodgson believed it perfectly appropriate to ask Macmillan to procure tickets to see Ellen Terry. In comparison with Dodgson's other requests, however, these were unquestionably the simplest, and must have seemed like sheer bliss when they were received. For Dodgson it seemed natural to make requests of his publisher. He conveyed the impression that a large firm like Macmillan had limitless help available to perform mindless or menial tasks: it "may perhaps be a day's work for one of your men" he mentions in one letter (p. 121).

That Macmillan was willing to perform these services for Dodgson is not surprising. As the firm said in another context, "as your books were not infrequently reprinted we made a fair commission on the manufacture" (p. 283). There was no reason to jeopardize their relations with an old author over a detail as minor as the purchase of theater tickets. And Dodgson was unfailingly thankful and courteous for their efforts on his behalf. But this does not begin to touch the subject of the real relationship between author and publisher, and the one that makes this volume so intriguing and exasperating at the same time. For one thing, the contractual relationship that Dodgson established with Macmillan was, if not unusual, distinctive in its details. When Dodgson proposed *Wonderland* it was on the basis of his own underwriting of the project. He was even to carry the costs for advertising. Macmillan was taking no risk on the publication; they were simply to receive a commission on the sales. In effect, they would be accepting a royalty on the book while Dodgson assumed the expense of its publication. Cohen and Gandolpho contend that this was the pattern for most books, and they quote from the Society of Authors that by 1890 "'at least three-quarters of modern fiction was published on commission'" (p. 15). Looked at from a modern point of view this might be considered a form of vanity publication; from another point of view it made sense, for neither Dodgson nor Macmillan could have anticipated the success of *Alice's Adventures in Wonderland.*

If we begin with the contractual arrangement, with Dodgson underwriting the production and distribution of his own book (an arrangement that was to continue through his entire publishing career), we would expect to find a correspondence concerned with the details of Dodgson's books. And we are not disappointed. These letters are filled with the minutiae of publication: the selection of illustrators, the price and quality of paper, the establishment of selling prices, the preparation of wood-blocks and the quality of printing, the discounting to booksellers, the sales and reprinting of issues and editions, the quality of reproduction of the illustrations, the size and spacing of the type, the bindings and color of various editions. The correspondence is an analytic bibliographer's dream. No one involved with the manufacture and printing of books could fail to be gratified by this edition of Dodgson's letters to Macmillan.

Yet for all that Dodgson is involved with every facet of the physical production—at one point he wants to know the technical names for the blue and green ink and is informed that they have none—his letters tell us nothing of his imaginative life nor of the composition of his texts. That aspect of the creative process is altogether concealed. We do at least learn a great deal about Dodgson himself; in fact, much of what we learn is different from that depicted by his editors. To take one of the most fascinating issues, there is the matter of Dodgson's personality. It is well known that he sustained a stammer throughout his life, a fact often given as a reason for his never pursuing a curacy. Along with the stammer goes the declaration that Dodgson was "a shy man" (p. 8). But it is simply impossible to read these letters and retain that view of his personality. Dodgson was a man who maintained absolute control over his life, certainly over his imaginative and intellectual compositions, and he brooked no contravention when it came to questions about the production of those texts. Everyone who had any professional relations with him testified to the fact that he was extremely demanding. The term that was used then was "particular." Walter Crane, an illustrator who had some correspondence with Dodgson about a possible collaboration, recalls: "His letters gave one the impression of a most particular person, and it is quite possible that he may have led Tenniel anything but a quiet life" (p. 134). Frederick Macmillan, who assumed the lion's share of the correspondence with Dodgson after his uncle, Alexander Macmillan, retired from the firm, said he was "a rather pernickety man to deal with" (p. 27). For Tenniel, whose illustrations for the first edition of *Wonderland* have become virtually synonymous with the text itself, Lewis Carroll was "impossible," according to the reports of Anne Clark.[5] Dodgson even characterized himself as "most exacting" in an inscribed copy of one of his books (p. 111).

Many critics and biographers of Dodgson have charged him with fussiness, particularly as they have examined much of this correspondence prior to its publication in this form. But Cohen and Gandolpho attempt to deflect the charge, and are convinced that the criticism is too harsh. They declare that Dodgson's exactingness was merely "the result of his devotion to the Evangelical ethic and his high aesthetic standards" (p. 18). This raises his meticulousness to the level of a religious impulse, and offers it as both a moral and an aesthetic virtue. The reality, however, is a good deal more problematic. Derek Hudson said Dodgson was "incessantly engaged in a struggle for perfection . . . fussy, difficult, touchy . . . all generosity and kindness" (p. 101). The reason the issue is of such critical importance is that Dodgson's habits—his exactingness, his meticulousness, his attention to detail—are the driving force behind his correspondence, which is another way of saying they are what determine his relations with Macmillan and explain much about the production of his texts. He was involved in his books at every stage of their production. These letters are virtually a primer for studying the publishing process from the initial design through the printing and promotion of individual texts. Dodgson was in actuality his own small press, using Macmillan as an imprint, and anticipating the movement toward beautiful book design in the *fin-de-siècle*.

It is astonishing to realize how much Dodgson knew and/or learned about printing and publishing, or technology and business. Not an aspect of the enterprise, from the duplication of ink color to the cost of an edition calculated on pence per copy, escaped his attention. The editors stress the point that Dodgson was not concerned with money, that his primary interest was the quality of the books. Indeed, the letters are filled with Dodgson's declarations that he cares for nothing else: "As to how many copies we sell I care absolutely nothing: the one only thing I *do* care for is that all the copies that *are* sold shall be artistically first-rate" (p. 195). But one must not conclude that Dodgson was uninterested in money. In fact, his letters are filled with shillings and pence—they can be used as confirmation of Herman Wouk's observation in *Youngblood Hawke* that writers' letters are always "about almost nothing but money." If at the beginning of his career Dodgson may simply have wanted to see *Alice* published, at some point he began to count on his books as a source of income. "My last receipts from you were, financially, a most disappointing amount. I had hoped for *hundreds* more: and it was a very serious deficiency, and difficult to meet" (p. 311). One of the central themes in his correspondence focuses on the money he can expect to realize from his books.

It is true that for many of Dodgson's books there was very little to be made, particularly his mathematics texts. It is also true that he secured the publication of separate editions of the *Alice* books for charity, bound with more expensive and durable covers and distributed freely to children's wards and hospitals. This was unquestionably a generous gesture, but it was also an integral part of Dodgson's management of his literary career. For example, he was always alert to any error in the list of titles printed in his books, and if there was a new publication or a later edition which did not update all the titles of his work he called attention to the mistake. As for the distribution of free books to children's wards, these were never done without printed declarations that the copies were not for sale. Ostensibly this was to insure that books printed more cheaply (except for the bindings) would not reach the booksellers and then be sold to the buying public—a way of maintaining quality control, distinguishing the product he was selling from that which he was giving away. His refusal to allow anything to get into print if it did not meet his approval, if it had the slightest appearance to his eye (although often to no other) of being imperfect, helped develop an indisputable reputation for quality. Dodgson deliberately sought to have his name identified with books that were first-rate in their production. Indeed, it is often hard to know whether the intellectual or the physical text was the more important. He insisted upon the wholesale consignment to America of editions that were carelessly produced or that did not meet his standards. "I would rather that these Oxford copies were not sold in England *at all.* But they will do very well for the Americans, who ought not to be very particular as to *quality,* as they insist on having books so very cheap" (p. 217).

Dodgson's unwillingness to sacrifice quality in any detail largely accounts for his reputation for being difficult. From a modern point of view, however, the perspective is reversed and he is seen as the artist who refuses to compromise his integrity for the marketplace, willing to sacrifice publication for the sake of perfection. Yet there may well be another view of this facet of Dodgson's behavior. He repeatedly refers to poorly produced editions as "disfigured" or "spoilt" or "worthless." It is as if his books were children, and just as he could not bear an imperfect child he could not tolerate a flawed text. Unlike children, however, who turned pubescent, or moved away, books were subject to absolute control. The attention lavished on their design insured their immortality. Unquestionably Dodgson's desire for visible perfection in life, achievable only through photography and writing, generated his obsession with the production of his texts. He was his own publisher just as he was his own photographer and writer and inventor and theorist. No one else could be expected to provide a clearer replication of perfection. The world of wonderland and child-friends and nonsense verse and nude photography enabled Dodgson to slip away from Oxford and enter an infinitely more pleasurable place. In the beginning Macmillan may have been an equal partner in a cooperative publishing venture, but in the end the firm was nothing more than a public instrument for Dodgson's re-creation of his private world.

Notes

1. William Charvat, *The Profession of Authorship in America, 1800–1870*, ed. Matthew J. Bruccoli (Columbus: Ohio State Univ. Press, 1968).

2. For examples of the former, see Robert L. Patten, *Charles Dickens and His Publishers* (Oxford: Clarendon, 1978); Barry Menikoff, *Robert Louis Stevenson and* The Beach of Falesá: *A Study in Victorian Publishing with the Original Text* (Stanford: Stanford Univ. Press, 1984); examples of the latter are N. N. Feltes, *Modes of Production of Victorian Novels* (Chicago: Univ. of Chicago Press, 1985), and Nigel Cross, *The Common Writer: Life in Nineteenth-Century Grub Street* (New York: Cambridge Univ. Press, 1985).

3. Morton N. Cohen with R. L. Green, eds., *The Letters of Lewis Carroll* (New York: Oxford Univ. Press, 1979).

4. Hudson, *Lewis Carroll* (New York: C.N. Potter), p. 84.

5. Clark, *Lewis Carroll: A Biography* (London: Dent, 1979), p. 242; Clark is quoting Harry Furniss, who quotes Tenniel in *Some Victorian Men* (London: John Lane, 1924), p. 77.

A New Biography of Sherwood Anderson

James Schevill

Kim Townsend. *Sherwood Anderson: A Biography.* Boston: Houghton Mifflin Company, 1987. 323 pp.

Hilbert H. Campbell, ed. *The Sherwood Anderson Diaries 1936–1941.* Athens: University of Georgia Press, 1987. 348 pp.

In our statistical age of facts and personality worship, biography has somehow become a more popular genre than the novel. This change provokes some important questions: Is biography becoming a substitute for the naturalistic novel because so many facts are available from the plethora of record-keeping today? Does it seem possible to illuminate a character in depth more in a biography than in a novel? Can the mass of facts help to explain why so many modern novels turn away from naturalism, even from character portrayal, to focus more on style and structural, narrative experiments? One fact is clear. It is not possible in fiction to write literally anymore in our world of nuclear weapons, genocide, and concentration camps. The maze of facts overwhelms us. New styles must be sought and found to cope with unrelenting facts. Paradoxically, the biographer's problem remains that the facts, no matter how extensive, are really subservient to the mysteries of personality and creativity. The dreams and fantasies that control our lives remain secret enigmas, difficult to perceive and record.

Sherwood Anderson's life is a good example of these problems. In his well-written, sympathetic new biography, Kim Townsend maintains correctly that Anderson's life was a unique struggle that shaped and often shattered his work. A fine cultural historian, Townsend writes that Anderson "dared—as he put it—to proclaim himself the American man." Townsend goes on to say that Anderson was "representative in his efforts to realize the American dream—but even more representative in his failures" (p. xi). As a cultural historian, then, Townsend's aim is to use Anderson's life as a focus that reveals the successes and failures of "the American dream" during Anderson's life from 1876 to 1941. In pursuing this aim, instead of recording the commonplace details of Anderson's life that would have required a thick, stolid volume in the fashion of many biographies today, Townsend writes a tightly constructed, selective book that concentrates on key transitional events in Anderson's wanderings.

In reviewing Townsend's biography, I should first admit the background of my opinions. In 1951 I published the first biography of Sherwood Anderson. I wrote the book in my late twenties after four years in the army during World War II. After the army I wanted to continue writing, as I had already written a good many poems and plays. My uncle, Ferdinand Schevill, offered to subsidize me while I wrote the Anderson biography. He had been a close friend of Anderson through all of Anderson's four marriages. Through my uncle, I became friendly with Anderson's widow, Eleanor, and she, generously, gave me access to and permission to use quotes from the Anderson papers which she had deposited in the Newberry Library in Chicago. Unfortunately, Townsend did not contact me and does not write much about Anderson's relationship to my uncle. Even in my biography, I didn't say much about the strength of this relationship as my uncle insisted that he remain in the background. Usually Anderson was wary of academics because of his lack of a formal education. However, my uncle was an extraordinary writer and teacher who was born in Cincinnati, Ohio, and his midwestern background was similar to Anderson's. As one of the first faculty members of the University of Chicago, my uncle delighted in forming friendships amongst creative people outside of the academic community. Consequently, his close friends, in addition to Anderson, were the architect Frank Lloyd Wright, the poet and playwright William Vaughn Moody, and my uncle's brother-in-law, the New York sculptor Karl Bitter. Far from being just a

"Professor of History at the University of Chicago," my uncle was one of the outstanding American historians, the author of *The History of Florence* (which Anderson admired greatly), *Siena: The History of a Medieval Commune*, *The History of the Balkan Peninsula*, *The Great Elector*, and other books. As an outstanding teacher, who decided finally to teach only undergraduates at the University of Chicago, he was a celebrated lecturer who also had the patience and modesty to listen to students. As a well-known writer himself, published by Harcourt, Brace and Company in New York, he could talk to Anderson on his own terms, about the vagaries of publishers and the difficulties of the American cultural scene. They enjoyed together beer-drinking in whatever bar was available, intensely competitive games of croquet, and bouts of story-telling with bursts of laughter that revealed a warmly shared sense of humor. As a patient friend, my uncle could listen to Anderson's problems, particularly his marital upheavals, and support Anderson even if he disagreed with him. Gratitude for this deep friendship led Anderson to dedicate to my uncle the important late book of short stories entitled *Death in the Woods*. During the final period of Anderson's life, my uncle was close to Anderson's depressive moods and saw how poignant and pathetic was his futile proposal of "a new brotherhood of artists." In the letters I have that my uncle wrote to me while I was working on my Anderson biography, I find the following excerpt written in August, 1950:

> For myself I can hardly bring myself *not* to acknowledge *a failure of the sense of mission*, temporary of course. [He is talking about the late period in Anderson's life between *Dark Laughter* and the *Memoirs*.] In any case he no longer acted with the dedication to a "call" that sounds the effective note of the *Winesburg-Poor White* period.
>
> I would even have you point out the dispersion of energy resulting from the restlessness that kept him on the road for months and months of every year....
>
> By my way of looking at life this fatal dispersion cannot be blamed on American society. It has its origin in *himself*, and Sherwood in his healthy work acknowledged as much by insisting on a high-minded individualism, by declaring in express words that every man, in last analysis, shapes his own fate.

Here his appeal for help, in his letter to Dreiser, comes in. This proposed brotherhood of artists is pure hokum. Of course there must be warm contact among writers, painters etc., precisely but not otherwise, as there must be cordial contact and fusion with the common folk that have constituted the world in every age of history. But associated artists promptly become a coterie, and exactly in measure as they are vital, resort to howling each other down as in a general dogfight.

At the source of this restless depression, as Townsend shows in perhaps the best part of his book, was Anderson's childhood. Townsend writes brilliantly about the town of Clyde, Ohio, where Anderson lived in the crucial years from 1883 to 1895:

By the time the Andersons arrived, Clyde's social calendar was full. The town offered everything from Episcopal ladies' entertainments or a concert by the Slave Cabin Jubilee Singers at Terry's Opera Hall, to a meeting of the Clyde Political Senate or a reunion of Civil War veterans at the Armory; the curious could find anything from a performance by a troupe from the Madison Square Theater of New York, to a meeting of the Chautauqua Literary and Scientific Circle that featured Mrs. Everett's reading a long poem she had written to celebrate the life of Clyde's Civil War hero, General James Birdseye McPherson.

Yet the town still betrayed traces of the unsettled West. A generation earlier, in Martin's Ferry, in the eastern part of the state, the young William Dean Howells could still gawk at Indians in the street. There were none in Clyde, but for most of Anderson's years there, the streets were dirt, and at night they were only dimly lit. They "were lighted by kerosene lamps set on posts," he wrote in *Tar: A Midwest Childhood*. "They were far apart, at the street corners mostly, and between the lamps was darkness." He did not see paved streets until he went to Cleveland; and riding the rails a few miles west to Fremont, he saw his first electric street lights. Clyde was still a frontier town. There were seventeen saloons catering to its 2500 citizens, and at least two houses of ill-repute. The quality of life, as it was represented by the goings-on at Hamer's tavern, earned Clyde another nickname: "Bang-All." [p. 6]

Townsend describes movingly the decline of Anderson's father, Irwin, as he lost his harness-making profession due to the new factories specializing in agricultural products, and became a disillusioned itinerant housepainter and paperhanger. He

A New Biography of Sherwood Anderson

bought a cart and had his name painted proudly on it: *I. M. Anderson*. But as Townsend says:

> He was not one to persevere. When he took his oldest boys along to help in the work, he would stop everything to tell them stories about the Civil War. On one occasion Sherwood got so impatient that he threw down his brush and walked away. When on his own, Irwin might just walk off the job or, supposedly scouring the countryside for work, disappear for days on end. [p. 9]

Like father like son; that was always Anderson's fear whenever a crisis occurred. Caught in this anxiety, he depicted his father's problems over and over again in his stories and novels. The shiftless father, afraid of yet devoted to women, became a familiar figure in Anderson's fiction. Yet he was forced to admit in time that he respected his father's frustrated storytelling ability and his love for parades, performances, and amateur theatricals. It was his father who used to read to the family at night from the few books that he possessed, books such as the Bible, *Robinson Crusoe,* and Tennyson's *Poems*. Somehow it was the mesmerizing tone of his father's voice that Anderson retained and that he struggled with in the tone of his own prose, as if he were struggling constantly with a ghost. As for Anderson's mother, her influence was even more crucial. Townsend writes of her:

> Emma died when Sherwood was eighteen years old. He had never been able to draw near enough to her. As he said quite freely of himself, "he was in love with her all his life." To him she *was* a "bound girl." She was oppressed, stifled, long-suffering. She was kept, kept from living life fully by the burden of her many children. For her he made up Italian ancestry, because it was "so wonderfully comforting to think of one's mother as a dark, beautiful and somewhat mysterious woman," and into her silence he read her power. He would always think of her as Woman, a figure who inspired him to do good, to write. If he could not approach her when she was alive, he would approach her through his works. [p. 13]

And he did. Not only did he dedicate *Winesburg* to her, but she is a leading character in the book and in much of his other work.

From her he learned the feminist principle that informs his best work and makes it influential today for its unusual perceptions of women's problems. In Clyde, Anderson earned the nickname "Jobby" out of "love and out of necessity," as Townsend puts it well. As a boy, Anderson developed a desire for money and a talent for salesmanship, as Townsend shows, that led to Anderson's future success in the new business world of advertising.

If Clyde was where Anderson's continuous life conflicts began—the weak father and strong mother, the androgynous conflicts that made Anderson a pioneer in this important and critical area with such fine stories as "The Man Who Became A Woman"; also the business conflict between selling a product openly or cleverly if not dishonestly—what about the business world that dominated the next phase of Anderson's life? Anderson's life has been especially romanticized because in books like *A Storyteller's Story*, he dramatized inaccurately how he left forever the world of business for the world of writing. The fact is that he never completely left the world of business because he suffered from money problems, ending his life as a journalist and the owner of two small-town newspapers, one Republican and one Democrat. He remained always a shrewd operator, which he recognized as a cause of his melancholia and restlessness. Yet he gave up his chance for the big money and the country-club life. By 1911, through his skill at copywriting (a process that came to eat at his conscience because he had to warp his writing into images and metaphors he scorned), he had become President of the American Merchants Company in Elyria, Ohio. He was a committed family man and he and his wife, Cornelia, had a new son. Even though he was marking up his Roof-Fix paint 500 percent and "was not above substituting cheaper ingredients as they came along," as Townsend says, he still believed in what he called "Commercial Democracy," his version of an ideal paradise for workers and owners such as Shaw satirized in *Major Barbara*. His one main recreation, ironically, was golf and the 19th hole session afterwards in the clubhouse with business associates that he came to hate for its money talk. To escape from business, he created a hideaway in an upstairs room in his house and fitted the door with a lock that kept out his family too. There, Townsend tells us, he tried desperately to write and to regulate his life with a strange game of commanding toy soldiers. Such actions pointed to his impending breakdown. He could not stand the make-believe of his life. The breakdown that Anderson suffered at the end of November 1912 was certainly a mental collapse that he feared the rest of his life. Using Anderson's own notes to Cornelia, which have become available in recent years, Townsend writes:

> The term that comes closest to describing Anderson's condition is "fugue state," a state of flight, something like those Anderson had experienced as a youth when parts of his body, or the landscape, or his very life, seemed to float away. But this time Anderson's state of mind was organized or composed in such a way as to make uncanny sense. Strictly speaking, a person in such a state knows nothing of his previous life, does not realize that he does not know, and does not even appear conspicuous to people who did not know him in his former state. Anderson knew enough to send his notes to Cornelia; his muddy suit and unshaven stubble must have raised suspicions, but no one who did not know him need have been alarmed by the man who went about doing what he described himself as doing in his notes and in the notes he dictated on Sunday at the hospital. What is most significant about the "fugue state" is that a person enters it when too many "strivings, affects, and attitudes . . . become contradictory to each other and become replaced by a single striving. . . ." Wandering to Cleveland, Anderson was a man who wanted to get out of business, to leave—if not destroy—his wife, but in his imagination, all he wanted to do was live in writing, be a writer. [p. 81]

From this point on, Anderson's primary concern would be his own writing, his personal "search for truth" as he called it, despite whatever jobs he had to take for a living. In 1915, living alone in a Chicago boarding-house room, when he was still in advertising working for the Taylor-Critchfield firm, Anderson wrote the first of his great *Winesburg* stories, "Hands," about the teacher, Wing Biddlebaum, who was almost lynched because his grotesque hands, fluttering affectionately over his students, were interpreted as homosexual advances.

Since he is writing a biography, and not a literary study, Townsend does not go at length into Anderson's concept of "grotesque." He mentions how the term was "in the air" at the time in such works as Poe's *Tales of the Grotesque and Arabesque;* Arthur Davison Ficke's short sequence of poems in the *Little Review,* "Ten Grotesques"; and Edgar Lee Master's *Spoon River Anthology,* which influenced Anderson greatly. But Townsend does not delve deeply into how the concept of the "grotesque" shaped Anderson's best work.

In *Winesburg, Ohio,* Anderson defines "grotesque" in his preface, "The Book of the Grotesque," with the Emersonian insight that "the moment one of the people took one of the truths to himself, called it his truth, and tried to live his life by it, he became a grotesque and the truth he embraced became a falsehood." It is significant that this definition of "grotesque" is formulated by the old writer in the preface. Townsend thinks this old writer is merely a projection of Anderson, who "introduces himself as an old man, lying in a bed just like Anderson's, one that has been raised to the level of his window." Clearly, though, the old writer is also a symbolic, Mark Twain-like figure, with his white mustache, heavy cigar-smoking, and his Joan-of-Arc fantasies hovering in his memories. Anderson felt deeply how the frustrations in his life and work were related to Mark Twain's: both men coming from agricultural, small-town backgrounds found their writing and their lives grotesquely split between frustrating commercial ventures and private desires to develop their unique talents in less ruthless ways.

In *Winesburg* Anderson was trying to define "American Grotesque" in terms of his own experience. Much has been written in recent years about the European background of the "grotesque style," particularly in the important work of Wolfgang Kayser. After the destruction of World War II and the dark revelation of the concentration camps, European artists and writers tended naturally to reflect a grotesque world in works such as Camus' *The Stranger* and Beckett's *Waiting for Godot,* in which man has become an absurdist cipher. The problem with "American Grotesque," as Anderson sensed it, is that our country remains tuned to optimistic change and continues to scorn "grotesque" with the literal definition of "distorted and ugly." Publicly, we ignore the increasingly grotesque elements in politics, religion, sports, and the media that are central concerns of the writers today who follow in Anderson's pioneering direction. Since World War II, a mixed tone of compassion and savagely ironic humor underlie our best fiction—from Heller's *Catch-22* through Flannery O'Connor, Eudora Welty, Thomas Pynchon, John Hawkes, Stanley Elkin, Bernard Malamud, Donald Barthelme, Joyce Carol Oates, Robert Coover, Ann Beattie, and Raymond Carver. No matter how different their styles, these writers and many others are exploring versions of a new "American Grotesque" subject matter and treatment.

Often the relationship between the subject matter and the treatment involves rhythmical experiments and a looser, fragmented approach to the novel, as in *Winesburg, Ohio*. For Townsend, *Winesburg* is "not a novel, not just a collection of stories." Rather, it is "precisely what Anderson called it in a subtitle that many editions omit: 'A Group of Tales of Ohio Small Town Life.'" But the fact is that Anderson came to think of it more as a novel and favored the elimination of the subtitle. At the end of his life, when he was writing his *Memoirs* in the form of a novelistic autobiography, he wrote to Roger Sergel: "Suddenly I decided to go back to the *Winesburg* form. That is really a novel. It is a form in which I feel at ease. I invented it. It was mine. 'Why not use it,' I told myself. Since then I have been happier."[1] In a review of Hemingway's *In Our Time*, D. H. Lawrence wrote in the *Calendar of Modern Letters* for April 1927: "*In Our Time* calls itself a book of stories, but it isn't that. It is a series of successive sketches from a man's life, and makes a fragmentary novel." Unfortunately, Townsend ends his biography with Anderson's death and does not discuss the posthumous publication of the *Memoirs*, which were badly edited by Paul Rosenfeld.[2] But the sense of the *Memoirs* as a "fragmentary novel" is important to consider. Anderson's reputation has sagged during recent years and Townsend, with his perceptive, knowledgeable portrayal of Anderson's life in relationship to his work, should help to restore the value of Anderson studies.

In a fine chapter on Anderson's relationships with Hemingway and Faulkner, Townsend shows how Anderson encouraged and influenced these two writers, and how, as writers will, they turned on him to satirize his style and pursue their own careers. Unfortunately, hurt by Hemingway's and Faulkner's actions and sensitive to criticism about his "naive" approach to small town "grotesques," Anderson sought to change his style in much of his later work from *Dark Laughter* on. In a letter to Ferdinand Schevill in early 1925, when he was working on *Dark Laughter*, he wrote:

> In the novel I am trying to get and give just the slow after-effect of war hatred on the emotions of people. You can see how elusive such a theme. I have had to create a style for it . . . I can't go on writing always in an old mood—the naive people of a small town.
> My own feeling is that there has been—in America since the war—a new influx of Europe. It is not so much people coming now as European moods. Cynicism with a sharper tang—the beginning of sophistication here.[3]

This "new cynicism with a sharper tang, the beginning of sophistication here," resulted in an artificial, experimental style that did not suit Anderson's compassionate nature and deep feeling for small-town country life. During his final restless wanderings in the 1930s, he achieved at last a successful marriage with Eleanor Copenhaver and a better understanding of his problems and special gifts as a man and a writer. Using much new material, Townsend illuminates these late years in two final chapters, "The Political Years" and "Finally At Ease." As Townsend says at the end of "Finally At Ease":

> Anderson made the "small town" serve several purposes. He said that it was still the testing ground of democracy, the place where we started, and where we could still prove ourselves as a nation and as individuals. It was also the place, the very image of smallness itself, to which he wanted to return in spirit. [p. 314]

The fact remains that there is still much to do in Anderson research. Especially, there needs to be a *Collected Short Stories*, which will show the mythical range of Anderson's conception of "American Grotesque," as Malcolm Cowley revealed the extraordinary imaginative range of Faulkner's Yoknapatawpha County in the *Portable Faulkner*. Also, with the advantage of time and Ray Lewis White's scholarly critical edition of *Sherwood Anderson's Memoirs* in 1967, a new edition of the *Memoirs* should be published that will show its merits both as a final pursuit of his vision of "American Grotesque" and as a "fragmented novel." Only then, despite Townsend's valuable new biography, will the true originality of Anderson's work be recognized.

The Sherwood Anderson Diaries: 1936–1941, well-edited by Hilbert H. Campbell, are a welcome addition to the available Anderson material. In these curt, sometimes cryptic daily entries covering the last five years of his life (Campbell's detailed notes are extremely helpful in deciphering these entries), Anderson notes hurriedly the key surface events of these years. Alas, he does not write about the nature of his work, for him the most important part of his life. Thus we read in one entry in Acapulco, Mexico, on 15 March 1938: "It is almost impossible to keep up notes in this place. All days seem the same. I wrote a beautiful short story. As usual, work, siesta, the sea (p. 164).

How frustrating not to learn more about the short story! Anderson's work was always a very private matter, an entrance into his fantasies of "the grotesque," which he created with his poetic vision from his accurate observations of the distortions of the American democratic dream.

The South American voyage with his wife, Eleanor, on which Anderson died in 1941, might have put him in touch with the new style of Magic Realism that was developing. This style has brought many Latin American fiction writers such as Miguel Angel Asturias, Julio Cortazar, and Gabriel García Márquez to the forefront of contemporary literary style. It is a way of writing that bears a distinct relationship to Anderson's concept of "American Grotesque." In any case, with Townsend's sympathetic, understanding new biography, there is now an opening again for Anderson studies that will show us, after years of critical silence, his important place in American literature.

Notes

1. James Schevill, *Sherwood Anderson: His Life and Work* (Denver: Univ. of Denver Press, 1951), p. 346.
2. *Sherwood Anderson's Memoirs*, ed. Paul Rosenfeld (New York: Harcourt, Brace, 1942).
3. Schevill, p. 208.

Correspondence

To the Editors:

I must question Richard Finneran's review of my *A Descriptive Catalog of W. B. Yeats's Library* which appeared in the 1987 number of your journal. In essence, I believe that Finneran misrepresents my work, faulting the *Catalog* for what it was never intended or advertised to be. He also makes judgments about my competence to convey accurately Yeats's annotations based on some dubious examples. I respond to his criticisms under three broad headings.

Accuracy of transcriptions: That some inaccuracies of transcription are included in the *Catalog*, I admit and deplore, but I leave it to other researchers to determine what percentage of the large number of complex annotations included *are* faulty. Further, I deny that the examples he cites, apart from one, are faulty transcriptions, and I reject his conclusion which questions my ability to make accurate transcriptions of Yeats's annotations. As to his specifics:
1) "T. March" (2381c) for "Mark," Yeats's editor at Macmillan, is in fact my error in transcription.
2) Yeats's reported inscription ("September 1913") in the 1928 edition of *The Tower* (2430f) is a misprint introduced by the typist in preparing the camera-ready copy. My note card has the accurate "September 1933."
3) Most crucially, as his prime example, Finneran corrects the misprinted inscription in 2335b to the accurate "An aimless joy is a pure joy," but then proceeds, on the basis of this misprint, to question my general competence to transcribe Yeats's annotations. In fact, I know (and knew) perfectly well the wording and the source of this inscription. It *is* one of Yeats's "standard inscriptions," and the reader will find it cited accurately elsewhere, as at 2402a where I write: "Has T. S. Moore's bp. of Helen emerging from egg with 'An aimless joy is a pure joy' WB Yeats." (I have also provided the editors and Professor Finneran my original typescript which has the accurate inscription which was then mistyped on the final copy.) *Of course* I admit my respon-

sibility for finding and correcting these typing errors, and I regret that I did not as I am sure *any* editor would under the circumstances.

Distinguishing handwriting: Finneran writes, "O'Shea's ability to accurately transcribe Yeats's handwriting or to discriminate between it and that of Mrs. Yeats—both difficult tasks—is open to question." He cites two examples of my indiscrimination (1827 and 2323b), though only by number, and concludes: "material which is ascribed to Yeats seems clearly the work of his wife." Surely Finneran intends "*is* clearly" if he is to retain the force of the adverb in this sentence? Or is he admitting, again, that the handwriting is often very close, that when one examines a few lines on a scrap of paper (2323b) or a scattering of corrections on thirteen typescript pages (1827,) it is difficult to differentiate W. B. Yeats from Mrs. Yeats, and he must write "seems clearly"? I believe he should at least have acknowledged the very scant evidence he is using in these two examples. But with item 1827 just cited, circumstantial evidence can provide more certainty than judgments about handwriting. The thirteen-page typescript entitled "Samhain 1908/First Principles" (of which I possess photocopies of only the first two pages) is lightly edited in a hand I judged in the *Catalog* and still judge to be WBY's. The two substantive revisions on these two pages (an added and a deleted word) have both been followed in the printed text of the 1908 *Samhain*. Now, if one concludes from this evidence that the typescript provided the copy-text for the 1908 *Samhain* as printed, these revisions could *not* have been Mrs. Yeats's since she was still some years in WBY's future. One could construct a scenario in which a typescript was made from the printed 1908 text and then corrected by Mrs. Yeats for a reprinting, but given the nature of the changes and the inefficiency of the procedure, it seems very unlikely. Additionally though, the printed 1908 text does not follow a deletion of a mark of punctuation and drops a word from the typescript, both plausibly oversights of the printer. But the revised text of the typescript *has* been followed in the 1908 *Samhain* as printed in *Explorations*, selected by Mrs. Yeats and published after W.B.'s death. Apparently, in this case at least,

Mrs. Yeats has scrupulously passed over a corrupted text and chosen a more authoritative one, a procedure Finneran would, presumably, approve.

Inclusiveness: This assertion I deny categorically. Finneran faults the *Catalog* for not including information about Cuala Press books sold at auction by Michael Yeats and others scattered in public and private libraries throughout the world. This was never my scope. I state in my preface: "This catalog provides at a minimum a basic bibliographical entry for each item in W. B. Yeats's private library as it is maintained by his daughter Anne Yeats in Dalkey, Ireland" (ix). The Dalkey library is very rich in material indeed, enough to keep this researcher and others busy for many years. If I had taken Finneran's path, the *Catalog* would be still unpublished. The items included that subsequently went to Michael Yeats were cataloged because I was told by Anne Yeats that they originated from the library she maintains. My information about Cuala books at Michael Yeats's came from two excellent sources with direct knowledge of his collection and was later confirmed for me from Michael Yeats by an American Yeats scholar, though, I conclude now, only after the books had already been sold at auction. I must, nevertheless, accept responsibility for what I wrote, and I regret the misinformation.

Finneran's reference to the "1920's Catalogue" is even more dubious. It exists as a card file at Dalkey made by an unknown indexer. The 500 missing items presumably were in Yeats's library at one time, but these cards do *not* have the same status as items still physically in the library which can be consulted and verified, and I saw a real danger in users of the catalog confusing the two different kinds of evidence. In any case, the list has now long been published in the British *Yeats Annual, No. 4*, and is readily accessible. I do not believe purchasers of the catalog have somehow been cheated by this arrangement (the book is in fact an excellent "value" for what it contains, if we must look at it as a commodity). To Garland's credit, they readily accepted the book for publication despite the obviously slim market for items of this kind. Still on the question of inclusiveness, I am compiling a supplement to the *Catalog* which will include information on books that have left the library. In fact I make a request for such information at the end of my introduction, and Warwick Gould has also offered to periodically update items in the *Catalog* in the *Yeats Annual,* but as I have said, a listing of scattered items was *never* my intention in the present *Catalog,* and this will be clear to anyone reading my preface.

No researcher, including this one, can object to having misprints or faulty information corrected as Finneran has done in this review. But I do expect that judgments about my competence and the integrity of the item under review be based on accurate inferences. I also look for an academic review to be more than a tabulation of corrections and omissions. I, for one, would like to have Professor Finneran comment on the directions Yeats scholarship might now take based on the kinds of information in the *Catalog.* Perhaps we can hear from him on this subject yet.

> Edward O'Shea
> State University of New York
> College at Oswego

Professor Finneran Responds:

Accuracy of transcriptions: O'Shea admits to all three errors, blaming two of them of his typist. But reviewers review, and readers read, books, not typescripts. A reviewer's responsibility is surely to note error if such there be, not to speculate on its origins. Moreover, O'Shea does not comment on my citation of George Bornstein's review of his volume (*Yeats,* 4 [1986], 219–21). Checking a relatively small body of material, Bornstein noted "several substantive errors in addition to numerous minor ones" (220) and concluded that the work contains "transcriptions that are not always reliable" (221). Quite so.

Correspondence 301

Distinguishing handwriting: My use of "seems clearly" was to remind readers that, as stated in the review, the hands of Yeats and his wife are not always distinct. But I accept O'Shea's criticism and would now like to substitute "is clearly," as he is wrong in both cases. He seems to admit his error with item 2323b but still maintains that the 1908 typescript of *Samhain* was corrected by Yeats himself. Unfortunately, materials in the British Library and in the archives of Macmillan (London) demonstrate otherwise. Briefly: after Yeats's death, it was discovered by Allan Wade that the *Edition de Luxe* proofs of *The Irish Dramatic Movement* did not include the 1908 *Samhain*. Thomas Mark (O'Shea's "March") communicated this fact to Mrs. Yeats, who replied as follows on 9 July 1939: "Mr Wade is quite right: that last *Samhain* essay was not included in *The Irish Dramatic Movement* when WBY republished with Macmillan. I shall send you a typed copy tomorrow (I have only one printed copy available which does not belong to me, so cannot send it)" (Macmillan). A copy of the typescript is in fact found in British Library Add. Ms. 55897. Mrs. Yeats's markings on both copies of the typescript either correct her typing errors or "improve" the text; she also silently introduced some variant readings into her typescript, such as "said that it" for "said it" in the opening sentence. Thus O'Shea's 1827 "is clearly" posthumous.

Inclusiveness: If O'Shea would look again at my review, he will find that I did *not* argue that his work should have cited stray items. Rather, I suggested that in the revised edition which we still require, he might consider including such of them as are known, especially those that have been cited and commented on in the published scholarship (as with my example). Of the three omissions that I *did* criticise, O'Shea appears to admit to two of them, though he blames his haphazard citation of only some of the items held by Michael Yeats on Anne Yeats, and his omission of the Cuala Press collection formerly held by Michael Yeats on "two excellent sources" and "an American Yeats scholar." As for the Cuala Press volumes, I can only say that someone who would rely on a trio of Deep Throats rather than on the published Sale

Catalogue provides a cautionary tale for one's next course in Research Methods.

The most important difference between us concerns the omission of the 1920s listing. Since O'Shea now admits that he should have included the volumes presently or previously held by Michael Yeats (and in fact did cite some of the former), he can hardly cling to the defense that his work cites only those books in the possession of Anne Yeats. More to the point, his published reason for excluding the list was *"for reasons of space"* (ix; italics mine) and that alone. The basic question is whether the catalogue should have attempted to list all volumes which Yeats is known to have owned, as I would argue, or should have contented itself with citing only those volumes in a particular collection at a particular point in time, as O'Shea has (more or less) done.

Finally, I do not think that other scholars are greatly in need of my advice on the obvious—and important—uses to which *A Descriptive Catalogue* can be put. But they *do* need to be aware that the volume in front of them is incomplete and inaccurate.

Contributors

PANTHEA REID BROUGHTON is Professor of English at Louisiana State University.

JEROME H. BUCKLEY is Gurney Professor Emeritus of English Literature at Harvard University.

SIDNEY BURRIS is Assistant Professor of English at the University of Arkansas.

WILLIAM E. CAIN is Professor of English at Wellesley College.

VINCENT CARRETTA is Associate Professor of English at the University of Maryland.

W. G. DAY is Assistant Editor of the *Annual Bibliography of English Language and Literature*.

DWIGHT L. EDDINS is Professor of English at the University of Alabama.

CARL FICKEN is Professor of Theology and Culture at Lutheran Theological Southern Seminary.

PHILIP L. GERBER is Professor of English at the State University of New York, College at Brockport.

ANDREW GORDON is Associate Professor of English at the University of Florida.

T. H. HOWARD-HILL is Professor of English at the University of South Carolina.

JAMES M. HUTCHISSON is Assistant Professor of English at Washington and Jefferson College.

RICHARD S. KENNEDY is Professor of English at Temple University.

THOMAS M. LEITCH is Associate Professor of English at the University of Delaware.

JAMES J. MARTINE is Professor of English at St. Bonaventure University.

A. E. WALLACE MAURER is Professor of English at Ohio State University.

BARRY MENIKOFF is Professor of English at the University of Hawaii.

MAXIMILLIAN E. NOVAK is Professor of English at the University of California, Los Angeles.

WALTER J. ONG, S. J., is Emeritus University Professor of Humanities at St. Louis University.

HERSHEL PARKER is H. Fletcher Brown Professor of English at the University of Delaware.

JEFFREY M. PERL is Associate Professor of English and Comparative Literature at Columbia University.

JAMES SCHEVILL is Professor Emeritus of English at Brown University.

JAMES GRANTHAM TURNER is Professor of English at the University of Michigan.